J O U R N A L · O F
M · O · R · A · L
T H E O L O G Y

VOLUME 5, NUMBER 1
JANUARY 2016

GRACE AND PEACE
IN THE EARTHLY CITY

Edited by David Matzko McCarthy

J O U R N A L · O F
M · O · R · A · L
T H E O L O G Y

Journal of Moral Theology is published semiannually, with issues in January and June. Our mission is to publish scholarly articles in the field of Catholic moral theology, as well as theological treatments of related topics in philosophy, economics, political philosophy, and psychology.

Articles published in the *Journal of Moral Theology* undergo at least two double blind peer reviews. Authors are asked to submit articles electronically to jmt@msmary.edu. Submissions should be prepared for blind review. Microsoft Word format preferred. The editors assume that submissions are not being simultaneously considered for publication in another venue.

Journal of Moral Theology is indexed in the ATLA Catholic Periodical and Literature Index® (CPLI®), a product of the American Theological Library Association.
Email: atla@atla.com, www: http://www.atla.com.

ISSN 2166-2851 (print)
ISSN 2166-2118 (online)

Journal of Moral Theology is published by Mount St. Mary's University, 16300 Old Emmitsburg Road, Emmitsburg, MD 21727.

JOURNAL OF MORAL THEOLOGY
VOLUME 5, NUMBER 1
JANUARY 2016

CONTENTS

J O U R N A L · O F
M · O · R · A · L
T H E O L O G Y

EDITOR
David Matzko McCarthy
Mount St. Mary's University

ASSOCIATE EDITOR
Jason King, *St. Vincent College*

EDITORIAL BOARD
Melanie Barrett, *University of St. Mary
of the Lake/Mundelein Seminary*
Jana M. Bennett, *University of Dayton*
Mara Brecht, *St. Norbert College*
Meghan Clark, *St. John's University*
David Cloutier, *Mount St. Mary's University*
Christopher Denny, *St. John's University*
John J. Fitzgerald, *St. John's University*
Mari Rapela Heidt, *Waukesha, Wisconsin*
Kelly Johnson, *University of Dayton*
Warren Kinghorn, *Duke University*
Kent Lasnoski, *Quincy University*
Ramon Luzarraga, *Benedictine University, Mesa*
M. Therese Lysaught, *Loyola University Chicago*
Paul Christopher Manuel, *Mount St. Mary's University*
William C. Mattison III, *The Catholic University of America*
Christopher McMahon, *St. Vincent College*
Rev. Daniel Mindling, O.F.M. Cap., *Mount St. Mary's Seminary*
Joel Shuman, *Kings College*
Matthew Shadle, *Marymount University*
Msgr. Stuart Swetland, *Donnelly College*
Christopher P. Vogt, *St. John's University*
Brian Volck, *University of Cincinnati College of Medicine*
Paul Wadell, *St. Norbert College*
Greg Zuschlag, *Oblate School of Theology*

Journal of Moral Theology, Vol. 5, No. 1 (2016): 1-36

Catholic Moral Traditions and Energy Ethics for the Twenty-First Century

Erin Lothes Biviano, David Cloutier, Elaine Padilla, Christiana Z. Peppard, Jame Schaefer

IN THE PAST TWO HUNDRED YEARS, the rapid extraction and combustion of fossil fuels have contributed to anthropogenic interference in global climate systems, while also increasing net global wealth and some forms of economic development. In the twenty-first century, it is now clear that fossil fuel sources have both positive and negative impacts on economies, livelihoods, and environments worldwide. What might formal Catholic teaching and theological-moral reflection offer to this situation?

The institutional Catholic Church has engaged energy issues in multiple documents, ranging from papal encyclicals to the U.S. Bishops' 1981 statement on energy.[1] So too have discussions of fossil fuels, climate change, and ethics occurred within broader scholarly discourses of Catholic theology and ethics.[2] Catholic organizations dedicated to the global common good and to countering the effects of climate change have proliferated in the U.S. and worldwide. This essay builds upon the growing ecclesial, scholarly, and practical attention to these issues by revisiting the U.S. Bishops' 1981 statement on energy, "Reflections on the Energy Crisis," in recognition that the question of what powers societies in the twenty-first century is not merely an issue of technology or economics: It is also an issue of energy ethics. A Catholic energy ethics requires attention to current energy realities

---

[1] "Reflections on the Energy Crisis: A Statement by the Committee on Social Development and World Peace" (Washington, D.C.: United States Catholic Conference, 1981), http://catholicclimatecovenant.org/catholic-teachings/energy-statements/#Energy Statement.

[2] See, for example, Richard W. Miller, ed., *God, Creation, and Climate Change: A Catholic Response to the Environmental Crisis* (Maryknoll: Orbis Books, 2010); Jame Schaefer, ed., *Confronting the Climate Crisis: Catholic Theological Perspectives* (Milwaukee: Marquette University Press, 2011); and Jame Schaefer and Tobias Winright, ed., *Environmental Justice and Climate Change: Assessing Pope Benedict XVI's Ecological Vision for the Catholic Church in the United States* (Lanham, MD: Lexington Books, 2013).

with scientific and technological precision, and can offer unique clarity about the specifically moral character of the problem.

Today economies and cultures are increasingly globalized. Few actions have strictly local effects. Thus globalization increasingly interlinks the private and social spheres of action, forming the present reality of "moral globalization," which increases the moral responsibility of all persons to act with integrity and recognize the global impacts of their personal and collective actions. The environmental crisis of today is the unintended result of the history of these impacts. As Pope Saint John Paul II wrote, "Today the environmental crisis has reached such proportions as to be the moral responsibility of everyone."[3]

In light of the impacts of fossil fuels on climate systems, and the differential distribution of economic and environmental benefits and burdens, we believe that the wise and appropriate use of energy sources is necessary to generate a sustainable and just energy future. Insofar as the United States represents a considerable proportion of global energy consumption as a "super-developed" nation, it is essential for the U.S. to show prudence and responsibility in its long-term energy policies.[4] One resource for public discussion and consideration about the shape of twenty-first century energy policies is the 1981 U.S. Bishops' statement on energy.

This article first contextualizes the U.S. Catholic Bishops' 1981 report, articulates its enduring principles, and notes developments in the global energy situation since 1981. Subsequent sections constructively engage the Bishops' document, analyzing energy sources and technical, economic, and ethical considerations in a parallel structure to the 1981 statement: Energy of the Past (Fossil Fuels); Energy of the Present (Bridge Fuels); Energy of the Future (Renewables). For each category, we offer an overview of opportunities and challenges, articulate distinct issues, offer important guiding principles, and suggest ways forward in making the transition to a more sustainable, just, and renewable energy future. The essay concludes with suggestions about global leadership and intergenerational responsibility.

The primary authors are United States residents and scholars of Catholic theology, Catholic social teaching, and environmental ethics at five universities whose integrative, analytic, and constructive work

---

[3] John Paul II, "The Ecological Crisis: A Common Responsibility," www.vatican.va/holy_father/john_paul_ii/messages/peace/documents/hf_jp-ii_mes_1989-1208_xxiii-world-day-for-peace_en.html/.
[4] John Paul II, *Sollicitudo rei socialis,* www.vatican.va/holy_father/john_paul_ii/encyclicals/documents/hf_jp-ii_enc_30121987_sollicitudo-rei-socialis_en.html; Benedict XVI, *Caritas in veritate,* www.vatican.va/holy_father/benedict_xvi/encyclicals/documents/hf_ben-xvi_enc_20090629_caritas-in-veritate_en.html; Francis, *Evangelii gaudium,* http://w2.vatican.va/content/francesco/en/apost_ex-hortations/documents/papa-francesco_esortazione-ap_20131124_evangelii-gaudium.html.

here builds upon a series of working group meetings and reports by contributing authors made at the Catholic Theological Society of America since 2012. The first sections were drafted as commentaries on ten individual themes within the statement by ten scholars.[5] These commentaries were shared with outside experts for independent review, and the primary authors crafted these commentaries into the current article. Additional scientists, economists, policy experts, and industry leaders gave their time generously to review sections of this essay for scientific accuracy and interdisciplinary rigor.[6]

REFLECTIONS ON THE ENERGY CRISIS: CONTEXTS AND PRINCIPLES (1981 TO 2014)

The context for the Bishops' 1981 "Reflection on the Energy Crisis" was the growing scarcity of oil, geopolitical tensions, price shocks,

---

[5] See The Catholic Theological Society of America, www.ctsa-online.org/discipleship_commentaries.html. The authors of the commentaries on various sections of the Bishops' statement are Meghan Clark, David Cloutier, Christine Firer Hinze, Erin Lothes Biviano, Richard Miller, Elaine Padilla, Christiana Z. Peppard, Nancy Rourke, Jame Schaefer, and Matthew Shadle.

[6] The reviewers listed here read one or more of the original commentaries or the draft of the final synthesized document, and the authors express their gratitude to each for their comments and insight. These are: Dr. Shahzeen Attari, Indiana University School of Public and Environmental Affairs, Purdue University; Dr. Sandra Baptista, Senior Research Associate, Center for International Earth Science Information Network, Columbia University; Patrick Doherty, Senior Fellow of the International Security Program. New America Foundation; Rev. Fletcher Harper, Executive Director, GreenFaith; James E. Hug, S.J., Spiritual Life Department, Adrian Dominican Sisters, Adrian, Michigan; David Lochbaum, Director of the Nuclear Safety Project of the Union of Concerned Scientists; Dr. John Mutter, Professor of International and Public Affairs; Professor, Earth & Environmental Sciences, Columbia University; Dawn M. Nothwehr, OSF, Ph.D., The Erica and Harry John Family Endowed Chair in Catholic Ethics, Catholic Theological Union; Dr. Robert Pollack, Professor of Biology, Columbia University; Dr. Veerabhandran Ramanathan, Distinguished Professor of Atmospheric and Climate Sciences at the Scripps Institution of Oceanography, University of California, San Diego, Council member of the Pontifical Academy of Sciences; Dr. Sunny Ramchandani, Global Energy Initiative and Falcon Energy; Dr. William H. Rauckhorst, Professor Emeritus of Physics at Miami University of Ohio; Natabara Rollosson, consultant for United Nations Development Programme, United Nations Executive Office of the Secretary-General, United Nations Climate Change Secretariat; Dr. Kristin Shrader-Frechette, Ph.D., O'Neill Family Endowed Professor, Departments of Philosophy and Biological Sciences, University of Notre Dame; Dr. Anthony Strawa, NASA Research Scientist, Lead- Aerosol and Cloud Microphysics Group, Atmospheric Physics Branch, Earth Sciences Division; Rear Admiral David W. Titley, USN (Ret) past leader of the U.S. Navy's Task Force on Climate Change, now Director of the Center for Solutions to Weather and Climate Risk at Pennsylvania State University and Adjunct Senior Fellow at the Center for New American Security; Dr. Pablo Wangermann, Client Principal, Aerospace & Defense, HP Enterprise Services. All analyses, opinions, and errors are our own and do not reflect the views of any of our expert reviewers.

and looming threats of economic and social chaos in the face of peak oil (the concern that the world's oil resources were being tapped to their limits, would soon peak, and decline, leaving an energy shortage). Thus "Reflections on the Energy Crisis" emphasized conservation to preserve this finite source for the future, while developing alternative sources to assure energy availability for all people. The document was structured to address past, present, and future energy sources in light of foundational principles and practical queries.

Climate change was already recognized by scientists when the Bishops wrote in 1981, but it was at the margins of public awareness. In 1988 the Intergovernmental Panel on Climate Change formed, and in the following year the prominent educator and environmental activist Bill McKibben wrote the first mainstream book on climate change.[7] Public awareness of the causes and scope of climate change have amplified dramatically in the intervening decades. Even in their 1981 statement, the Bishops recognized that "it would be the height of folly to tamper in ignorance with the ecology of the entire planet." In 2014, that folly is fact. Attempts at global protocols, emissions caps, and mitigation schemes have been numerous, yet not well supported by the United States and some other highly industrialized nations. So too has the threat of diminishing fossil fuels shifted somewhat since 1981, as unconventional sources (such as tar sands and shale oil reserves) have become more economically feasible to tap. Moreover, an ethical concern has emerged forcefully: Human-induced changes to the climate system bring multiple consequences, including unequal global patterns of distribution of the fossil fuel economy's benefits and burdens. The Fifth Assessment Report of the United Nations Intergovernmental Panel on Climate Change (IPCC) reports that without a change in society's dependence on fossil fuels, severe disruption of ecological, social, and political systems will occur worldwide. The IPCC concludes that a world temperature increase of 2°C or more will create climate instability, diminished environmental resiliency, human suffering and displacement, and geopolitical strife as conditions such as drought, storms, and biodiversity loss alter traditional human lifestyles, habitations, cultures, and economies.[8]

While all humans will be affected by climate change, the lack of access to energy will make the poorest three billion especially vulnerable to extreme events with devastating consequences. This is additionally problematic since the developing world contributed the least

---

[7] Bill McKibben, *The End of Nature* (Random House, 1989).
[8] Working Group I: Contribution to the Fifth Assessment Report, "Climate Change 2013: The Physical Science Basis," (Intergovernmental Panel on Climate Change, 2013), www.ipcc.ch/report/ar5/wg1/.

to the build-up of the heat-trapping greenhouse gases in the atmosphere. The United States is responsible for 26% of the CO_2 emissions from 1751-2012, while China is responsible for nearly 11%, India is responsible for 3%, and the whole of Africa is responsible for 2.6%.[9] Long-term sustainable development must include the transition of existing fossil fuel economies to renewable energy systems, in both industrialized and industrializing contexts. Yet significant responsibility and leadership must fall to the developed nations who have already benefited from the exploitation of fossil fuel resources.

To be sure, communities in the United States face many challenges in the contemporary energy economy, including access to affordable, clean energy. Low-income and minority communities are disproportionately burdened by pollution and toxic waste sites, leading to asthma, learning disabilities, school absenteeism, and other illnesses.[10] Yet the United States also understands itself as a land of opportunity, ingenuity, entrepreneurship, and resourcefulness. Generations of people committed to civic life, technological innovation, and global participation have focused scientific resources on the technological triumphs that advance human comfort and wellbeing. Their efforts launched outer space exploration, generating that enduring image of the "Earthrise;"[11] revolutions in electronic and digital technologies have multiplied global interconnections. These and other scientific, technical, economic, and political developments created new possibilities for reframing human societies' relationships. We think that energy is the necessary revolution for the present generation; and not only is it possible, its foundations are already present.

What the U.S. Bishops recognized in 1981 as largely a problem of finite supply is now augmented by problems of sustainable development and global justice for present and future generations in an era of population growth, economic globalization, and environmental degradation. Within this context, the 1981 Bishops' statement provides a moral framework that deserves attention and updating to address the current energy situation and urgent ethical concerns facing the world.

---

[9] J. Hansen, P. Sato M Kharecha, V. Masson-Delmotte, F. Ackerman, et al., "Assessing 'Dangerous Climate Change': Required Reduction of Carbon Emissions to Protect Young People, Future Generations and Nature," *PLos ONE* 8, no. 12 (2013), http://127.0.0.1:8081/plosone/article?id=info:doi/10. 1371/journal.pone.0081648.

[10] Robert D. Bullard, Paul Mohai, Robin Saha, and Beverly Wright, "Toxic Wastes And Race At Twenty 1987-2007: Grassroots Struggles to Dismantle Environmental Racism in the United States. A Report Prepared for the United Church of Christ Justice and Witness Ministries" (2007).

[11] NASA, "Earthrise," www.nasa.gov/multimedia/imagegallery/image_feature_124 9.html.

ENDURING MORAL PRINCIPLES FOR ENERGY ETHICS

Climate change already casts its shadow on our planet; the diverse impacts of pollution and the inequalities of energy access call for a new moral analysis, for an energy ethics. As many scholars have pointed out, climate change is complicated to theorize in existing moral frameworks. This is because its effects are indirect and non-localized; impacts occur at different places and times; those affected are often not those who cause the problem; carbon dioxide and other greenhouse gases (such as water vapor) are not necessarily in and of themselves "toxic," even while amplified atmospheric concentrations outstrip the earth's natural capacities to absorb these compounds. Furthermore, the processes that are driving climate change did not begin as deliberate attempts to harm the planet; indeed, the burning of hydrocarbons has accompanied most forms of human development. More recently fossil fuels have facilitated the industrial modernity that many residents of the globalized West inhabit.

Yet with today's ever-increasing knowledge about the modes and causes of anthropogenic climate change comes a moral responsibility to address the worst of its impacts as well as its root causes. While advanced nations have made great strides in containing and minimizing localized pollution, international agreements have faltered, effective carbon reduction has been minimal, and industrializing nations accelerate the pace of atmospheric change catalyzed by developed nations. Given this complexity and scale, what can be said morally about the situation?

The Catholic Church is well positioned to provide a coherent energy ethic to its many practitioners around the world. Moreover, as privileged North Americans, we think that solidarity requires that those living within the upper echelons of economic globalization respond to the global situation while acting in our geographical and national context. Our essay addresses itself squarely to U.S. Catholics; indeed, it may be said that middle and upper-middle class Americans are the single most important group of people to "convert" on issues of energy ethics, because—as many contemporary ethicists agree—they "probably have much more economic power than the vast majority of people on the planet."[12]

The Catholic Church has with increasing frequency pointed out that climate change is not a partisan issue; neither is it solely a political, economic, or technological issue. Instead, climate change is a human

---

[12] James Garvey, *The Ethics of Climate Change* (New York: Continuum, 2008), 141. See also Willis Jenkins, *The Future of Ethics* (New York: Oxford University Press, 2013).

issue, linked to the security and flourishing of all the families and living communities of the earth.[13] From this perspective, moral and religious traditions have significant resources to offer to grounding and framing an energy ethics. Official, institutional Catholic social teaching (CST)—a tradition dating in its modern form to 1891—does not provide alternative economic or scientific theories, but rather engages social realities by applying moral principles and moral vision emphasizing the one human family and the unity of creation. Since at least 1967, Catholic social teaching has explored intersections among social well-being, economic development, and environmental degradation; it includes speeches and writings by papal authorities, from the Pope himself to various agencies such as the Pontifical Council for Justice and Peace, as well as subsidiary ecclesial bodies such as national conferences of Bishops. Climate change has been increasingly attested in this literature. In 2001 the U.S. Bishops remarked: "At its core, global climate change is not about economic theory or political reforms... it is about the future of God's creation and the one human family."[14]

Theological traditions seeking justice need prophets as well as careful, sophisticated analysts who are accountable to the most authoritative data and that attend to specific contexts. Thus a Catholic energy ethics needs to be tough-minded in at least two senses: it needs to be based on the most rigorous scientific understanding, and it needs to be pragmatic. While CST as formally understood refers to a body of texts generated by the magisterium, the broader conversations about Catholic social thought and environmental ethics are crucial sites of agency for lay people with multiple forms of expertise.

The call to live out an energy ethics proceeds from the universal call to holiness. The Vatican II document *Lumen gentium* insists that the laity, just as much as those called to ecclesiastical vocations, have a "vocation to perfection" (no. 32), one in which they together "seek the kingdom of God by engaging in temporal affairs and by ordering them according to the plan of God" (no. 31). The laity are to "learn the

---

[13] Pontifical Council for Justice and Peace, *Energy, Justice and Peace: A Reflection on Energy in the Current Context of Development and Environmental Protection* (Libreria Editrice Vaticana, 2014); Pontifical Academy of Sciences, "Statement of the Joint PAS/PASS Workshop on Sustainable Humanity, Sustainable Nature: Our Responsibility: Stabilizing the Climate and Giving Energy Access to All with an Inclusive Economy," www.casinapioiv.va/content/accademia/en/events/2014/sustainable/statement.html; Pontifical Academy of Sciences, "Protect the Earth, Dignify Humanity. The Moral Dimensions of Climate Change and Sustainable Humanity," www.casinapioiv.va/content/accademia/en/events/2015/protectearth.html.

[14] United States Conference of Catholic Bishops, "Global Climate Change: A Plea for Dialogue, Prudence, and the Common Good," www.usccb.org/issues-and-action/human-life-and-dignity/environment/global-climate-change-a-plea-for-dialogue-prudence-and-the-common-good.cfm.

deepest meaning and the value of all creation, as well as its role in the harmonious praise of God," as well as "remedy the customs and conditions of the world, if they are an inducement to sin" (no. 36). Thus, the vocation of the laity combines intense learning with forthright criticism of structures of sin.[15]

In 1981, the U.S. Bishops aimed "to situate energy issues in a moral context, to arouse sensitivity to human considerations that are often ignored." The statement develops that claim by laying out six principles to guide reflection on specific aspects of that crisis. These foundational principles provide the starting point for our reflection and can be summarized as follows:

1. Cherishing and protecting life as a gift from God.
2. Accepting an appropriate share of responsibility for the welfare of creation.
3. Living in solidarity with others for a common good, namely, the sustainability of an abundant earth.
4. Striving for justice in society.
5. Giving special attention to the needs of the poor and members of minority groups.
6. Widespread participation in decision-making processes.

The energy ethics framework set forth here builds upon these principles, and adds a seventh from more recent magisterial teaching. We express the principles adapted to developments in the Catholic social teaching tradition and today's specific energy contexts as follows:

1. *Cherishing and protecting life, health, and the conditions that support human and ecosystemic well-being in the present and for future generations.* The protection of life and health requires affordable, accessible energy and clean, safe water. Energy systems that destroy the homelands and livelihoods of people in diverse places around the world contradict the protection of life. Life itself relies on a broader ecological balance that transcends geographic and temporal boundaries, and includes the conditions that support all of life on earth, now and in the future.[16]
2. *Accepting an appropriate share of responsibility for climate change, with a strong sense of duty to ameliorate its worst effects as well as to address its root causes.* Accepting an appropriate share of responsibility means that U.S. residents and communities must acknowledge their historical contribution to the accumulation of greenhouse gases, including current per capita usages and

---

[15] Vatican II, *Lumen gentium,* www.vatican.va/archive/hist_councils/ii_vatican_council/ documents/vat-ii_const_19641121_lumen-gentium_en.html.
[16] The natural order and balance of creation is often expressed in Catholic teaching as the "grammar" of creation; see Benedict XVI, *Caritas in veritate,* no. 48.

political-economic structures that benefit vested interests instead of the common good.[17] Our duty is to address root causes by means that are not merely economic or technical, but also moral and educational.

3. *Seeking a common good that lives in solidarity with others to promote genuine, shared flourishing.* Preserving the common good calls us to recognize that energy systems are changing, and must be changed. We must immediately take every action to shape energy systems that support flourishing communities. We believe that our ultimate happiness and security comes from God, who has endowed us with the privilege and responsibility to be the guardians and protectors of creation. As a spiritual invitation, this is a call to refocus on family and community, on time spent in recreation, not endless overwork, consumption, and economic expansion. A genuinely shared common good comes from a shared life of balance, sufficiency and seeking joyful living with friends and family. "Super-developed nations" have a special obligation to stand in solidarity with other nations and marginalized peoples. Contributing to the development of new energy systems and economies is an important task of solidarity that shapes communities in which all flourish.

4. *Promoting distributive justice: In striving for a more just society, Catholics are called to create energy systems that are both fair and sustainable.* The 1981 statement paraphrases Pope John XXIII, insisting that "the economic prosperity of any people is to be assessed not so much from the sum total of goods and wealth possessed as from the distribution of goods according to norms of justice, so that everyone in the community can develop and perfect themselves" (no. 74).[18] This standard of distributive justice suggest that our current measures of economic prosperity be adjusted. Rather than promoting individual maximizing of excess luxury, everyone should be enabled to live a decent life. We have enough energy to go around, but currently it is distributed in unjust ways.

5. *Orienting justice towards a preferential option for the poor and future generations to ensure universal access to sustainable energy for basic needs.* Current measures of economic prosperity should be adjusted towards integral development that provides

---

[17] For dialogue between scientific and religious leaders on the multiple causes of the ecological crisis, see John E. Carroll and Keith Warner, eds., *Ecology and Religion: Scientists Speak* (Quincy, IL: Franciscan Press, 1998), vii-xv.

[18] Pope John XXIII in *Mater et magistra* (http://w2.vatican.va/content/john-xxiii/en/encyclicals/documentshf_j-xxiii_enc_15051961_mater.html) elaborates on the point: "From this it follows that the economic prosperity of a nation is not so much its total assets in terms of wealth and property, as the equitable division and distribution of this wealth" (no. 74). Pope John XXIII references similar teaching from Pope Pius XII, underscoring the consistent magisterial teaching that prosperity must include the equitable distribution of wealth.

sufficient resources for the poorest members of society. This is vital because the greatest effects of climate change impact poor nations whose members have contributed virtually nothing to the problem. Moreover, in our own society, we must address the problem that environmental action too often appears as a cause for the wealthy, without placing heavier burdens for change on those already suffering from relative energy poverty. Access to sustainable energy systems should be available to all, so that the poor are not forced to rely on the energy of the past.

6. *Enabling participation through subsidiarity and ensuring transparency when accounting for the benefits and burdens of energy options.* Sufficient participation in energy decisions requires transparency and full-cost accounting of the impacts of various energy options. Energy firms have a legitimate right to reasonable profit, but not to a maximum profit made possible by minimizing safety regulations and overlooking the common good. Transparent communication of energy risks and costs is essential and any manipulation of information infringes upon the rights of citizens to self-determination.

7. *Developing technological prudence.* Recent Catholic thought has put a new emphasis on the limits of technological solutions. Pope Benedict XVI taught that "the development of peoples goes awry if humanity thinks it can recreate itself through the 'wonders' of technology" (*Caritas in veritate*, no. 68). Technological innovation is a marvelous human capacity, but unintended consequences are common, and technical interventions are only as good as the social frameworks within which they are deployed. A misplaced conviction of technological determinism—what CST has called an idolatrous "faith in progress"—believes science will allow humans to create "a totally new world."[19] This trust that any and all ecological problems can be met by some future technological solution, however fantastic or dangerous, is misplaced. As a result, the precautionary principle should guide energy ethics.

ENERGY OF THE PAST: FOSSIL FUELS

Fossil fuel extraction and combustion have supported a world unimaginably transformed from even a few centuries ago. The energy produced from these sources has been transformed into health, light, comfort, and reduced labor for billions of people around the world. Energy is an essential, life-giving reality that creates industrial modernity as we know it. However, fossil fuel infrastructures, their processes of extraction and combustion, cause irreversible damage to our climate and our earth. Transitioning to an economy that bridges fossil fuels and renewables is an enormous challenge, but an essential task. What

---

[19] Benedict XVI, *Spe salvi*, no. 17, www.vatican.va/holy_father/benedict_ xvi/encyclicals/documents/hf_ben-xvi_enc_20071130_spe-salvi_en.html.

do we make of fossil fuels that have powered societies and economies for the past several hundred years, and why might they rightly be seen as "energy of the past"?

Fossil Fuels and Carbon Budgets

The Catholic Church recognizes the scientific consensus that human-induced changes to climate are measurable, attributable to the burning of fossil fuels, and that an ethical response is required. While the Bishops' 1981 statement focused on the context of peak oil, today the global carbon budget and amplified feedback cycles (meaning the intensification of effects in the coming decades and centuries) are of chief concern.[20] Atmospheric carbon dioxide (CO_2) would decline rapidly if fossil fuel emissions were to be instantly terminated—a counterfactual proposal, to be sure, but an important baseline for calculations. Halting emissions in 2015 would allow atmospheric CO_2 to decline to 350 parts per million (or "ppm," signifying a ratio of carbon dioxide molecules to all of the other molecules in the atmosphere) at century's end. Some scientists argue that with a tightened carbon budget and improved forestry and agricultural practices, global temperature rise might only be 1° C by the end of the century as long as there is no net increase of non-CO_2 greenhouse gases.[21] Thus scientists and policymakers increasingly speak of a carbon budget for meeting certain temperature targets.[22]

---

[20]Johan Rockström et al., "Planetary Boundaries: Exploring the Safe Operating Space for Humanity," *Ecology and Society* 14, no. 2 (2009), http://pdxscholar.library.pdx.edu/ cgi/viewcontent.cgi?article=1063&context=iss_pub.

[21] Keith Kloor, "The Eye of the Storm," *Nature Reports Climate Change* (November 26, 2009), www.nature.com/climate/2009/0912/full/climate.2009.124.html.

[22] The World Bank, "CO_2 emissions (metric tons per capita)," http://data.worldbank.org/indicator/EN.ATM. CO2E.PC. One calculation of the global carbon budget is expressed in terms of carbon dioxide as 750 Gt CO_2. By dividing this budget of 750 Gt CO_2 among all countries on an equal per-capita basis based on their population for 2010, national CO_2 budgets are identified. With a global population of 6.9 billion in 2010, the U.S.'s average annual per-capita emissions is 2.7 tons of CO_2 until 2050. For comparison, the U.S. per capita emissions in 2009 was 17.3 tons.

When viewing the carbon budget in terms of per capita emissions, the United States' carbon budget is almost exhausted.[23] There are proposals to create an international trading emissions system that would allow the U.S. to buy carbon credits from other developing countries. Proponents suggest such proposals would allow developed countries like the United States leeway in its process of radical emissions reduction, while allowing developing countries the possibility of economic benefit.

> Carbon companies can become partners within a clean, prosperous, and healthy economy as energy companies, not fossil fuels companies. The conventional fossil fuels that remain within a safe global carbon budget must be directed toward building a clean energy infrastructure. The stable pricing of carbon is a widely-recognized and recommended means to incentivize sustainable choices. Currently available technologies can assist developing nations.

Carbon budgets demonstrate the practical and ethical necessity of transitioning away from carbon-based energy sources. Continued expansion of unconventional fuel sources such as tar sands and tar shale, hydraulic fracturing (commonly referred to as "fracking") for oil and gas,[24] coal mining, and drilling in the Arctic, Amazon, deep ocean, and other remote regions must be named for what they are: profit-seeking and polluting practices that do not contribute either to carbon reductions or to the transition to a renewable energy situation. The transition will entail both opportunities and costs to the current functioning of fossil fuel companies and economies, as social and environmental sustainability—not corporate profits that shift the costs of pollution to society—is the fundamental value that must be achieved. Thus U.S. energy policy at both govern-

---

[23] The U.S. population as of 2010 is estimated to be 4.6% of the world's population. With that population as a reference the U.S. share of the global carbon budget between 2010 and 2050 is 35 Gt CO_2. Estimated U.S. emissions in 2008 were 6.1 Gt CO_2. If we assume annual emission do not increase or decrease from 2008, the United States' carbon budget would be exhausted in a little less than 6 years. In sum, the carbon budget analyses from multiple scientists make vividly clear the implications of delaying a rapid transition away from fossil fuels. If emissions reduction had begun in 2005, reduction at 3.5%/year would have achieved 350 ppm at 2100. Now the requirement is at least 6%/year. Richard Miller, "Discussion of 'Reflections on Energy'," conference paper, Catholic Theological Society of America (June 8, 2014).

[24] "Fracking" is used as an overall term to encompass vertical and horizontal drilling as well as the hydraulic fracturing process. Technical discussions make additional distinctions and seismologists note the hazards associated with injection wells where waste water is disposed of, including triggering small and moderate earthquakes. John Mutter, personal communication (October 4, 2014).

mental and corporate levels must drive a necessarily ambitious, purposeful path to a low carbon economy—what some theorists have referred to as a new "grand strategy."[25]

Making the Transition in the United States: Proposals and Technologies

In addition to addressing carbon budgets and permit trading, some policymakers propose that nations provide financial support proportionate to their historical emissions for mitigation and adaptation measures in developing countries.[26] The cumulative historical emissions of a particular country are significant because of the long life of CO_2. A widely-accepted policy proposal at present is a price on carbon, which raises the price on coal-fired electricity compared to solar, wind, hydro, or nuclear power, reducing demand for carbon-emitting products, reducing profits of fossil fuel producers, and incentivizing reduced consumption. While consumers would pay higher prices for fossil-fuel based electricity or home heating, the revenues gained by pricing carbon can be returned to the public through a dividend or by reducing payroll taxes. In contrast to subsidies, which are financed by the public, pricing carbon creates lower costs for those who purchase non-carbon emitting products and increases profits of those who produce them. Nor do carbon prices identify favorites among emerging technologies.[27]

A carbon price eliminates uncertainty, creates a level playing field as it applies across the board, and avoids the question of whether too many permits in too few sectors are issued. Carbon prices incentivize sustainable behavior and disincentivize polluting behavior. One policy suggests a revenue-neutral upstream carbon tax, which returns money through tax reductions to corporations and individuals. This option reduces the corporate tax rate, reduces individual taxes, and compensates individuals for energy costs. Other policies advocate returning a dividend to consumers alone. However structured, the price must be high enough to drive down CO_2 emissions.[28] Historically, policies that

---

[25] Patrick Doherty, "A New U.S. Grand Strategy," *Foreign Policy* (January 9, 2013), http://foreignpolicy.com. According to Doherty, "For the United States, a grand strategy is a generation's plan to create the global conditions necessary for the country to pursue the great purposes set forth in the preamble of the U.S. Constitution."

[26] See the German Advisory Council on Global Change, "The WBGU Budget Approach" (2009), 3, www.wbgu.de/en/factsheets/factsheet-3/.

[27] Michael J Graetz, "Energy Policy: Past or Prologue?" *Daedalus: the Journal of the American Academy of Arts & Sciences* 141, no. 2 (2012): 37.

[28] George Frampton, Partnership for Responsible Growth, argues that returning carbon revenues to corporations and individuals increases GDP, growth, jobs, competition, and avoids new spending by government. See www.partnershipforresponsible

kept oil and gas prices artificially low "not only decreased incentives to conserve energy but also diminished the prospects for successfully developing and marketing alternative energy sources."[29]

The Principles of Protecting Life and Solidarity
Climate change is a tremendous threat to life, health, and wellbeing that affects Americans and our neighbors around the globe, necessitating a transformation to a low-carbon economy. Catholic teaching affirms that climate change is a life issue. Yet solidarity also requires that developing nations that have minimal access to fossil fuels—yet still emit dangerous short-lived climate pollutants—are able to climb out of energy poverty.[30] Globally, the poorest billion depend on solid biomass or solid coal for their basic energy needs of lighting, cooking and home heating.[31]

Clean energy for cooking and lighting for the "bottom" three billion people is currently available in advanced cook stoves and solar lighting.[32] What is necessary is continued small-scale innovation, attention to political-economic realities, and technology transfer and access based on principles of justice and the preferential option for the poor. Micro-grid and off-grid solar power for accessing drinking water and irrigation water will reduce CO_2 and black carbon emissions from diesel generators. These technologies also empower women and contribute to positive economic growth through education and microfinance, since the new technologies save each woman or girl about one to five hours of lost time collecting firewood.[33]

---

growth.org/team/. Eduardo Porter, "Climate Deal Badly Needs a Big Stick," *New York Times,* June 2, 2105.
[29] Graetz, "Energy Policy: Past or Prologue?" 39.
[30] The Kevin Anderson and Alice Bows carbon budget notes that some greenhouse gases (i.e. methane and nitrous oxide) cannot be reduced to zero because of their necessary role in feeding a growing population. See Kevin Anderson and Alice Bows, "Beyond Dangerous Climate Change," *Philosophical Transactions of the Royal Society* 369, no.1934 (January 2011): 31.
[31] Veerabhadran Ramanathan, "The Two Worlds Approach for Mitigating Air Pollution and Climate Change," in *Pontifical Academies Workshop: Sustainable Humanity, Sustainable Nature, Our Responsibility* (Vatican City, 2014), 2. For some in the highest 1.1 billion of the top four billion, this may mean reductions from as much as 50 tons/year.
[32] Ramanathan, "The Two Worlds Approach for Mitigating Air Pollution and Climate Change," 12. Ramanathan proposes a voluntary carbon market by which the top 1.1 billion earn credits in a carbon market by paying about $22 per person to purchase these clean technologies.
[33] Nicholas D. Kristof and Sheryl WuDunn, *Half the Sky: Turning Oppression into Opportunity for Women Worldwide* (New York: Vintage, 2010).

Action Items
The principle of subsidiarity requires that institutions and agents act at the most local level of society, then at incrementally higher levels, and petition for action at increasingly higher levels of governance to minimize the use of fossil fuels and mitigate their effects. Moreover, living out an energy ethics invites us to recognize ourselves as Catholics who are working for justice in our communities, in solidarity with people everywhere, for and with the poor who are most adversely affected by human-forced climate change, now and in the future. We must also recognize ourselves as working in solidarity with other species, their habitats, and our shared ecosystems toward a planetary solidarity.[34]

All educated residents need to understand the full costs of energy and the present and future risks to climate and health. Counterfactual lobbying by science-denying groups and fossil fuel corporations must be exposed and ended. The full and transparent accounting of all costs of energy systems should be made available as a requirement of justice. Transparency means that the price of gas at the pump reflects the worldwide market price of oil, the costs of transporting oil safely worldwide, the costs of coal pollution, and the costs of the impacts of climate change. Policy leaders must also manage the risks of stranded hydrocarbon assets. Local leaders should work to identify effective solutions with input at the local level that support national goals.[35] All should place the common good of the nation and earth above local interests and private luxury if its costs include climate impacts upon more vulnerable neighbors.

Twenty-four percent of the U.S. population identifies as Catholic.[36] This community, its ecclesial governance, and all its leaders can draw on our traditions of moral reasoning to be a significant leader in the visible vanguard of a renewable energy revolution.

ENERGY OF THE PRESENT: BRIDGE FUELS
In 1981, the Bishops rightly pointed out that, "cheap oil and natural gas not only powered the dramatic transformation of Western society in the 20th century, they underlie much of the material progress developing countries have made." The question in 1981—and even more

---

[34] "Vatican official calls for shared responsibility in protecting planet," *Catholic News Service* (September 24, 2014), www.catholicnews.com/data/stories/cns/1403959.htm.
[35] "Fact Sheet: U.S.-China Joint Announcement on Climate Change and Clean Energy Cooperation," The White House Office of the Press Secretary (November 2014), https://www.whitehouse.gov/the-press-office/2014/11/11/fact-sheet-us-china-joint-announcement-climate-change-and-clean-energy-c.
[36] "U.S. Catholics: Key Data from Pew Research." *Pew Research Center* (February 25, 2013), www.pewresearch.org/key-data-points/u-s-catholics-key-data-from-pew-research/#popsize.

prominently today—is: what kind of energy framework will human societies deploy to build the future? This section considers two types of energy currently viewed as "bridge fuels:" shale gas via horizontal hydraulic fracturing and nuclear power.

Natural Gas Extraction via Horizontal Hydraulic Fracturing

Today, the escalating role of natural gas extraction via horizontal hydraulic fracturing is an example of unconventional development, which calls for moral values to clarify thinking about the future of the U.S. energy economy. In particular, the clear values of the precautionary principle, of informed and transparent decision-making, and of the Church's advocacy about fresh water and human health are central considerations.[37]

Geological imaging has indicated that the natural gas and oil shale resources buried beneath the domestic U.S. are quantitatively dramatic, and some commentators predict that the fuel sources could power the entire U.S. for at least another century.[38] Whether shale gas supplies are abundant or will diminish is difficult to predict. According to a geological expert cited in *Bloomberg View*, "Production from shale is not a revolution; it's a retirement party."[39] If shale and gas decline due to the increasing cost of accessing it, as some predict, energy independence will require a more thorough diversification of the nation's energy portfolio.[40] Either way, the use of shale oil and natural gas found within the landmass of the U.S. is viewed by many as a desirable step towards energy sovereignty and global exports, thereby contributing in new ways to the U.S. economy. Energy companies are keen to develop more robust portfolios of fuels and fuel sources, especially with the advanced technologies and permissive regulatory climate which supports widespread fracking only in the U.S. and its northern neighbor, Canada.

---

[37] Christiana Z. Peppard, "Fresh Water and Catholic Social Teaching—A Vital Nexus," *Journal of Catholic Social Thought* 9:2 (2012): 325-51; and Peppard, *Just Water* (Maryknoll: Orbis Books, 2014), 36-67.

[38] Tom Zeller Jr., "Is the U.S. Shale Boom Going Bust?" *Bloomberg View* (August 22, 2014), www.bloombergview.com/articles/2014-04-22/is-the-u-s-shale-boom-going-bust.

[39] The average decline of the world's conventional oil fields is about 5 percent per year. By comparison, the average decline of oil wells in North Dakota's booming Bakken shale oil field is 44 percent per year. Individual wells can see production declines of 70 percent or more in the first year. Shale gas wells face similarly swift depletion rates, so drillers need to keep plumbing new wells to make up for the shortfall (Zeller, "Is the U.S. Shale Boom Going Bust?").

[40] John H. Cushman, Jr., "As Oil Prices Erode, Tar Sands Become Riskier Investments," *Inside Climate News* (November 5, 2014), http://insideclimatenews.org/news/20141105/oil-prices-erode-tar-sands-become-riskier-investments.

While it is valuable to pursue the goal of energy sovereignty, any responsible conversation about fracking must ask: What scientific data do we have about fracking and its effects? What do we lack, why do we lack it, and what do we need to be sufficiently informed? At present, U.S. discourse on this extractive technology does not sufficiently meet the criteria of honest conversation. The permissive regulatory culture centers on a 2005 amendment to the National Energy Act—known colloquially as the "Halliburton Loophole"— that explicitly excluded fracking solutions from regulation, by the Environmental Protection Agency, by rendering the chemical contents of those solutions as "trade" secrets. This amendment has profoundly limited the regulatory and even investigative powers of the EPA and other entities into the downstream, potential long-term effects of whatever chemicals are used in fracking solutions. For environmental and public health reasons, it is important to know what is in fracking solutions, but by and large this information is unavailable.[41] What is known is that between 2005 and 2009—that is, the first four years following the Halliburton Loophole—gas companies actively used over 2500 different fracking solutions, 650 of which included "29 chemicals that are (1) known or possible human carcinogens, (2) regulated under Safe Drinking Water Act for their risks to human health, or (3) listed as hazardous pollutants under the Clean Air Act."[42]

Transparency: Full and Honest Disclosure

Chemicals used in fracking operations, the exact sites of usage, short and long-term toxicological and environmental effects, and the current limitations of our knowledge all need to be part of transparent, public conversation. This information needs to be available far enough in advance for the public to engage in meaningful research and reflection, and thereby to make decisions that reflect standards of informed consent.[43] Chapter 10 of the *Compendium of the Social Doctrine of the Church* clearly states: "In the realm of technological-scientific interventions that have forceful and widespread impact on living organisms,

---

[41] The registry, FracFocus (fracfocus.org), is largely voluntary or mandated on a state-by-state basis and cannot be searched in terms of chemical components of the fracking solution.

[42] United States House of Representatives Committee on Energy and Commerce, Minority Staff, "Chemicals Used in Hydraulic Fracturing," (April 2011), http://democrats.energycommerce.house.gov/sites/default/files/documents/Hydraulic-Fracturing-Chemicals-2011-4-18.pdf.

[43] An excellent legal overview is available from David Allen Himes, "The 'Halliburton Loophole': Exemption of Hydraulic Fracturing Fluids from Regulation Under the Federal Safe Drinking Water Act" (March 8, 2012), http://energy.wilkes.edu/PDF-Files/Laws%20and%20Regulations/Halliburton%20Loophole%20Essay%20Final.pdf.

with the possibility of significant long-term repercussions, it is unacceptable to act lightly or irresponsibly."[44] The document also notes that "politicians, legislators and public administrators" must encourage—fairly and without special interest lobbying—"a correctly informed public opinion and make decisions that are best suited to the common good," and not merely for the profit of corporations.[45] Several practical implications follow. Insofar as the lack of scientific evidence is the result of the Halliburton Loophole, that loophole must be eliminated. Ongoing disclosure and stringent regulation of fracking chemicals at federal and state levels must follow. Until more is known definitively about the downstream effects of fracking, the precautionary principle holds that operations should desist. Only by looking at the big picture of value—not just short-term, shareholder-focused economic value—are we likely to achieve the human and ecological well-being that undergird any meaningful, long-term economic growth and independent, sustainable, energy future.

> Natural gas will continue to play a major role in the global economy, with potentially grave risks to the climate and environment, unless society acts to make it transitional by building renewable infrastructure. Natural gas can be a bridge to a clean, prosperous, and healthy economy if directed towards the right ends, and not viewed as an end in itself. Policy leaders must establish correct incentives with monitored timelines to ensure that transition.

Nuclear Energy

In "Reflections on the Energy Crisis," the Bishops questioned whether the United States should continue to rely upon nuclear fission to generate electricity. Approximately 12% of the electricity used in the United States in 1981 was generated by nuclear fission, whereas nuclear reactors generate 20% of the electricity used in the United

[44] Pontifical Council for Justice and Peace, *Compendium of the Social Doctrine of the Church* (June 29, 2004), no. 473, www.vatican.va/roman_curia/pontifical_ councils/justpeace/documents/rc_pc_justpeace_doc_20060526_compendio-dott-soc_en.html.

[45] Pontifical Council for Justice and Peace, *Compendium*, no. 479. See also Robert Gronski, National Catholic Rural Life Conference, "Fracking: Injecting Ethics into the Process," www.ncrlc.com/news.aspx?ID=348. Bishop Paul D'Etienne of Wyoming has said that "the public needs more information than is currently being provided about the chemicals in this mix that is currently being injected into the earth." See the series by Dennis Sadowski in the *National Catholic Reporter,* "Catholic Voices Raise Moral Concerns in the Country's Fracking Debates," (January 2014) http://ncronline.org/blogs/eco-catholic/catholic-voices-raise-moral-concerns-countrys-fracking-debates.

States in 2014.[46] The Bishops' 1981 document raised many important questions about nuclear fission as a source of energy, several of which persist as particularly problematic.

Highly Radioactive Waste
   The key moral problem with nuclear generated electricity is the accumulation of highly radioactive spent fuel at nuclear power plants throughout the United States because a system for isolating the used fuel from the biosphere has not been provided throughout the 60 years that nuclear plants have been generating electricity. In the absence of long-term disposal, most of the pools into which the used fuel is stored have been retrofitted to accommodate more densely packed spent fuel assemblies, while others have been placed in dry casks on concrete slabs where they continue to dissipate heat into the air. Federal officials have tried to identify a method for isolating the spent fuel for the long term, settled theoretically on a geological formation for a repository, and sought to site one that would prevent entry of the radiation into the biosphere.[47] However, the burial of the spent nuclear fuel is fraught with difficulties that range from geological to ethical considerations. Before any more nuclear generating plants are constructed, a system for isolating highly radioactive used fuel must be functioning and capable of accepting all the used fuel that has been accumulating at existing facilities as well as the used fuel to be yielded by new facilities. The development and implementation of this requisite system must be accomplished in ways that protect the integrity of local communities and ecosystems now and into the future.

Safety Concerns
   Also problematic today are safety concerns about nuclear leakage, spills, and explosions. The bishops raised these considerations even before the accidents at Chernobyl, Ukraine (1986) and at Fukushima, Japan (2011). Beyond the possibility of sudden catastrophes, the effects of low-level radiation on the health of uranium miners and others

---

[46] Frank Rusco, Director, Natural Resources and Environment, U.S. General Accounting Office, "Commercial Spent Nuclear Fuel: Observations on the Key Attributes and Challenges of Storage and Disposal Options," Testimony before the Subcommittee on Energy and Water Development and Related Agencies, Committee on Appropriations, House of Representatives (April 2013), GAO-13-532T, p. 7. A one million year period was specified for disposition in the now-cancelled repository in Yucca Mountain in Nevada; see U.S. EPA, "Fact Sheet: Public Health and Environmental Radiation Protection Standards for Yucca Mountain, Nevada, Final Rule (40 CFR Part 197), Final Rule," www.epa.gov/radiation/yucca/2008factsheet.html#ts.
[47]U.S. General Accounting Office, *Commercial Nuclear Waste: Effects of a Termination of the Yucca Mountain Repository Program and Lessons Learned*, GAO-11-229 (April 2011), www.gao.gov/assets/320/317627.pdf.

exposed to this element also correlate with increased rates of lung cancer and diseases in uranium miners and negative effects on DNA.[48] Finally, the increased proliferation of nuclear weapons from the five nations noted by the bishops in 1981(among the United States, France, China, the United Kingdom, and the Russian Federation) looms large in the present day, including in highly volatile areas of the world (India, Pakistan, North Korea, and Israel).[49]

MAKING THE TRANSITION:
"BRIDGING" TO A MAXIMALLY SUSTAINABLE ENERGY SYSTEM
The Carbon Savings of Natural Gas?

While natural gas is often touted as being a "cleaner" energy source than traditional fossil fuels like coal, some scientific studies show that methane emissions from leaking gas wells counteract those benefits and may in fact amplify short-term global carbon concentrations.[50] Unless such concerns are addressed, natural gas, which appears to be a "bridge" forward, may instead amount to business as usual.[51] And while the shale gas boom has had a modest impact on emissions relative to the cuts needed to address climate change, some commentators suggest that perhaps "the greatest impact of shale gas may turn out to

[48] U.S. Center for Disease Control and Prevention, "Worker Health Study Summaries: Research on long-term exposure: Uranium Miners," www.cdc.gov/niosh/pgms/worknotify/uranium.html; U.S. Environmental Protection Agency, "Radiation Protection: Health Effects," www.epa.gov/radiation/understand/health_effects.html.

[49] Stockholm International Peace Research Institute, "World Nuclear Sources," www.sipri.org/yearbook/2013/06 (accessed March 28, 2014); Julian Borger, "The truth about Israel's secret nuclear arsenal," *The Guardian* (January 15, 2014), www.theguardian.com/world/2014/jan/15/truth-israels-secret-nuclear-arsenal; and, International Atomic Energy Agency, "IAEA and Iran," www.iaea.org/newscenter/focus/iaeairan/index.shtml.

[50] Eric D. Larson, "Natural Gas & Climate Change" (Princeton: Climate Central, 2013), http://assets.climatecentral.org/pdfs/NaturalGas-and-ClimateChange.pdf. Another study from the National Center for Atmospheric Research concluded that unless leaks can be kept below 2 percent, gas lacks any climate advantage over coal. See Tom M.L. Wigley, "Coal to Gas: The Influence of Methane Leakage," *Climatic Change* 108, no. 3 (2011).
A 2013 study by Climate Central, a group of scientists and journalists studying climate change, concluded that the 50 percent climate advantage of natural gas over coal is unlikely to be achieved over the next three to four decades.

[51] Anthony R. Ingraffea, "Gangplank to a Warm Future," *New York Times* (July 28, 2013), www.nytimes.com/2013/07/29/opinion/gangplank-to-a-warm-future.html?_r-=0.

be changing the political economy of introducing strong climate policy, making it easier for the Obama administration, for example, to propose regulations to reduce power plant emissions."[52]

The Carbon Savings of Nuclear Energy?

Nuclear energy has been vaunted as a low-carbon energy solution,[53] which is desirable in the context of climate change since carbon-free energy solutions are essential to keep emissions below 450 ppm and global temperature increase below 2 degrees C. Because the IPCC predicts that under a business-as-usual scenario, the atmosphere will reach 450 ppm by 2030, nuclear power seems attractive from a carbon perspective. Yet given global historical trends in construction delays and costs, it is very unlikely that nuclear power can be brought to adequate scale by the IPCC's target date of 2030.[54] As Cornell engineering professor and former gas industry consultant Anthony Ingraffea warns, "unfortunately, we don't have that long to address climate change—the next two decades are crucial."[55] In addition, there are dynamics internal to energy economies that shape the pace of development: U.S. Energy Secretary Ernest Moniz has opined that not Fukushima but shale gas has put the brakes on a U.S. nuclear renaissance.[56]

Though some new nuclear technologies appear promising because they are anticipated as more cost-effective and safer than previous generations of infrastructure, these remain largely in concept or pilot

---

[52] Jason Bordoff, "Why the Shale Revolution is More Boon than Bane," *Financial Times* (June 8, 2014), www.ft.com/cms/s/0/fcea14a2-e66d-11e3-bbf5-00144feabdc-0.html#axzz3bHj54Z2N.

[53] James Hansen, *Storms of My Grandchildren* (New York: Bloomsbury, 2009), 194.

[54] The Keystone Report, a fact-finding report written jointly by nuclear industry and environmental leaders, states that maintaining the low-carbon benefits of international plants, many of which are scheduled to retire, requires an aggressive reactor building program. To build enough nuclear capacity to meet the carbon reductions of a Pacala/Socolow wedge, which is 1 GtC/year or 700 net GWe nuclear power, a rapid period of growth is needed that matches the industry's most rapid historical period of growth (1981-1990), and then maintains this growth for 50 years. See Robert Socolow and Stephen Pacala, "Stabilization Wedges: Solving the Climate Problem for the Next 50 Years with Current Technologies," *Science* 305 (August 13, 2004): 968-72. The Keystone Report assesses this projected rate of growth to be more optimistic than proposed plant construction validates, or that is forecast by the Energy Information Administration. Notable emissions result from mining activities, fuel fabrication (if not based on centrifuge enrichment), the transportation of fuel, materials and waste: see Sustainable Development Commission, "The Role of Nuclear Power in a Low Carbon Economy" (May 3, 2006), 19.

[55] Ingraffea, "Gangplank to a Warm Future."

[56] "Special Report—Nuclear Energy: The Dream That Failed," *The Economist* (March 10, 2012), www.economist.com/sites/default/files/20120310_nuclear_power.pdf.

stages and unready to serve in immediate strategies to reduce CO_2 by 2030.[57] Private financiers and private industry continue to invest in the research and development of advanced, fourth-generation, small modular reactors.[58] This is an appropriate role for private industry. However, public funding of costly and unproven technologies warrants high levels of transparency and public scrutiny, lest the public adopt the costs of stalled investments.[59]

Nuclear power plants that are currently generating electricity can serve as a limited bridge to a more efficient and renewable energy future. However, intergenerational justice requires that additional conventional nuclear capacity be restricted until an operating system is in place for isolating the highly radioactive used fuel that has been accumulating for sixty years. Given global historical trends in construction delays and costs, it is very unlikely that nuclear power can be brought to adequate scale by the IPCC's target date of 2030.

Even *The Economist* is skeptical about the potential for the development of a large market for small, rapidly mass-produced reactors theoretically free of construction delays, as such a market for competition does not exist.[60] Finally, it is feasible that massive government investments in nuclear power may compete in deleterious ways with development of cleaner, renewable technologies. Especially if undertaken in the public sector, the massive sunk costs of multi-year investments in nuclear plants may lock out investments from decentralized technologies that already show significant advances, and divert funding from renewable technologies.[61] Cognizant of some of these trends, *The Economist* concludes that "in a low-emissions world, the role for nuclear will be limited to whatever level of electricity demand remains when renewables are deployed as far as possible."[62] Indeed, scientists urge rapidly deploying the many renewable wind, water, solar, and energy-efficiency technology options available now.

---

[57] Six technologies were selected in 2003 by the Generation IV International Forum as representing the future of nuclear energy. They may be ready by 2030. "Current and Future Generation Fast Neutron Reactors," www.world-nuclear.org/info/Current-and-Future-Generation/Fast-Neutron-Reactors/.

[58] Stewart Magruder, Division of Advanced Reactors and Rulemaking Projects Branch, Office of New Reactors, "Status of SMR Reviews and Issues in the United States" (United States Nuclear Regulatory Commission, 2012), www.uxc.com/smr/Library%5CLicensing/2012%20-%20Status%20of%20SMR%-20Reviews%20and%20Issues%20in%20the%20US.pdf.

[59] Bruce Henderson, "Protesters Target Duke Energy Meeting" (May 6, 2011), www.newsobserver.com/2011/05/06/1178675/protesters-target-utility-meeting.html.

[60] "Special Report—Nuclear Energy," *The Economist,* 16.

[61] Sustainable Development Commission, "The Role of Nuclear Power," 13.

[62] "Special Report—Nuclear Energy," 17.

The Principles of Participation and Prudence

In reference to both hydraulic fracturing and nuclear fission (as well as many other emerging types of energy generation), participation requires transparency, full cost accounting, and implementation of the "polluter pays" principle. Markets for energy should be shaped so that both producers and consumers pay the full cost of the energy they produce and use, thus incentivizing cleaner energy and conservation, but this must be done in ways that allow for a just distribution of energy resources. People living in poverty should not bear disproportionate burdens of increased energy costs.

For both fracking and nuclear technologies, problematic byproducts pose real toxicological threats. Natural gas and nuclear energy may provide bridges to a renewable energy future if, and only if, the virtues of prudence and justice are engaged by the U.S. to counter the imprudence and intergenerational injustice that has thus far prevailed. Environmental historians and contemporary demographers demonstrate that people living in poverty bear the biggest burden of environmental changes related to fossil fuel extraction, and negative externalities are unlikely to be shared evenly. With regard to natural gas extraction as well as nuclear fission, these "bridge fuels" must be built wisely and with attention to the ultimate destination of renewable, minimally-polluting energy sources and infrastructures that facilitate human and ecosystem flourishing.

Action Items

The precautionary principle enacts an appropriate concern about the integrity of water sources and human health, placing the pursuit of profit and economic growth as a secondary consideration. Citizens and policy makers must insist upon transparency regarding toxicological risks and other environmental, economic, and carbon-related externalities. The practical and prudent course is to deploy all renewable technologies as rapidly as possible, without waiting for a technological silver bullet, and to support distributed energy production in the developing world.[63]

---

[63] Joe Romm, "Socolow Re-Reaffirms 2004 'Wedges' Paper, Urges 'Monumental' Levels of Clean Energy Deployment ASAP," *Climate Progress* (September 11, 2011), http://thinkprogress.org/climate/2011/09/30/333435/socolow-wedges-clean-energy-deployment/; see also Jeff Spross, "How Renewables in Developing Countries Are Leapfrogging Traditional Power," *Climate Progress* (November 4, 2014), http://thinkprogress.org/climate/2014/11/04/3588512/bnef-renewables-developing-countries/.

ENERGY OF THE FUTURE: RENEWABLES
  The economic and technological capabilities of renewable energy have improved significantly since 1981. From an ecological standpoint, renewable energy is the most sustainable because it is generally cleaner than fossil fuels or nuclear energy, and some forms of renewable energy (especially wind and solar) are potentially inexhaustible. As the Bishops decreed in 1981, renewable energy "possesses key advantages over the rest of the field." Certainly in the past, as in the present and future, technological and economic limitations have been barriers to the full implementation of renewable energies; yet in many instances, renewable energy is now approaching cost-parity, and significant policy resources exist to incentivize developments of renewable energy technologies on multiple scales.[64]

Renewable Energy and Questions of Scale
  Simply put, renewable energy is needed at an enormous scale if carbon emissions are to be minimized by 2030 and the most dramatic temperature-related effects are to be avoided. (According to a national defense advisor, it is necessary to start thinking about "Plan B" if we do not make the transition at some speed.[65]) Scientists have suggested a range of models for energy generation that indicate scenarios in which coal, gas, oil, biomass, solar, wind, and nuclear energy might be used—and in what proportions—for power generation by 2100. By comparing multiple models, one study reaches well-grounded conclusions about the profile of energy use needed in 2100 to remain below a 2°C temperature increase.[66] They argue

> Renewable energy must comprise 50-75% of the global energy mix in order to have a 70% chance of remaining below a 2-degree Celsius temperature increase. The clean energy systems of the future can be created by investments that bring currently available technology to the necessary scale of deployment. This will require a revolution in the political and economic valuation of fossil fuels as well as concentrated civic and international effort to achieve transitions to renewable energy sources. Renewable energy sources are not perfect, but they represent the most ethical direction for global action on "what powers us" in the present and future.

---

[64] Diane Cardwell, "Solar and Wind Energy Start to Win on Price vs. Conventional Fuels," *New York Times* (November 3, 2014), www.nytimes.com/2014/11/ 24/business/energy-environment/solar-and-wind-energy-start-to-win-on-price-vs-conventional-fuels.html?_r=0.
[65] Rear Admiral David Titley (ret.), personal communication (July 29, 2014).
[66] B.C.C. van der Zwaan, H. Rösler, T. Kober, T. Aboumahboub, K.V. Calvin, D.E.H.J. Gernaat, G. Marangoni, D.L. McCollum, "A Cross-Model Comparison of

that if the planet is to have a 70% chance of remaining below a 2°C temperature increase by 2100, then by 2100 the global energy supply must use 50%-75% renewable energy. This is a significant shift from current practice: for example, in the United States in April 2014, renewable energy provided about 10 % of total energy produced.[67] Haste in moving toward renewable energy is essential—yet reform in energy sectors is blocked at various levels of governance and confounded by lobbying and corporate action.

Thus deploying existing technologies is only part of the problem; a considerable aspect of U.S. recalcitrance in moving towards renewable energy sources has to do with political economy, existing infrastructure and management of utilities, and an entrenched fossil fuel lobby in the United States. These social, economic, and political realities represent resistance from an energy regime whose growth is decelerating relative to renewable energies.[68] According to a 2013 U.S. Department of Energy report, four technology revolutions have occurred in the last five years, namely: onshore wind power, a variety of new polysilicon photovoltaic modules for solar power generation, LED lighting, and electric vehicles.[69] These advances have been accompanied by "dramatic reductions in cost" and surges in consumer, industrial, and commercial deployment. Although these four technologies still represent a small percentage of their total markets (e.g. electricity, cars, and lighting), they are growing rapidly. Hydropower has also been put forward as a renewable energy source, as have emerging sources such as biofuels. Though treatment of these sources is beyond the scope of this paper, it is important to note that there are significant sustainability and resource-use concerns about both hydropower and biofuels.[70]

Global Long-Term Technology Diffusion under a 2'C Climate Change Control Target," *Climate Change Economics* 4, no. 4 (November 2013).

[67] U.S. Energy Information Administration, "Monthly Energy Review" (November 2014), www.eia.gov/totalenergy/data/monthly/pdf/mer.pdf.

[68] Tom Randall, "Fossil Fuels Just Lost the Race Against Renewables," *Bloomberg Business* (April 14, 2015), www.bloomberg.com/news/articles/2015-04-14/fossil-fuels-just-lost-the-race-against-renewables. Randall holds that: "The race for renewable energy has passed a turning point …And there's no going back."

[69] Levi Tillemann, "Revolution Now: The Future Arrives for Four Clean Energy Technologies," (U.S. Department of Energy, 2013), http://energy.gov/sites/prod/files/2013/09/f2/200130917-revolution-now.pdf.

[70] Christiana Z. Peppard, *Just Water*, 115-41; and Diane Cardwell, "Cleveland Indians Have Home-Field Advantage on Recycling," *New York Times* (May 1, 2015), www.nytimes.com/2015/05/02/business/energy-environment/cleveland-indians-have-home-field-advantage-on-recycling.html.

Wind and Solar
   Use of wind energy is growing at an approximate rate of 25% annually. The Department of Energy estimates that 10-20% of projected U.S. electricity demand could be met by wind power by 2030. Deployed wind power has the equivalent generation capacity of about sixty large nuclear reactors, and it accounted for more new electrical generation capacity than any other source in 2012. Advances in both technology and management/distribution structures are needed to address intermittencies and the disincentives limiting municipal or regional utilities' shifts to clean power. Yet wind has great promise: "Wind is the first non-hydro renewable energy source to begin to approach the same scale as conventional energy forms like coal, gas, and nuclear."[71]
   Solar photovoltaic technology is rapidly approaching cost parity with traditional electrical generation in many parts of the world and the U.S. Through these cost reductions and technological revolutions, formerly real barriers of renewable energy's cost are becoming merely perceived barriers. Here, too, electricity storage and intermittencies are present challenges (though battery technology is rapidly improving), as is the challenge of lost income for utility companies under conditions of distributed electricity generation. In addition, while solar and wind "burn" more cleanly than fossil fuel sources, the mechanisms and infrastructure for transmission and storage require mining of finite, rare earth materials. Truly renewable energy sources will need to account for the full costs of such technologies beyond the solution of the carbon problem.

Powering Vehicles and Improving Energy Efficiency
   Clean vehicles are essential since vehicles create 28% of greenhouse gases.[72] A clean vehicle transition thus has a non-trivial effect. To support wider use of electric cars, a more robust electrical grid and network of EV charging stations will be needed, which are already visible on some highways.[73] Lower-carbon synfuels provide cleaner transportation options as well, though biofuels involve their own sets of complications, as does compressed or liquid natural gas. Public

---

[71] Office of Energy Efficiency and Renewable Energy, "Revolution Now: The Future Arrives for Four Clean Energy Technologies," (U.S. Department of Energy, 2014), http://energy.gov/eere/downloads/revolution-now-future-arrives-four-clean-energy-technologies-2014-update.

[72] U.S. Environmental Protection Agency, "Sources of Greenhouse Gas Emissions," www.epa.gov/climatechange/ghgemissions/sources.html

[73] Julie Wernau, "Electric vehicle charging stations ready to roll after long delay," *Chicago Tribune* (November 14, 2014), www.chicagotribune.com/business/ct-charging-stations-1115-biz-20141114-story.html.

transportation should be expanded and developed in alignment with standards of renewability and sustainability.

Energy efficiency is also an important area of growth and innovation. Energy experts consider improved energy efficiencies to be equivalent to a new source of energy since they decrease the amount of fuels required. A major example is improvements in new and existing buildings, which create a significant proportion of greenhouse gases. Sustainable developers are working toward zero-emission or even negative-emission buildings, while polls show that many U.S. residents increasingly choose walkable communities over long commutes for life satisfaction.[74]

The Necessity of Policy Support

A 2013 Department of Energy report notes the critical role of government support to create energy options for the future, citing how "the U.S. federal government's production incentives for shale gas and support for new drilling technologies laid the foundation for that industry's dramatic rise" between 1980 and 2002. In the same way, "well-designed federal and state incentives and investments in research and development have the potential to stimulate significant energy transformations."[75] Surveys indicate considerable public support for these government initiatives.[76]

Access to Affordable Energy

"Energy poverty" is a reality, even in the United States; it means that a household spends 10% of its income on energy. Households enduring extreme energy poverty spend 20% or more of their income on energy. In 1981, the Bishops emphasized that "given the inequalities that pervade American society, fairness may also require active assistance to those whose voice is rarely heard in policy discussions." In current political debates, the option for the poor is referred to in terms of the "Matthew 25 criteria" that budgetary

> Catholic social teaching strongly endorses the goals of creating affordable, clean, secure energy and supporting working families and low-income households. Energy costs must be accessible and allocated fairly in light of the needs of the materially poor and the development of economies globally.

---

[74] Charles Montgomery, *Happy City: Transforming Our Lives Through Urban Design* (NY: Farrar, Straus and Giroux, 2013).

[75] Tillemann, "Revolution Now," 4.

[76] Yale Project on Climate Change Communication, "Politics and Global Warming" (Spring 2014), http://environment.yale.edu/climate-communication/article/politics-and-global-warming-spring-2014/.

decisions should be evaluated upon the basis of how they affect persons in or near poverty.

From a civic and moral perspective, affordable energy is essential for lower-income households. Households making less than \$60,000 a year spend a higher percentage of their income on home heating and transportation, and have less capital available to invest in efficiency or new technologies; these households often change their food buying habits due to higher energy prices.[77] Initiatives including vouchers, guaranteed loans, and other incentives empower consumers to purchase energy-efficient cars, appliances, and home renovations. Such initiatives have reduced families' energy bills by more than 20%, reduced demand on the power grid, and created jobs.[78] Faith communities can play a vital role by advocating for efficiency programs and enrolling low income households in them.[79]

Conservation can be as valuable as efficiency, but concern for high profit margins frequently obstructs energy-conservation measures.[80] Positively, utilities that provide periodic reports to homeowners comparing their usage to other regional users encourage energy conservation.[81]

MAKING THE TRANSITION:
MOVING TOWARD NECESSARY DEPLOYMENTS

A low-carbon world requires both disinvestments in fossil energy infrastructure, and increased investments in solar and wind power. Estimates suggest that global society needs to invest \$800 billion annually to avoid widespread, intense climate disruption. The United States has an investment gap of \$110 billion annually.[82] Delay will only increase the cost. "We cannot afford to lose another decade," says Ottmar Edenhofer, a German economist and IPCC report co-chair. "If

---

[77] Lisa Margonelli, "Practical Pieces of the Energy Puzzle: Energy Security for American Families," *Issues in Science and Technology* 15, no. 2 (Winter 2009).

[78] Margonelli, "Practical Pieces of the Energy Puzzle."

[79] Rev. Fletcher Harper, GreenFaith, personal communication (August 6, 2014).

[80] Education and incentives for sustainable renovations are also needed to support contractors' knowledge of sustainable building with standards, licensing and testing.

[81] William Rauckhorst, personal communication (July 21, 2014). Center for Research on Environmental Decisions, "The Psychology of Climate Change Communication: A Guide for Scientists, Journalists, Educators, Political Aides, and the Interested Public" (2009), https://coast.noaa.gov/digitalcoast/_/pdf/CRED_Psychology_Climate_ Change_Communication.pdf.

[82] See also Mark Fulton and Reid Capalino, "Investing in the Clean Trillion: Closing the Clean Energy Investment Gap," *Ceres* (2014), www.ceres.org/resources/reports/investing-in-the-clean-trillion-closing-the-clean-energy-investment-gap/view.

we lose another decade, it becomes extremely costly to achieve climate stabilization."[83]

While $800 billion for investment in renewables is a very large figure, it is put into context by comparison with current subsidies for fossil fuels. The International Monetary Fund and International Energy Agency report that direct subsidies for fossil energy and fossil electricity totaled at least $480 billion in 2011—six times the subsidies for renewables in 2011.[84] The latest IEA reports show that subsidies in 2014 amounted to $550 billion.[85] This is a large pool of funds whose better use in renewable energy investment must be evaluated. Super-developed nations like the United States must step into leadership roles in advocating for a shift away from fossil fuel subsidies and towards renewable energy subsidies. "Business, investors, activists, and scientists alone cannot change the way we produce and use energy.... Public policies that create markets, remove barriers, level the playing field, and establish clear objectives and targets for renewable energy and energy efficiency help shape the future."[86]

Consider, too, that the costs of shifting to renewable energy globally have been assessed at between 2-6% of GDP. By comparison, the Apollo project cost 4% of GDP. Digging London's sewer system after its third deadly cholera outbreak in 1864 took 2% of GDP. The justification for investing in a sustainable planet is equally valid, and from the point of view of Catholic moral teaching, an essential response in justice and stewardship.[87]

Moreover, these are technologically feasible transitions with energy-positive outcomes for many generations: "The world is tapping only a small amount of the vast supply of renewable energy resources

---

[83] Justin Gillis, "Climate Efforts Falling Short, U.N. Panel Says," *New York Times* (April 13, 2014), www.nytimes.com/2014/04/14/science/earth/un-climate-panel-warns-speedier-action-is-needed-to-avert-disaster.html.

[84] David McCollum et al., "Energy Investments Under Climate Policy: A Comparison of Global Models," *Climate Change Economics*, LIMITS Special Issue (2014), 20. Ben Sills, "Fossil Fuel Subsidies Six Times More Than Renewable Energy," *Bloomberg News* (November 9, 2011), www.bloomberg.com/news/articles/2011-11-09/fossil-fuels-got-more-aid-than-clean-energy-iea.

[85] Tim Worstall, "As the IEA Says, the $550 Billion a Year Subsidy to Fossil Fuels Restricts Renewables," *Forbes* (2014), www.forbes.com/sites/timworstall/2014/11/12/as-the-iea-says-the-550-billion-a-year-subsidy-to-fossil-fuels-restricts-re-newables/; Ambrus Bárány and Dalia Grigonytė, "ECFIN Economic Brief: Measuring Fossil Fuel Subsidies," in *Economic Analysis from European Commission's Directorate General for Economic and Financial Affairs* (2015), http://ec.europa.eu/ economy_finance/publications/economic_briefs/2015/pdf/eb40_en.pdf

[86] Mohamed T. El-Ashry, "National Policies to Promote Renewable Energy," *Daedalus: The Journal of the American Academy of Arts & Sciences* 141, no. 2 (2012): 110.

[87] Mogens B. Mogensen, "Closing the Carbon Cycle with Air Capture," Annual Conference, Lenfest Center for Sustainable Energy (Columbia University, April 2014).

worldwide, with the technical potential of renewable energy several times greater than global energy demand."[88] If properly incentivized and developed, renewable energy could provide up to 77% of global energy needs by 2050.[89] Studies increasingly demonstrate that barriers are not technological, nor even always economic, but are significantly socio-political.[90]

Insofar as "one of the biggest hurdles to overcome on the path to energy system transformation and the 2°C target will be to mobilize the necessary investment flows, particularly in light of competing demands for capital within the energy sector," then this hurdle represents an opportunity for moral leadership and moral conscience in Catholic communities.[91]

Developed nations will need to assist the developing nations in their transition to more sustainable technologies. The International Energy Agency confirms that "managing this transition will be more difficult for some countries or power systems than others…. Integration is not simply about adding wind and solar on top of 'business as usual'. We need to transform the system as a whole to do this cost-effectively."[92] Because of varied geography, nations vary in their capacity to produce wind and solar energy, just as they do in their access to oil and natural gas. For these reasons, it has become increasingly necessary for the nations of the European Union to collaborate in linking their energy networks if they are to meet their goals for sustainable energy. Fair technological transfer mechanisms are essential.

The United States should lead by example in developing its own sustainable technologies and assisting developing nations fairly, conscious of its carbon debt and the significant ingenuity and investments of developing nations. Against a paltry U.S. legacy in international climate negotiations, positive steps have begun to emerge. In November 2014, the United States and China announced long-range efforts to achieve deep decarbonization of the global economy. These actions

---

[88] El-Ashry, "National Policies to Promote Renewable Energy," 112.

[89] Working Group III: Mitigation of Climate Change, "Special Report on Renewable Energy Sources and Climate Change Mitigation" (Intergovernmental Panel on Climate Change, 2001), http://srren.ipcc-wg3.de/.

[90] Mark A. Delucchi and Mark Z. Jacobson, "Providing All Global Energy with Wind, Water, and Solar Power, Part I: Technologies, Energy Resources, Quantities and Areas of Infrastructure, and Materials," *Energy Policy* 39, no. 3 (2011).

[91] Delucchi and Jacobson, "Providing All Global Energy with Wind, Water, and Solar Power," 29.

[92] Maria van der Hoeven, "IEA Technology Roadmaps for Solar Electricity" (International Energy Agency, 2014), www.iea.org/newsroomandevents/pressreleases/2014/february/name,47513,en.html#.Uw9u-qnrKq8.twitter.

signify the mutual cost-sharing and commitment needed to create a successful new climate agreement in Paris in 2015.[93]

In future negotiations, the United States must play a leading role in advocating for emissions reductions and the adoption of more sustainable technologies, while also allowing for the integral development of the developing nations. Solidarity calls for assisting the developing nations of the world to achieve the economic growth needed without unduly contributing to climate change. Finally, the U.S. must collaborate with its neighbors to promote the free flow of sustainable energy.

The Principles of Justice and Subsidiarity

In a recent statement on energy from the Pontifical Council for Justice and Peace, Bishop Mario Toso stressed that "in view of the realization of peace—and peace includes several goods—it is necessary that energy be thought of, produced, distributed, and used, according to a new paradigm."[94] This new paradigm calls for assessing social cost in tandem with economic cost. The category of social cost should be further studied and highlighted as an essential component of authentic and honest energy calculations.[95]

Protecting Catholic values of life, human health, dignity, and participation in decision-making requires the full accounting of social costs and strict externality pricing.[96] Communities of color in the United States and many industrializing regions in the global South bear disproportionate impacts of climate change and environmental toxins.[97] Externality pricing is especially essential to accurately and fairly register the impact of climate change upon those most vulnerable. The Bishops acknowledge in their 1981 statement that the energy

---

[93] "Fact Sheet: U.S.-China Joint Announcement on Climate Change and Clean Energy Cooperation," The White House Office of the Press Secretary (November 2014), https://www.whitehouse.gov/the-press-office/2014/11/11/fact-sheet-us-china-joint-announcement-climate-change-and-clean-energy-c.

[94] Andrea Gagliarducci, "Pontifical Council Considers Energy's Relation to Justice, Peace," *Catholic News Agency* (April 13, 2014), www.catholicnewsagency.com/news/pontifical-council-considers-energys-relation-to-justice-peace/. See also Erin Lothes, "A New Paradigm for Catholic Energy Ethics," *Catholic Moral Theology* (January 28, 2015) http://catholicmoraltheology.com/a-new-paradigm-for-catholic-energy-ethics/.

[95] Scott Barrett, "Some Thoughts on Air Capture and Climate Policy," Annual Conference, Lenfest Center for Sustainable Energy (Columbia University, April 2014).

[96] For externality pricing of major energy sources, see U.S. Energy Information Administration, "Levelized Cost of New Generation Resources in the Annual Energy Outlook 2012" (June 2012), www.eia.gov/forecasts/archive/aeo12/.

[97] Robert D. Bullard, Paul Mohai, Robin Saha, and Beverly Wright, "Toxic Wastes and Race at Twenty 1987-2007: Grassroots Struggles to Dismantle Environmental Racism in the United States," (United Church of Christ Justice and Witness Ministries, 2007), www.weact.org/Portals/7/toxic20.pdf.

crisis involves socioeconomic systems and structures that are affected by human sin and finitude. Since then, CST has only amplified these analyses[98] to describe how structural sin has ecological, political and cultural dimensions.[99] Christians seeking to respond actively to this crisis must therefore clear-sightedly analyze ways that structural sin is incentivized within the socioeconomic energy status quo, while also articulating how the structural dimensions of energy connect ethically to the responsibilities of particular persons and communities. U.S. residents are especially called upon to assess the meaning of solidarity in an era of structural sin, particularly with regard to the valuation of profit over human life or ecosystem integrity.[100]

Action Items

Every American makes energy decisions within his or her sphere of influence. Individuals personally and with others should consider how they use energy and how to use it more wisely and appropriately in their residences, workplaces, parishes, neighborhoods —wherever they can make decisions. Such discussions provide significant and transformative local leadership.[101] All can strive to increase the proportion of renewable energy they purchase and increase the energy efficiency of their homes and purchases, as well as choose lower-carbon transportation and local food. To support the right and obligation to make informed and ethical energy decisions, energy suppliers should transparently account for the full social cost of energy, while public leaders and legislators should work to prevent suppression of information.

At their most robust, regional and national policies should also strive to support walkable communities, help low-income consumers purchase renewable energy, expand public transit, support innovation and regional growth, and rebuild the middle class with high-wage,

---

[98] Public understanding of corporations' infrastructures, profit strategies, and interactions with governments is much greater than in 1981, evident in Occupy movements and public discussions of "the 99%."

[99] See John Paul II, *Sollicitudo rei socialis*; Benedict XVI, *Caritas in veritate*; Pope Francis *Evangelii gaudium*. See also Jame Schaefer, "Environmental Degradation, Social Sin, and the Common Good" in *God, Creation, and Climate Change*, ed. Richard W. Miller (Maryknoll: Orbis Books, 2010), 69-94.

[100] The concept of solidarity and an awareness of its good has since 1981 become a much more broadly discussed concept, both within and outside of Catholic social thought. See the historic overview of solidarity in Jame Schaefer, "Solidarity, Subsidiarity, and Preference for the Poor" in *Confronting the Climate Crisis: Catholic Theological Perspectives*, ed. Jame Schaefer (Milwaukee: Marquette University Press, 2011), 389-425.

[101] Erin Lothes Biviano, "Come With Me into the Fields: Inspiring Creation Ministry Among Faith Communities," *New Theology Review* 26, no. 2 (March 2014), http://newtheologyreview.org/index.php/ntr/article/viewFile/998/1359.

skilled jobs, which are produced by the advanced engineering and manufacturing of an economy driven by a revolution in low-carbon productivity. Similar policy revolutions must take root in the agricultural sector as well, given the intersections between industrial agriculture and the fossil fuel economy.[102]

GLOBAL LEADERSHIP

Cooperation over resources and the goal of renewable energy societies and economies can build bonds between nations.[103] As the Bishops stated in 1981, the U.S. is called to "open-hearted cooperation in the effort to develop a global policy to bring about future energy security." More recently, Pope Benedict XVI warned that "the risk for our time is that the de facto interdependence of people and nations is not matched by ethical interaction of consciences and minds that would give rise to truly human development," and—referring specifically to the energy problem—he adds that "there is a pressing moral need for renewed solidarity."[104] Solidarity is, in the famous words of Pope John Paul II, "a firm and persevering determination to commit oneself to the common good; that is to say to the good of all and of each individual, because we are all really responsible for all."[105] U.S. energy policy, foreign policy, and the actions of all citizens should encourage collaborative efforts to face and solve these global challenges.[106] The Catholic Church in the U.S. has a unique capacity to be prophetic in this complex situation, by clearly linking principles and exhortations to solidarity to strategies that help Christians to undertake sustained reformations of energy policy. Such clear moral leadership demands a more piercing analysis of "institutional inertia" and its power over everyday life and a serious dedication to transformative pedagogy and practices at all levels of the church's institutions and among its people. This essay has sought to be one such contribution towards an energy ethic.

---

[102] Doherty, "A New U.S. Grand Strategy." About 56% of Americans are already seeking smaller homes in walkable, convenient, transit-oriented communities in their next housing purchase. See also Fred Kirschenmann, *Cultivating an Ecological Conscience: Essays from a Farmer Philosopher* (Lexington: The University Press of Kentucky, 2010), and David Cloutier, *Walking God's Earth: The Environment and Catholic Faith* (Collegeville, MN: Liturgical Press, 2014).

[103] The Israel-Jordan water agreement shows how water scarcity can be viewed as a "common threat" that drives cooperation between states otherwise in conflict. India-Pakistan's water agreements have survived multiple kinetic conflicts. David Titley, personal communication (July 29, 2014).

[104] Benedict XVI, *Caritas in veritate*, nos. 9 and 49.

[105] John Paul II, *Sollicitudo rei socialis*, no. 38.

[106] Working Groups I, II, and III: Contribution to the Fifth Assessment Report, "Synthesis Report of the Fifth Assessment Report" (Intergovernmental Panel on Climate Change, 2014), www.ipcc-syr.nl/.

34   *Erin Lothes*, et al.

CONCLUSION: GENUINE HUMAN FLOURISHING

The commitment to building an energy future is not simply a technical one, nor is it simply a matter of policy agreement. It also requires, in many ways, a kind of spiritual recognition of a necessary religious response and ethical transformation. The hope that dwells in concepts such as the "American dream" is actualized with the dreams of other human beings, their rights to a clean environment, and the flourishing of the planetary whole.

The 1981 statement exhorts U.S. Catholics not to "heedlessly exploit" and "destroy" nature but rather to "communicate with nature as an intelligent and noble master and guardian." Our most egregious practices of energy consumption and distribution were not intended to destroy nature. Nonetheless, the practices in our present energy paradigms commit us to the exploitation of finite resources and climate change. And while fossil fuels are central to the lifestyle and economy of the contemporary United States and most countries worldwide, and energy sovereignty is a worthy goal, there are energy alternatives to fossil fuels. Thus, while fossil fuels are currently inextricable from contemporary life, they need not always remain so. In principle and increasingly in practice, other kinds of energy sources—such as wind or solar—can fill the energy-generating niche.

The present energy crisis presents a moral call to renew our freedom and inventiveness and community spirit to build the global, national, and local communities we desire. Within that call is the summons to examine our understanding of genuine human flourishing.

Genuine Human Fulfillment

The American dream expressed in our national hymn, "America the Beautiful," is about genuine human fulfillment, seeking prosperous and just communities in our beautiful land. It is not about overconsumption and waste, its commercialized substitutes. Recall the magisterial critiques of super-development, which John Paul II called "an excessive availability of every kind of material goods," which makes people "slaves of possessions and immediate gratification, with no other horizon than the multiplication or continual replacement of the things already owned with others still better."[107] This message about what truly fulfills us as individuals is increasingly reinforced by the scientific literature of happiness studies, which stresses that we are

---

[107] John Paul II, *Solicitudo rei socialis*, no. 28. He offers similar critiques in *Centesimus annus*.

fulfilled by relationships and a sense of skill and empowerment in our own lives.[108]

Addressing overburdened working families, social recession, unemployment, and a loss of social capital depends on an ecological macroeconomics based on a "new economic and social logic."[109] This secular statement of economic pragmatism and community solidarity echoes the Bishops' call for freedom in altering our lifestyles and reimagining the structures of healthy and just families and communities.

In addition, gratitude for life is a starting point for religious renewal that draws on joy. The Psalms reflect on the spacious skies as the heavens which proclaim the glory of God, the sacramentality of our beautiful earth through which we experience the presence of God. Environmental writers like John Muir,[110] Aldo Leopold[111] and Rachel Carson[112] have demonstrated the power of gratitude as they described their environments with overflowing enjoyment. In that way they were able to awaken Americans to their own interconnectedness with the land.

> The American dream is not about excess, consumerism, and waste. The authentic foundation of the American dream is that God prospers our hopes for a better life, for peaceful, fair and prosperous communities.

American Catholics can also look to virtue ethics' focus on flourishing to re-envision our relationship with energy in the context of creation.[113] The mindful practice of interdependence centered on God as sustainer and giver of life enables us to see, judge, and act vis-à-vis

---

[108] Tim Kasser, *The High Price of Materialism* (Cambridge, MA: MIT Press, 2002). Barry Schwartz counsels the need to "curtail social comparison," "control expectations," and even "learn to love constraints." See Barry Schwartz, *The Paradox of Choice* (HarperCollins, 2004), 233-236. For a useful summary of research on economics and happiness, see Aaron Ahuvia, "Wealth, Consumption, and Happiness," in *The Cambridge Handbook of Psychology and Economic Behaviour*, ed. Alan Lewis (Cambridge: Cambridge University Press, 2008), 199-226.

[109] Sustainable Development Commission, *Prosperity Without Growth? The Transition to a Sustainable Economy* (London, 2009), 90.

[110] See, for instance, John Muir, *Nature Writings: The Story of My Boyhood and Youth; My First Summer in the Sierra; The Mountains of California; Stickeen; Selected Essays* (New York: Penguin Books, 1997).

[111] Aldo Leopold, *A Sand County Almanac, and Sketches Here and There* (New York: Oxford University Press, 1987).

[112] Rachel Carson, *The Edge of the Sea* (Boston: Houghton Mifflin, 1955); and *The Sea around Us* (New York: Oxford University Press, 1989).

[113] See Ronald D Sandler and Philip Cafaro, eds., *Environmental Virtue Ethics* (Lanham, MD: Rowman & Littlefield Publishers, 2005); and Jame Schaefer, "The Virtuous Cooperator: Modeling the Human in an Age of Ecological Degradation," *Worldviews: Environment, Culture, Religion* 7, nos. 1-2 (2003): 171-95.

energy scarcities "as creatures and as fellow creatures," as the Bishops' statement characterized humanity.

Seeking to bring these insights into practice, Catholics may strive for the anticipated, just and sustainable future through the spiritual practices that rekindle a passion for the flourishing of all life—characterized by equity. The faces of those who lack the resources to meet even their most basic needs, or the traces left by extinct populations of animal and plant life, echo this plea to encounter God so that we claim our true identity as creatures.[114] Created in the image of God, we are also called to image God's creativity, as co-creators of beauty and sustainable forms of living—across geographic boundaries as well as with respect for future generations. ▥

---

[114] On encountering God through rest, renewal, and reverence for the Sabbath, see Matthew Sleeth, *24/6: A Prescription for a Healthier, Happier Life* (Carol Stream, IL: Tyndale House Publishers, 2012). On creative self-giving as a Christian vocation, see Erin Lothes Biviano, *The Paradox of Christian Sacrifice: The Loss of Self, the Gift of Self* (New York: Herder and Herder, 2007), esp 228-231; on Catholic and universal expressions of self-giving love, see Robert J. Daly, *Sacrifice Unveiled: The True Meaning of Christian Sacrifice* (London: T&T Clark, 2009), esp. 230-231. On creaturely poverty and diversity, see the website of the United States Census Bureau, www.census.gov/hhes/ www/poverty/about/overview/. See the website for the UN Refugee Agency, www.unhcr.org/pages/49c3646c10a.html; See the Center for Global Diversity, www.biologicaldiversity.org/programs/biodiversity/elements_of_ biodiversity/extinction_crisis/.

Journal of Moral Theology, Vol. 5, No. 1 (2016): 37-64

Human Capacities and the Problem of Universally Equal Dignity: Two Philosophical Test Cases and a Theistic Response

Matthew Petrusek

EW WORDS IN CONTEMPORARY MORAL DISCOURSE have the same immediate traction as the term "human dignity." Politicians, lawyers, preachers and priests, human rights advocates, academic theorists, and campaigners of all stripes regularly appeal to dignity as the foundational warrant for their manifold causes, even when they bitterly disagree with each other. It may not always be the first claim in the chain of reasoning, but, if all else fails, it frequently ends up being the last. Why, for example, should poverty be eradicated? "Because it is an affront to human dignity," activists tell us. Why should foreign dictators be toppled? "So the universal yearning for human dignity can break free," say opposition leaders and their international supporters. Why should this healthcare, or housing, or debt-forgiveness bill be passed? "Because dignity calls for no less," protestors clamor. Or why should stem cell research be funded? "Because it advances human dignity," say researchers. Why should it be prohibited? "Because it undermines human dignity," respond church leaders. Many agree that animal-human hybrids pose a threat to human dignity. But some also maintain that alleged unfair labor practices, which, depending on the political platform, may include insufficient paid vacation time, do the same. An organization called "Dignitas" in Switzerland offers its clients what it calls "death with dignity," a common euphemism for assisted suicide. Opponents argue that such a practice constitutes a grave violation of human dignity itself.

Indeed, human dignity not only lies at the heart of a potpourri of moral disputes—often with each side claiming that it is the one "true" defender or advancer of human worth—but also serves as the foundational ballast of entire charters and declarations. The first article of the *Charter of Fundamental Human Rights of the European Union*, for example, asserts, "Human dignity is inviolable. It must be respected and protected."[1] The earlier and more internationally recognized

---

[1] "Charter of Fundamental Rights of the European Union," *Office Journal of the European Communities* 364 (2000):9.

United Nations document, *The Universal Declaration of Human Rights,* commences similarly: "[the] recognition of the inherent dignity and of the equal and inalienable rights of all members of the human family is the foundation of freedom, justice and peace in the world."[2] Confirming the ethical centrality of dignity to the document, article one goes on to affirm, "All human beings are born free and equal in dignity and rights." Remarkably, when the final form of *The Declaration* was approved in December of 1948, only eight nations abstained from approving it, and not one dissented.[3] Though divided into Communist and non-Communist blocks and still ravaged by the effects of World-War II, almost the entire world came together (at least on paper) to recognize the existence of universal human worth. Rarely has the global community seen such consensus—a consensus that over 60 years later appears to continue growing, at least on empirical grounds.[4]

To be sure, some prominent naysayers have emerged along the way. The utilitarian philosopher Peter Singer has long provided readers with a meticulously crafted case against the existence of human worth, arguing that it amounts to an unjustified form of discrimination he calls "speciesism."[5] The Harvard psychologist Steven Pinker has also

---

[2] The United Nations, "The Universal Declaration of Human Rights," www.un.org/en/documents/udhr/.

[3] The United Nations, "History of the Document," www.un.org/en/documents/udhr/history.shtml. It is also interesting to note that article one of the 1949 and 1990 German Constitutions (the text was amended in part after the 1990 unification of West and East Germany) reads, "Die Würde des Menschen ist unantastbar. Sie zu achten und zu schützen ist Verpflichtung aller staatlichen Gewalt." Translated: "Human dignity is unassailable. To respect and protect it is the duty of all state authority." See The German Government, "Grundgesetz für die Bundesrepublik Deutschland," www.gesetze-im-internet.de/bundesrecht/gg/gesamt.pdf. Even if one agrees with the claims in the German Constitution and The Universal Declaration of Human Rights—and I think most people would— the conception of dignity in these documents remains deeply problematic because it is in no way clear, in either document, how or why human dignity can be both universally and inherently equal while also being something that needs to be protected. Certainly declarations and constitutions do not bear the burden of exhaustively justifying their first principles; but the problem is that the first principles, in these cases, appear to be contradictory—at least without substantial additional elaboration and explanation.

[4] The 1989 United Nations Treaty, "Convention on the Rights of the Child," for example, also includes language recognizing the "fundamental....dignity and worth of the person" (see The United Nations, "Convention on the Rights of the Child," www.ohchr.org/en/professionalinterest/pages/crc.aspx). According to the United Nations website, 194 countries are currently a party to the treaty. Interestingly, the United States has signed the treaty, but has not yet ratified it (see The United Nations, "Treaty Collection," https://treaties.un.org/Pages/ViewDetails.aspx?src= TREATY&mtdsg_no=IV-11&chapter=4&lang=en).

[5] Singer's writing provides a multitude of quotable material on this point, but here is a succinct expression: "The doctrine of the sanctity of human life, as it is normally

recently come out against the validity of human dignity as an ontological or ethical principle; in 2008 he wrote an influential article in *The New Republic*—polemically entitled, "The Stupidity of Human Dignity"—that lambastes the use of dignity as a basis for making moral judgments, especially in bioethics.[6] So it is certainly inaccurate to say that the *belief* in human dignity is anywhere near universal, either inside or outside the academy.

But it is certainly widespread, even global. Just imagine getting elected or holding a prominent position—or, for that matter, being accepted among polite company—in most parts of the world while publically denying the existence of equal human worth. Not even far left environmental parties who see humanity as a threat to the planet or far right cultural purity parties who see certain ethnic, religious, or racial groups as a threat to civilization make that claim, at least openly. Call it, to borrow from John Rawls, an overlapping consensus.

But why the agreement? And what, exactly, is the agreement about? Peek beneath the near unanimity on human dignity's existence, and it quickly becomes apparent that there is a great diversity, if not cacophony, of viewpoints on dignity's origin, specific character, and ethical implications. Indeed, like many other deeply loaded moral terms ("fairness" is another good example), what human dignity enjoys in general acceptance, it frequently lacks in clarity and coherence, a reality this article's introductory examples seek to capture.[7]

---

understood, has at its core a discrimination on the basis of species and nothing else" (see Peter Singer, *Unsanctifying Human Life*, ed. Helga Kuhsé [Malden, Ma: Blackwell Publishing, 2002], 221). Singer offers a sustained critique in this text not only of the claim that humans have *unique* value—his understanding of that which bestows worth on a living being has roots in Jeremy Bentham's famous query: "The question is not can they reason? nor Can they talk? but Can they suffer?"—but also of the claim that humans have uniquely *equal* worth. All attempts by theologians and philosophers to establish universally equal human dignity have left him thoroughly unconvinced: "[The] appeal to the intrinsic dignity of human beings appears to solve the egalitarian's problems only as long as it goes unchallenged. Once we ask *why* it should be that all humans—including infants, mental defectives, psychopaths, Hitler, Stalin and the rest—have some kind of dignity or worth that no elephant, pig, or chimpanzee can ever achieve, we see that this question is as difficult to answer as our original request for some relevant fact that justifies the inequality of humans and other animals" (Singer, *Unsanctifying Human Life*, 91).
[6] Pinker writes, for example, "The problem is that 'dignity' is a squishy, subjective notion, hardly up to the heavyweight moral demands assigned to it." He argues that "autonomy," in contrast, has an objective, fixed meaning, and should be used in moral discourse rather than "dignity." See Steven Pinker, "The Stupidity of Human Dignity", *The New Republic,* May 28, 2008, http://pinker.wjh.harvard.edu/ articles/media/The%20Stupidity%20of%20Dignity.htm.
[7] Another instructive way to see the conceptual elasticity of human worth in action is to search for "human dignity" on the White House's webpage. There are not only hundreds of results from different speeches, remarks, executive orders, etc., but the

Several books and articles have recently emerged addressing this
basic definitional problem. The more prominent include political theorist Michael Rosen's *Dignity: Its History and Meaning,* philosopher
George Kateb's *Human Dignity,* and theological ethicist Gilbert Meilaender's *Neither Beast Nor God: The Dignity of the Human Person,*
as well as an excellent series of essays in *Human Dignity and Bioethics.* Each text distinctively addresses the problematic status of "human
worth" in contemporary moral discourse, especially with regards to its
definitional elasticity and the frequency with which it appears in support of various causes without a systematic defense of its meaning or
moral validity.[8]

---

contexts in which the President uses the term also vary widely. Those contexts include: national security, sexual assault awareness, regulatory impact analysis, health
care, torture, human rights, the rights of women and girls, the death of Osama Bin
Laden, economic growth, economic alliances, environmental initiatives, diplomacy,
foreign independence movements, combating sex trafficking, the National Day of
Prayer, and economic sanctions, among others.

Perhaps even more interesting than this topical diversity are the different forms that
human dignity takes within the *same* speech. For example, in prepared remarks to
honor the awarding of the Nobel Peace Prize to Lui Xiaobo, a Chinese human rights
activist and political prisoner, President Obama states just after the introduction, "All
of us have a responsibility to build a just peace that recognizes the *inherent* rights and
dignity of human beings—a truth upheld within the Universal Declaration of Human
Rights" (my emphasis). He then declares, a few lines later, "[Mr.] Liu reminds us that
human dignity also *depends* upon the advance of democracy, open society, and the
rule of law" (See Barak Obama, "Statement by President on the Awarding of Nobel
Peace Prize," www.Whitehouse.Gov/the-press-office/2010/12/10/statement-presi-
dent-awarding-nobel-peace-prize, my emphasis).

On the one hand, these sound like boiler-plate, non-controversial claims for this kind
of context, at least to an American audience. On the other hand, they contradict each
other: if dignity is *inherent* then it should not, conceptually, *depend* on anything. Likewise, if dignity *depends* on certain social and political circumstances (or anything
else), then it is not clear how it could be either inherent or, for that matter, universal.
This is not, I believe, a nit-picky distinction: human dignity lies at the core of the
argument President Obama employs to honor and defend Mr. Liu, and yet the two
uses of the term in the speech are incompatible, at least without substantial additional
elaboration. This kind of incompatibility, moreover, is not isolated to President
Obama's use of dignity. Claiming that human worth is both inherent and in need of
protection/advancement—without explaining how these two characteristics can coherently coexist—is common in contemporary moral discourse.

[8] I will be drawing from Martha Nussbaum's article in *Human Dignity and Bioethics,*
"Human Dignity and Political Entitlement" for this essay. Several other essays in the
collection effectively frame and reply to the question of human dignity's definition
and source. However, none, in my view, adequately respond to what I take to be one
of human dignity's fundamental questions: What, from a conceptual perspective, is
the condition for the possibility of defining dignity as both universal *and* equal? In
other words: What is conceptually necessary in order for "human dignity" to coherently apply to *all* human beings in equal measure? My answer, as the essay will seek
to demonstrate, is that dignity must be defined as "invulnerable." I believe it is this

Yet notwithstanding this relatively small body of literature, and despite the ubiquity of the term "human dignity" in contemporary moral discourse, there remains a problematic dearth of philosophical and theological work dedicated to systematically defining and defending dignity's full meaning. In particular, there remains a lack of clarity on what unique human characteristic, or characteristics, could coherently account for dignity's purported universality and equality. The normative definition of human dignity thus remains an open and pressing issue. Theory needs to catch up with practice.

To this end, this article seeks to help lay the theoretical groundwork for a normative definition of human worth by, first, identifying the conceptual parameters required to describe dignity as both 1) universal and 2) equal, and then, second, testing three substantive accounts of dignity—those present in the thought of moral philosopher Alan Gewirth, political theorist Martha Nussbaum, and theologian St. Pope John Paul II—in light of those parameters. It is important to stress at the outset that my goal is not to identify which conception of dignity is "true" in the sense of rationally necessary or otherwise persuasively demonstrable, though that is, of course, an important goal. Rather, I am seeking to establish which conception of dignity is *coherent* within the conceptual parameters of "universality" and "equality." And by "coherent" I only mean, in a minimal sense, not self-contradictory. It would be *incoherent*, for example, for a definition of dignity to affirm "all human beings sometimes have universally equal worth depending on their socio-historical circumstances." The claim contradicts itself; if something is universal, it cannot depend on any set of circumstances nor can it "sometimes" be the case. In this instance, we would have good reason to reject such a view of dignity on the grounds of its inconsistency.

However, to rule out a particular view of dignity in this way does not tell us what constitutes the *right* or *true* view of dignity. In this sense, the article only seeks to test the internal coherence of three different views of dignity, not to establish which, if any, is true. Put differently, I am seeking to identify a *valid* argument for the theoretical

---

conceptual requirement of invulnerability that contemporary philosophical and theological accounts of human dignity, including the other texts listed above, have either overlooked or underappreciated—a lacuna, I believe, that has led to substantial confusion with regards to dignity's definition and ethical implications. See Edmund Pellegrino, Adamn Schulman, and Thomas Merril, eds. *Human Dignity and Bioethics* (Notre Dame: University of Notre Dame Press, 2009), Gilbert Meilaender, *Neither Beast Nor God: The Dignity of the Human Person* (New York: New Atlantis Books, 2009), and George Kateb, *Human Dignity* (Cambridge: Harvard University Press, 2011).

foundations of universal and equal dignity, not, necessarily, a sound one.[9]

Given these preliminary parameters, I wish to advance the following argument: *if* we seek to define human dignity as universally equal among all human beings, *then* any account of human dignity that defines human worth according to human capacities must be understood as incoherent. The "if" here is crucial. I am not arguing that we ought to define human dignity as universally equal in this context or that definitions of dignity that are not universally equal are necessarily internally incoherent. I am, rather, deliberately *assuming* a starting premise, sidestepping the foundational question of its justification. The premise is that human dignity, whatever else it might be or entail, is both universal and equal among all beings whom we otherwise define as "human."[10] If we accept this claim, I argue, then we are com-

---

[9] In a basic sense, a valid argument is one in which the conclusion necessarily follows from the premises. A sound argument is valid, with the added criterion that the premises are also *true*. Take for example, the following argument: premise 1) all human beings have equal dignity; premise 2) equal dignity bestows human equal rights on all humans; premise 3) basic education is a human right; premise 4) Julia is a human being; therefore, the conclusion: Julia has a right to basic education. This is a valid argument; given the premises, we have no other option but to conclude that Julia has a right to basic education. To conclude otherwise would be, in a decisive sense, *incoherent* and, hence, *irrational.*
However, is the argument also sound in addition to being valid? That would depend on demonstrating the truth of each one of the premises, an immensely complex task that would include doing foundational work in both ethics and meta-ethics (that is, not only identifying foundational moral principles but also establishing the ultimate origin of those principles and how, epistemologically, they can be known). This article does try to do this kind of work. Thus, in claiming that I seek to establish a valid rather than sound argument for universally equal dignity, I am claiming that I will deliberately *not* seek to determine the truth of premise "human beings have universally equal dignity." I only seek, rather, to determine the valid conclusion that must follow, assuming this premise as a starting point.
[10] Insofar as this article seeks to establish the formal, conceptual grounds for defining dignity as universally equal, I do not seek to provide a specific, substantive definition of what normatively constitutes a human being. In other words, I am not seeking to substantively answer the question "what is a human?" either descriptively or normatively in this context.
That said, it is difficult to conceptualize human dignity as being universal and equal if it only applies to a subset of humanity. Indeed, if human dignity only applies to some human beings, or applies to all human beings but unequally, then it is, by definition, *not* universal and/or equal. The question would therefore be: what do we call those "entities" that are not human (or fully human) but also, apparently, not anything else in existence? Can something be both not (fully) human and not (fully) anything else? The logical principle of identity appears to preclude this claim. Thus, from a descriptive standpoint, at least, it seems necessarily to be the case that something is either uniquely a human or not uniquely a human, and one of the main points this article is seeking to advance is that if human dignity is universally equal, then, by

mitted to rejecting all accounts of human dignity that find their justificatory warrant in some form of human capacities, which includes the accounts of both Alan Gewirth and Martha Nussbaum.[11]

In light of this argument, I will conclude by arguing that John Paul II's theistic account of dignity *can* coherently support the claim that dignity is universally equal because it is grounded in a divine-human relationship, a relationship that recognizes the value of human capacities yet is not dependent upon them.

GEWIRTH AND NUSSBAUM: DIGNITY BASED ON HUMAN DOING

Before establishing and defending what constitutes "universality" and "equality" as they apply to a general conception of human dignity, it is important to identify and exposit the specific accounts of dignity in Alan Gewirth and Martha Nussbaum, letting them speak for themselves, as it were, before I seek to impose a conceptual framework on their thought. The reason I have chosen to engage Gewirth and Nussbaum in particular is because each represents a conception of human worth that finds its grounding in a human capacity or set of capacities: "agency," as we will see in Gewirth, and "capabilities" in Nussbaum. Let me first turn to Gewirth.

Gewirth, Human Agency, and the Supreme Principle of Morality

Gewirth lays out his systematic case for human dignity in his book, *Reason and Morality* (1978), though he also provides a condensed restatement of his position in a later work, *The Community of Rights* (1996). I derive my own treatment of Gewirth's argument for dignity chiefly, though not exclusively, from the latter work, despite the fact that he develops his position more extensively in the former. The reason is that Gewirth's basic argument can, as he demonstrates in the first chapter of *The Community of Rights*, be summarized concisely without sacrificing the argument's force and cogency.

The first step in Gewirth's argument requires him to establish and defend what he describes as an "agent." Gewirth argues that whatever we mean by action, we must at least mean that which is the object of

---

definition, all that which is uniquely human must fall under the umbrella of that worth—otherwise we are using the term "human dignity" incoherently.

[11] While neither Nussbaum nor Gewirth *explicitly* claim they are seeking to establish a universally equal definition of human dignity, their respective arguments certainly imply that their use of the words "human" or "person" morally include as many individuals as possible under the umbrella of equal human worth—all of those with "human capacities" for Nussbaum and all of those with "autonomy," or the potential for autonomy, for Gewirth. In this sense, each is *implicitly* suggesting that they view human worth as both universal and equal. On these grounds, I believe "universal equality" can serve as a fixed conceptual standard for evaluating the internal coherence of their respective moral theories.

all practical precepts, whether they are moral precepts or not—that is, whether the precepts apply to what one ought categorically do independently of one's interests (moral precepts) or what one ought do in order to pursue one's interests (prudential precepts). Yet any precept, he argues—that is, any statement that is made with the intention of guiding action—necessarily implies that the object of the precept, the person to whom the precept is addressed, is both 1) voluntary and 2) purposive. In other words, any practical precept, *qua* precept, necessarily implies that the object of the precept is both free (voluntary) and capable of acting for an end or goal (purposive). Gewirth also calls these two foundational characteristics the "generic features of action." The term "agent" thus applies to individuals who act voluntarily and with purpose.

Having defined agency, Gewirth then seeks to demonstrate how acting as an agent necessarily implies the existence and recognition of a supreme principal of morality, which includes within it both the existence of each agent's fundamental dignity and the existence of basic negative and positive rights based on that dignity. This conception of dignity and human rights is "necessary" for Gewirth, in the sense of being rationally necessary. As he explains, "Any agent, simply by virtue of being an agent, must admit, on pain of self-contradiction, that he ought to act in certain determinate ways."[12] These "certain determinate ways" reflect the existence and moral authority of the supreme principle of morality.

The movement from agency to the supreme principle of morality, or, to put it differently, the movement from the "is" of the agent to the "ought" that governs her action, takes place by a process of reasoning Gewirth calls "dialectical necessity." Put simply, dialectical necessity means establishing what any agent, *qua* agent, must necessarily affirm in performing any action at all. By means of this necessity, Gewirth seeks to establish what he calls "two theses," which, together, constitute the supreme principle of morality and the justification for human dignity. In his own words:

> The first thesis is that every agent logically must accept that *he* or *she* has rights to freedom and well-being. The second is that the agent logically must also accept that *all other agents* also have these rights equally with his or her own, so that in this way the existence of universal moral rights, and thus of human rights, must be accepted within the whole context of action and practice.[13]

---

[12] Alan Gewirth, *Reason and Morality* (Chicago: University of Chicago Press, 1978), 26.

[13] Gewirth, *Reason and Morality*, 17, author's emphasis.

These two theses ultimately entail the conclusion, for Gewirth, that human beings have rights by virtue of their agency. Any claim to the contrary is to engage in pragmatic self-contradiction.

Agency and Human Dignity

Although Gewirth rarely uses the term "dignity," he makes it clear that the supreme principle of morality that he derives from the agential structure of human action is tantamount to a supreme principle of dignity, a point he makes explicit when he recasts his entire argument in terms of human worth. The passage is worth citing at length:

> [A]ll agents attribute value or worth to the purposes for which they act. But since the agents are the sources or loci of this attribution of worth, they must also attribute worth to themselves. Their purposes are conceived as having worth or value because the agents themselves have worth. This attribution of worth to the agents encompasses not only their purposiveness as such but also the abilities of reason and will that enter into their agency. For acting for purposes agents use both will and reason: will in their freedom as controlling their behavior by their unforced choice and in their endeavors to achieve their purposes; reason in ascertaining the means to their ends, in attributing to themselves rights to the necessary conditions of their agency and in accepting that all other agents also have these rights. Even if they reason incorrectly or will what is wrong, each agent must recognize in herself and others *the general abilities that give worth to human life and action* and that ground her attribution of the rights of agency. Human dignity consists in having and at least potentially using these abilities, and human rights are derived from human dignity thus conceived.[14]

The passage reveals the deep interplay of agency—and in particular, agential *action*—and human worth in Gewirth's thought. To be an agent is to have worth, and to have worth means that one is an agent, or, at least, a prospective agent. More specifically, it appears that both reason and will—the capacities that underpin an agent's more general capacity to act voluntarily and with purposiveness—are that which ultimately bestow value on human beings. In other words, human beings have value because we are agents or prospective agents; but we are agents or prospective agents only because we have, or will have, the capacities of "reason" and "will." In this sense, then, agency broadly, and reason and will more specifically, are, in effect, the cause of human dignity; they are those characteristics that justify why human beings not only have worth, but also uniquely *human* worth.

---

[14] Gewirth, *Reason and Morality*, 66, emphasis added.

Nussbaum and the Dignity of Human Capacities

Martha Nussbaum takes a more comprehensive approach to defining human dignity. While she, like Gewirth, upholds the fundamental importance of agency as the ground of human worth—especially agency as it relates to the human capacity for rationality—she cautions against defining worth *exclusively* on agency and rationality. She writes in a recent essay, "Human Dignity and Political Entitlements," for example, "[It] is quite crucial not to base the ascription of human dignity on any single 'basic capability' (rationality, for example), since this excludes from human dignity many human beings with severe mental disabilities."[15]

Rationality and the capacity for agential action thus form only one component of Nussbaum's conception of dignity. Her full account of human worth includes several other "basic capabilities," as she calls them, and it is these capabilities, in turn, that provide the justification of her conception of human worth: "[F]ull and equal human dignity," she writes, "is possessed by any child of human parents who has any of an open-ended disjunction of basic capabilities for major human life-activities."[16] Indeed, she goes on to specify that human capacities not only confer dignity on humans, but also, more fundamentally, *possess* dignity themselves. The locus of human dignity, in other words, is within human capacities. As she writes while describing how rape violates dignity, for example, "A woman… has sentience, imagination, emotions, and the capacity for reasoning and choice; to force sexual intercourse on her is inappropriate, lacking in respect for *the dignity that those capacities possess.*"[17]

The capacities of "sentience," imagination," "emotions," "reason," and "choice" constitute only part of the list of central human capabilities. Others include life, bodily health, bodily integrity, affiliation with others, non-discrimination, contact with other species, play, and control over one's environment.[18] Taken together, it is this cluster of human capacities for what Nussbaum calls "major human life activities" that account for how and why human beings have worth *qua* human beings.

It is important to note, as Nussbaum acknowledges, that this conception of dignity has deeply Aristotelian roots; to be human is not only to be something ontologically static—a human being—but also to be something that *develops*, a "human becoming." And it is by

---

[15] Martha Nussbaum, "Human Dignity and Political Entitlements," in *Human Dignity and Bioethics*, eds E. Pellegrino, A. Schulman, and T. Merrill (Notre Dame, IN: University of Notre Dame Press, 2009), 362.
[16] Nussbaum, "Human Dignity and Political Entitlements," 363.
[17] Nussbaum, "Human Dignity and Political Entitlements," 359, emphasis added.
[18] See Nussbaum, "Human Dignity and Political Entitlements," 377-8.

means of exercising one's basic human capacities, she argues, that one can and does become fully human in the normative sense, a state of existence she also calls "human flourishing."

On this point it is important to stress, however, that Nussbaum does not seek to identify a single standard of normative humanity to which all human lives ought to conform. Here she departs from Aristotelianism to embrace something more akin to Rawlsian liberalism; we ought not seek to enforce one vision of the comprehensive good, be it religious or secular, in any given political community. "[It] is itself violative of human dignity," she argues, "to base political arrangements on a single comprehensive doctrine."[19] Her emphasis on grounding dignity on human capacities thus falls on the possession and exercise of the capacities themselves, not on what any given individual uses them for. To be human and have worth, that is, is to have basic human capacities; to be a unique person is to use those capacities to strive for any morally licit goal one chooses, insofar as there is not one normative goal that all humans ought to pursue. As she writes, "[H]uman beings have a worth that is indeed inalienable, because of their capacities for various forms of acting and striving."[20]

Nussbaum's conception of dignity thus rests on a broader theoretical foundation than Gewirth's. Humans not only have dignity because we are rational and purposive agents; we also have dignity because we have unique capabilities to become more human by exercising a broad array of distinctively human capacities. Each capacity is fundamentally related to what it means to be human. Indeed, Nussbaum goes far beyond a strictly agential account of dignity by additionally recognizing a deep connection between uniquely human needs and uniquely human worth: "There is a dignity not only in rationality," she writes, "but in human need itself and in the varied forms of striving that emerge from human need."[21]

THE CONDITION FOR THE POSSIBILITY OF UNIVERSAL EQUALITY

Notwithstanding the fundamental differences between Gewirth and Nussbaum, it is important to recognize that both ground their respective conceptions of dignity on human capacities. To be human in a moral sense is derived from human *doing*—or the potential to do—rather than human *being*; whether it is human purposiveness and rationality or human striving more generally, to have a capacity as it relates to human dignity, for both, is to have a power to do something distinctively human. Capacities in this sense certainly include rational capacities and the capacity for purposive action; yet they also include

[19] Nussbaum, "Human Dignity and Political Entitlements," 362.
[20] Nussbaum, "Human Dignity and Political Entitlements," 357.
[21] Nussbaum, "Human Dignity and Political Entitlements," 363.

the kinds of basic human capabilities that Nussbaum enumerates, capabilities that are related to rationality and purposive action, but not necessarily reducible to them. As Nussbaum in particular implies, human children have dignity-bearing capacities long before they develop agency.

The question I wish to address, then, is whether these capacity-grounded views of human worth can coherently account for a definition of dignity that purports to be both universal and equal. As noted above, I do not intend to examine or criticize the views of Gewirth or Nussbaum *per se*, or, even, to question whether or not they can coherently ground *some* conception of dignity. Rather, I seek to test them against a definition of dignity that affirms that dignity, whatever else it may be, belongs to all human beings without exception in equal measure. Can either Gewirth or Nussbaum coherently account for *this* kind of dignity?

Basic Definitions of "Universality" and "Equality"
As a starting point for making this evaluation, it is crucial to establish some basic meanings for both "universality" and "equality," and then to ask what these terms conceptually entail. The common, everyday uses of these words do sufficient work for the purposes of the argument. Describing something as "universal" means that it applies to *every* member of a given class or group, everywhere, all the time, with no exceptions. Not admitting of exceptions is particularly important for the conception of universality; if there is even *one* exception—that is, if even one member of a particular group or class does not share the otherwise "universal" characteristic defining the group or class—then, by definition, the characteristic cannot be described as universal. So to say "human dignity is universal" means that *all* humans have dignity *everywhere, all the time*; or, put again, of the class/group "human," all members universally have worth.

Given this definition, it would thus be conceptually incoherent to claim that "some humans have universal human dignity" or "all humans have universal dignity in some places or sometimes," or "all humans have human dignity depending on...." If dignity is universal—conceptually independent of *why* or *how* it is universal—then it must, in an absolutist sense, somehow inhere in, or otherwise apply to, every single human being without exception or the potential for an exception. Otherwise human dignity is not, by definition, universal.

Describing something as "equal," in turn, means claiming that it is quantitatively and/or qualitatively *identical* everywhere it exists. As with universality, equality also has absolutist conceptual implications: one cannot say coherently, for example, to paraphrase the famous line from *Animal Farm*, "all humans have equal dignity but some have more dignity than others." Conceptually, equality does not admit of degrees; there can be no "more" or "less." So to say that human beings have equal worth—again, independent of *why* or *how* it is equal—is to say that human beings have absolutely identical worth, worth that inheres in the same way, to the same extent, in every individual who has worth.

Combining the characteristics of universality and equality and applying them to a conception of human dignity thus entails the following affirmation: every human being—that is, every individual being otherwise defined as "human"—has worth in the same way and to the same extent as every other human being. If worth does not extend to all human beings then it is not universal. If that worth admits of any kind of degree, even if it is universal, it is not equal. Universally equal human dignity, therefore, is an exhaustive, absolutist conception, at least from a formal, conceptual perspective. It allows for no exclusions and admits of no degrees.[22]

It is important to note, here, that universality and equality do not necessarily conceptually imply each other. To say something is universal, in other words, is not necessarily to say that it is equal; likewise, to say something is equal, is not necessarily to affirm that it is universal. One could, for example, coherently profess a belief that humans with a certain kind of characteristic or group of characteristics have equal dignity, while those who do not possess that characteristic or group of characteristics do not have equal dignity. From such a perspective dignity would be defined as equal, but not universal.

A poignant example of this claim can be found in Aristotle's *Nicomachean Ethics*. Though Aristotle is often credited for making a distinctive, egalitarian-tinted break with pre-Socratic Greek thought by examining the function or final cause of *humans as such*, independently of their social status and role in the polis (see, e.g., 1097b, 21-27), he clearly categorizes a large swath of humanity as effectively non-human in a moral sense. Take, for example, this passage often overlooked or downplayed by contemporary admirers of Aristotle's thought:

> [Anyone] who is going to be a competent student in the spheres of what is noble and what is just—in a word, politics—must be brought

---

[22] I do not mean to claim, even from a formal perspective, that universally equal worth implies that all human beings must all be *treated* equally, only that they would have to be shown equal *moral regard*. This distinction between equal treatment and equal regard—substantively and persuasively developed, for example, in Gene Outka's book *Agape: An Ethical Analysis* (New Haven: Yale University Press, 1972)—is especially important for answering the question of how to *apply* a universally equal conception of human worth. One can easily imagine showing equal moral regard to a five year old and an eighteen year old, for example; but one hopes they would not be treated the same.

up well in its habits. For the first principle is the belief *that* something is the case, and if this is sufficiently clear, he will not need the reason *why* as well. Such a person is in the possession of the first principles, or could easily grasp them. Anyone with neither of these possibilities open to him should listen to [the poet] Hesiod:

> This person who understands everything for himself is the best of all,
> And noble is that one who heeds good advice.
> But he who neither understands it for himself nor takes to heart
> What he hears is a worthless man.[23]

Aristotle's claim about the potential value of a human being in this passage is not subtle. His claims for equality are hardly universal.

Aristotle essentially declares that any individual who has "not been brought up well" in "good habits"—which, means, we should be clear, those children not fortunate enough to have been born into the right kinds of households in the right kinds of civic environment—will *inevitably* not become virtuous, and thus inevitably fail to fulfill their proper function as a human being, which, according to Aristotle, renders them, borrowing Hesiod's words, "worthless." In other words, there are humans in Aristotle's world who, despite being classified as human (and therefore *not* classified as any other kind of animal), have *no intrinsic moral worth at all*. They may look like humans, act (in a non-moral sense) like humans, and communicate like humans, but they are not *morally* humans because they cannot realize their final cause or proper function: a life of virtue in service of the polis and in contemplation of the Unmoved Mover.

This exclusion of a large swath of humanity from moral recognition does not, however, prevent Aristotle from recognizing substantive moral equality among those *who do* have the good fortune to have been born and raised in a properly formed city-state. Indeed, in a way that might make him arguably more "egalitarian" than Plato, he even recognizes a kind of equality of opportunity to become authentically virtuous, and thus happy in the eudainomistic sense, among those who have been rightly habituated in the polis: "[For] all who are not maimed as regards their potentiality for virtue," he writes in the *Ethics*, "may win it by a certain kind of study and care."[24] Everyone, in other words, has a relatively equal chance to become virtuous and thus fully

---

[23] Aristotle, *Nicomachean Ethics*, trans. Roger Crisp (Cambridge: Cambridge University Press, 200), 1095b, 4-10. The quotation from Hesiod is found in *Hesiod: The Works and Days*, trans. Richmond Lattimore (Ann Arbor: University of Michigan Press, 1959), 293, 295-7.

[24] Aristotle, *Nicomachean Ethics*, 1099b, 19-20.

human—so long as we understand "everybody" as those formed in good habits. So while Socrates stands starkly isolated after explaining to his interlocutors how to ascend to the Form of the Good at the end of *The Symposium*, Aristotle depicts a *community* of the virtuous in the polis, going so far as to locate friendship, which is only possible among equals in his view, as essential to fulfilling one's final human purpose. Humans, therefore, can certainly be understood as morally equal to Aristotle, but not universally so. It is an example of how equality does not necessarily presuppose universality.

The opposite also holds true: universality does not necessarily entail full equality.[25] One could maintain, for example, that all humans, by virtue of being human, have some kind of objective worth that morally distinguishes us from all other forms of life. But that claim does not necessarily commit one to claiming that all humans have *substantively* equal worth. For instance, one could believe that all humans, no matter what their measurable level of intelligence, have some kind of basic dignity, but add that those who have IQ scores of at least 100, or those who come from a particular blood line, or those who share certain physical features have *more* dignity by virtue of belonging to an "enhanced" subset of humanity, which, the argument could then be made, entitles them to additional or enhanced rights and protections. It is one thing to say that everyone gets a slice of the pie, another to say that every slice must be the same size. It is for this reason, then, that my argument's starting point is the claim that dignity is universal *and* equal. The attribution of equality to universality is not redundant.

Universal Equality and Invulnerability

If, then, human dignity is both universal and equal, as I am assuming, what, then, also must be true about dignity so-defined from a purely conceptual perspective? The condition for the possibility of universal equality, I believe, takes the form of "invulnerability," and, specifically, invulnerability to harm (including ultimate harm or extirpation) and/or enhancement.

As with universality and equality, a basic understanding of the term "invulnerability" adequately illuminates the necessary point in this context. To say something is invulnerable is, drawing on the word's Latin roots, to say that it cannot be harmed or wounded. That is, the integrity and unity of that which is invulnerable cannot be qualitatively or quantitatively extirpated, effaced, or diminished in any way. The "cannot" here does not mean that one cannot *intend* or *try* to cause

---

[25] Universality does conceptually imply *some* measure of equality insofar as it is the case that if human worth is universal then every human must have at least some value—but that does not mean that everyone must have *substantively* equal value solely by virtue of being human.

harm to that which is invulnerable; rather, it applies to the efficacy of such an act: if something is invulnerable one cannot *effectively* cause harm to it. It is for this reason, too, that invulnerability also, according to the *Oxford English Dictionary*, means "unassailable;" that which is unassailable is that which cannot *successfully* be attacked. Conversely, if something *can* be effectively assailed, and thus harmed or diminished in some way, it is not, by definition, *in*-vulnerable.

What, then, does "invulnerability" mean when describing a conception of human worth, and why is it a necessary presupposition for universality and equality? Put simply, if dignity is not conceived of as invulnerable, then it cannot coherently be described as either universal or equal. Imagine, for example, a horrifying action or event that, we might say, causes severe or, even, irrevocable harm to those who experience it. Examples representing both "moral" and "natural" evils are, sadly, not difficult to think of: rape, torture, drug-addiction, incapacitating poverty, disfiguring disease, injuries that leave victims conscious but otherwise completely immobile, mental illness and the loss of one's personality, etc. It goes without saying that these kinds of experiences deeply wound individuals, perhaps even causing, in extreme cases, the loss of the person's *individuality* in the sense of those unique characteristics that define a human as a specific person. But do they cause individuals to lose their individual *dignity*? If so—again, purely from a conceptual perspective—we cannot therefore say that human dignity is universal. Recognizing the potential loss of dignity, for whatever reason, is to recognize possible *exceptions* to the universality of human worth and, therefore, to contradict the possibility and coherence of universality itself. *If* dignity can be eradicated or defaced in any way for whatever reason, in other words, *then* it is not something that can inhere in or apply to every human being without exception. It is, rather, something that is conditional, something whose integrity and unity depends on *whether or not* it is respected or violated by one's own actions, the actions of others, and/or good or bad fortune. [26] "Universality," however, cannot coherently accommodate

---

[26] Aristotle's thought, as noted above, cannot provide a coherent foundation for universally equal human worth (a conclusion that Aristotle would mostly likely not find problematic), but his conception of the normative human being and what defines human flourishing is, nevertheless, deeply insightful for understanding the distinction between vulnerability and invulnerability in this context. While Aristotle recognizes the possibility of living a fully-human life by cultivating both moral and intellectual virtue in service of the polis and/or in contemplation of the Unmoved Mover, he is clear that achieving such a life not only depends on being born into the right kind of community so that one can acquire, by absorption, the good habits necessary for moral virtue in particular, it also depends on what the philosopher Thomas Nagel would call "moral luck" (see Thomas Nagel, "Moral Luck," in *Ethics: History, Theory, and Contemporary Issues, eds. S. Cahn and P. Markie* [New York: Oxford University Press,

"conditionality," and so if dignity is conditional, *for whatever reason*, it is not universal. The only way to say that dignity is universal, therefore, is to say that it is *invulnerable* to any attempt to strip or efface it, whether the attempt comes from human hands, natural disaster, or the bad luck of the genetic draw.

A similar argument can be made with regards to the relationship between invulnerability and equality. Equality, recall, does not conceptually allow for degrees; to say that something has more or less of a given quality than other entities with the same quality is to say, by definition, that it is unequal. Thus, if there is a kind of event, action, or environment that has the capacity to quantitatively or qualitatively *diminish* human worth in any way—no matter how much or to what extent—then we cannot say coherently that dignity is equal. The same goes for any event, action, or environment that has the capacity to quantitatively or qualitatively augment or improve human worth, as well: *if* such a possibility exists, *then* dignity is not equal. Independently of how we define the origins and content of worth, in other words, to allow the possibility of any degree or gradation of dignity is to render it unequal. Thus, as with universality, the only way to say that dignity is equal is to say that it is invulnerable—invulnerable, in particular, to any kind of internal or external power that would have the capacity to destroy, degrade, or improve it.

It is for these reasons, therefore, that invulnerability is a necessary precondition for the claim that "dignity is universally equal in all human beings." If this claim is true about dignity, then the claim "human dignity is invulnerable" must also be true. Otherwise, we are committed to recognizing that human worth is somehow vulnerable; and if it is vulnerable, in any way for whatever reason, it is conceptually possible to eradicate and/or weaken (or strengthen) it, and, consequently, conceptually *impossible* to call it "universal" or "equal."[27]

2009], 752-61). Aristotle specifies that developing the virtues must take place "over a full life" in order for human life to flourish; if disaster strikes along the way—say a debilitating loss of a loved one, or a traumatic injury, or the emotional devastation of wrongly being accused of a crime—the humans of good habits may ultimately fall short of their potential, and thus fail to be fully human, by, in effect, no fault of their own. It is instructive to compare this conception of moral vulnerability with the implicit moral invulnerability found in Socrates's famous declaration before being put to death: "Wherefore, O judges, be of good cheer about death, and know this of a truth—that no evil can happen to a good man."

[27] It is important to note that "human dignity" and "human life" may be deeply interrelated, but the former cannot be reducible to the latter if dignity is to be understood as universal and equal. Life, of course, not only can be lost, it can also exist in degrees in terms of greater or lesser biological functioning in relation to the standard of healthy functioning. So while human dignity may include human life, it cannot be reducible to it—if, again, dignity is universally equal.

Is Any Human Capacity Invulnerable?

This brief foray into abstract conceptual territory leads us back to the substantive central question, namely, whether either Gewirth or Nussbaum can coherently account for universally equal dignity. And it appears we are arriving at an answer: if, indeed, invulnerability, as this article has defined it, is a necessary condition for universality and equality, then it appears to be the case that no human capacity, or set of capacities, can coherently serve as the ground for a definition of universally equal dignity. In order to support the opposite conclusion—namely, that capacities *could* provide such a justification—we would have to identify at least one human capacity that is invulnerable to all attempts to harm and/or enhance it. Can we?

Gewirth and Nussbaum provide helpful test cases. Gewirth, as noted above, founds his account of dignity on agency, which, in turn, he grounds in two characteristics of human action: 1) voluntariness or freedom, and 2) purposiveness or intentionality, which includes rationality (one must be able to *know* what one is acting for in order to be an agent). If a human being does not have these capacities, then a human is not an agent; and, by Gewirth's own reasoning, if a human is not an agent, then she or he does not have human worth.

Gewirth recognizes the morally troubling nature of this claim, and so adds what he calls "prospective agents" to the protective umbrella of human worth. By prospective agents, he primarily means children, who are not yet agents—because they do not yet have fully developed free will or rationality—but who one day will be agents. Setting aside the problematic derivation of prospective agency as grounds for moral worth (prospective agency is *not* part of the dialectically necessary structure of human action, and therefore it is not clear how, on rational grounds, the supreme principle of morality can apply to children), it is important to ask whether agency, either in its actualized or potential form, is invulnerable to harm and/or enhancement.

The question, I think, answers itself. Agency is not only something that can and does exist in degrees in the sense of some humans having more agency than others; think, for example, of children who are in the process of becoming full agents and full agents who are in the process of becoming diminished agents because of age, disease, or injury. Agency, it appears, can also be completely destroyed. We need not only think of the exceptionally difficult moral cases of individuals who are alive but in a coma; individuals who have acute mental diseases, or who have been tortured, or who have been severely emotionally abused—they, too, can utterly *lose* their agency as Gewirth defines it. Some individuals who suffer such disease and trauma may be able to regain their agency. But some won't. There are many classes of individuals whom we otherwise define as human, in other words, who are not, and never will be, "agents" in Gewirth's sense.

Again, my goal here is not to critique Gewirth's view of human dignity in and of itself, but, rather, to demonstrate that his account of agency, founded on the capacities of freedom and rationality, cannot coherently account for *universally equal* dignity. Agency is *deeply* vulnerable to harm and/or enhancement, and can and does exist in degrees. And insofar as it is vulnerable in this way, as I sought to establish above, we cannot coherently say a conception of human dignity founded on agency is universally equal. To be sure, Gewirth may be able to justify some conception of dignity—perhaps we might call it "personal dignity"—but he cannot coherently justify universally equal *human* dignity.

The same conclusion applies to Nussbaum's account of human worth. To be sure, Nussbaum seeks to ground dignity on more than agency. However, even if we broaden the scope of capacities eligible for justifying human worth, we are still founding it on *capacities*: sense, imagination, friendship, play, contact with nature, even having bodily integrity—these are things that human beings *do* or can potentially *do*. And insofar as they are things that we do, it is not only the case that some humans, even in potential form, can do them better or more effectively than others, which is to recognize, prima facie, that human capacities are profoundly unequal. It is also to recognize that these capacities can, put simply, be taken away. Indeed, it is in great part for this reason that Nussbaum highlights the moral importance of these capacities; she wants individuals and communities to protect them and help them to flourish. However, the very recognition of the vulnerability of capacities, and, hence, the need to safeguard them, necessarily leads to the conclusion that these capacities are neither universal nor equal and, therefore, cannot coherently ground a universally equal conception of dignity.

The more radical formulation of this claim goes beyond Nussbaum and Gewirth. It applies to all human capacities, however we might define them. The more basic claim is that *no* human capacity is unassailable. That is, there are no human capacities that do not in some way *depend* on any number of internal (an individual's own actions) or external (one's own genetics, the actions of others, the nature of one's surrounding environment) conditions for their initial existence, continued existence, and/or the degree to which they effectively operate for any particular purpose. If this claim accurately characterizes all human capacities, then all human capacities are vulnerable and, therefore, no human capacity is invulnerable. As such, no capacity can account for a universally equal, which, is to say, invulnerable conception of human worth. Put positively, any conception of universally equal human dignity that seeks to justify its universal equality based on a human capacity or set of human capacities is necessarily incoherent.

Human Capacities and the Problem of Human Dignity

This, then, is one of the fundamental problems inhering within the conception of human dignity. If no human capacity can coherently cause or otherwise warrant invulnerable human dignity, what else are we left with? What other "human something" might be able to account not only for how we are distinctively valuable, but also universally and equally so? If nothing humans *do* can account for dignity, perhaps, then, we can turn to what we biologically *are*. That is, perhaps human DNA, something that inheres universally and equally among all human beings, could provide the grounds for universally equal human worth.

The problem with this line of thinking is that even if DNA could account for a conception of dignity as such, it is not clear how it could account for *human* dignity in particular. The claim would essentially be that what makes humans valuable, the cause of our worth, is that we are all bio-chemically the same as a species. But how, then, are we morally different from any other species? How would human dignity be any different qualitatively from the dignity of dolphins, guinea pigs, mosquitos, or any specific kind of bacterium? If shared DNA constitutes the standard by which we attribute dignity to something, in other words, then *all life*, or at least every species of life, would have equal dignity, in which case the "human" in "human dignity" would be superfluous.[28]

We cannot, moreover, claim that DNA is invulnerable given ongoing scientific "advancements" in genetic engineering. Human DNA can be, and has been, altered, including attempts to combine it with the DNA of non-human animals. Whether such experimentation should be permitted and, if it is permitted, in what ways and under what conditions it should be allowed is a vital question. But the fact that it can happen *at all* challenges the status of human DNA as something that could account for a universally equal conception of human dignity. Even if human DNA could never be annihilated save for some

---

[28] In this sense, human life is radically similar to all other forms of biological life: we are contingent beings who come into material existence and leave material existence by forces we have minimal (and, ultimately, no) control over. We are part of the "giveness" of existence. In this respect, we are not unique, and, thus, cannot claim any moral distinctiveness on the grounds of this giveness. To be sure, humans, or most humans, can and do have a unique awareness of and response to this situation of giveness; to say that we are given is not to say that we do not have any freedom in relation to being given. Yet this freedom, and the awareness underlying it, describes a *capacity*; and any capacity or group of capacities, as I sought to argue above, cannot coherently serve as the grounds of universally equal dignity. In other words, "giveness" itself cannot account for makes human dignity "human," and the human response to givenness cannot account for what makes human dignity universal and equal. (I am indebted to Roberto Dell'Oro for the conception of "giveness" as a constitutive feature of human existence.)

catastrophic global event that eradicated all human life (in which case the question of what warrants universally equal human dignity would become moot), there is nothing intrinsic to the nature of DNA itself that prevents it from being corrupted in the sense of altering its original integrity. There is nothing, in other words, that conceptually or practically *guarantees* that all humans will, by virtue of their humanity, remain equal in terms of our shared genetic structure. So in addition to the problem of justifying how and why human DNA could generate worth in general and human worth in particular, it seems that even the very blueprint of human life is not, ultimately, invulnerable and thus not capable of accounting for a universally equal account of human worth.

The fundamental problem of human dignity, then, appears to be this: In order to claim that human dignity is universal and equal—which, again, is to claim that every being otherwise defined as "human" has equal worth *qua* human—we cannot appeal to anything that is *in* human beings or *of* human beings *qua* humans, including all human capacities, in order to justify that worth. This is doubly a problem because, as Gewirth and Nussbaum effectively illustrate, to be human from a moral perspective is, in a decisive sense, to possess and employ distinctively *human capacities* like freedom, and purposiveness, and imagination, and friendship. How could we conceive of human beings as valuable without reference to these kinds of capacities?

JOHN PAUL II'S THEISTIC CONCEPTION OF DIGNITY AS A POSSIBLE SOLUTION

The question, in other words, becomes whether it is possible to coherently conceive of human dignity as universally equal in a way that recognizes the value of human capacities yet is not ultimately dependent upon those capacities. There is at least one way, I believe, and it takes the form of a theistic conception of dignity, like, for example, that which we see in the thought of Pope John Paul II.

As a preliminary point, I wish to emphasize that I mean "theism" in its most basic and widely-accepted sense for the purposes of the argument in this context: namely, the affirmation of the existence of a transcendent and personal divine being. The qualities of "transcendence" and "personal" are both important here. To say that a being is transcendent is to say that it exists independently of everything else in existence, to say, that is, that it does not depend ontologically on any other being. In this sense, a transcendent being is also, by definition, a non-contingent being, and insofar as it is non-contingent, it is, therefore, also ontologically *invulnerable* to everything in existence—nothing in existence, in other words, has the capacity to eradicate, diminish, or enhance its existence.[29]

Yet this kind of ontological independence and invulnerability does not mean that a transcendent being cannot be in relation with that which is non-transcendent. It is not a definitional contradiction, in other words, for theism to claim that the transcendent being is also a *personal* being. As transcendent and, thus, ontologically independent, the divine does not *need* to be in relationship with non-contingent reality, including human beings; yet theism claims that the divine non-contingent being *chooses* to be in this kind of relationship. In this way, then, theism can affirm that the non-contingent and contingent—the divine and the human, in this context—can and do have a *relationship*.

Pope John Paul II presents this kind of theistic view of God-in-relation throughout his theological writings, but especially in his encyclical, *Evangelium vitae* (*The Gospel of Life*). The text commences with an affirmation that life, in its fullest sense, means eternal life in communion with the divine: "Man is called to a fullness of life," John Paul writes, "which far exceeds the dimensions of his earthly existence, because it consists in sharing the very life of God."[30] Yet he quickly and carefully qualifies this assertion by clarifying that humankind's final goal of communion with God does not diminish the value of temporal life. To the contrary, it is the very call to communion with the divine that endows temporal life with its worth and significance. As he writes, "The loftiness of this supernatural vocation reveals the *greatness* and the *inestimable value* of human life even in its temporal phase. Life in time... is the fundamental condition, the initial stage and an integral part of the entire unified process of human existence."[31]

This synthetic relationship between the transcendent and the temporal plays a crucial role in defining John Paul's conception of dignity. On the one hand, he seeks to ground the worth of the person in the individual's *supernatural* origin and destiny; human beings, he argues,

---

[29] It is important to note here that to say the divine is invulnerable to the created world (including human action) is *not* to say that the created world, especially including human action, can or does not *affect* the divine. Indeed, from within the thought of John Paul II specifically, and many strands of Christian thought more broadly, it *matters profoundly* to God whether or not human beings choose to accept God's invitation to relationship and communion. God, in this sense does not need, but God does *desire*—in this case, God desires fellowship—and it is meaningful to the divine whether or not human beings exercise their freedom to fulfill that desire (and, by doing so, to fulfill their own humanity). In this sense, human action does not "harm" or "improve" God from an ontological perspective, but it does *make a difference* to God.

[30] John Paul II, *The Gospel of* Life, (Boston: Pauline Books and Media, 1995), 12.

[31] John Paul II, *The Gospel of Life,* 12.

are created in the image of God and, though fallen, redeemed by Christ's death and resurrection, which enables humans to *return* to God, our one and only true home. Indeed, the very fact that God chose to redeem humanity despite our sin *by becoming human* both establishes and confirms the unparalleled value of humanity and of each human life. As John Paul avers, "Truly great must be the value of human life if the Son of God has taken it up and made it the instrument of the salvation of all humanity!"[32]

Yet John Paul also maintains that the process of returning to God, of being justified and sanctified, takes place in the concrete social and historical circumstances that each individual occupies during her specific lifetime. Dignity's *supernatural* origin and destiny, in other words, plays itself out in each individual's *natural* life. "[Life on earth]," he affirms, "remains *a sacred reality* entrusted to us, to be preserved with a sense of responsibility and brought to perfection in love and in the gift of ourselves to God and to our brothers and sisters."[33]

In recognizing these two poles of human existence, the natural and the supernatural, *The Gospel of Life* thus seeks to provide an account of dignity that is both transcendent and temporal in such a way that the transcendent—our origin in the divine and final destiny as communion with the divine—acts as both the ground and goal of temporal life. As John Paul explains, "The dignity of this life is linked not only to its beginning, to the fact that it comes from God, but also to its final end, to its destiny of fellowship with God in knowledge and love of him."[34]

This "dual citizenship" between natural and supernatural existence also helps explain John Paul's conception of how the image of God relates to human dignity. Humans have dignity because we are created in God's image, which, for John Paul, means that humans have *capacities* analogous to God's capacities, something that is unique in Creation. As he writes, "*The life which God offers to man is a gift by which God shares something of himself with his creature.*"[35] That which God shares with human beings not only includes stewardship over Creation, but also, as he specifies, "those spiritual faculties which are distinctively human, such as reason, discernment between good and evil, and free will."[36] To be human, in other words, is to be able to know the good as good and to be able to freely choose to act in accordance with it. Humans are unique in Creation, moreover, not only because

---

[32] John Paul II, *The Gospel of Life*, 59, document's emphasis.
[33] John Paul II, *The Gospel of Life,* 12, document's emphasis.
[34] John Paul II, *The Gospel of Life*, 65.
[35] John Paul II, *The Gospel of Life* 60, document's emphasis.
[36] John Paul II, *The Gospel of Life*, 60.

we possess these capacities, but also because we possess the potential to employ them for their intended purposes: attaining virtue in this life so that we may, by God's gracious gift, enjoy communion with God in the next. The value human beings have by virtue of these capacities associated with the image of God is thus attached both to capacities themselves and for the ends for which they can and ought to be used.

John Paul is careful, however—and this is crucial for the article's overall argument—to avoid the conclusion that either the image of God in humanity or the dignity associated with it is reducible to these capacities. Indeed, one of the greatest themes in the encyclical is John Paul's lamentation that the contemporary world regards those with diminished capacities as having less value than other human beings. As he writes, "It is clear that... there is no place in the world for anyone who, like the unborn or the dying, is a weak element in the social structure, or for anyone who appears completely at the mercy of others and is radically dependent on them, and can only communicate through the silent language of a profound sharing of affection."[37] The recognition of human dignity thus enjoins all individuals to recognize that *every* person has the same intrinsic worth as every other person, and that to be "a person" is not only defined by what we can do, but also, and more fundamentally, by who we *are*: individuals created in the image of God and redeemed by Christ's life, death, and resurrection.

---

[37] John Paul II, *The Gospel of Life,* 36. The relationship between the image of God as being valuable independently of human capacities and the image of God as being valuable *because* of human capacities is complex in John Paul II's thought. On the surface, it may appear to be a contradiction—how can he claim that human beings are both valuable because they have distinctively human capacities yet also deny that those capacities confirm value on human life? While a full exposition of this element of John Paul's conception of dignity falls outside the scope of this article, it is important to note that this need not necessarily be interpreted as a contradiction if we understand the image of God not only as an ontological constitutive feature of who human beings are, but also as a *potential to be realized*. Insofar as the image of God *ontologically* defines humans as dignified, it does so independently of any capacity or the exercise of that capacity; insofar, however, as the image of God defines dignity as a potential to be realized (so, for example, one can *become* more fully human from a moral standpoint by acting in accordance with the image of God and less human by acting in ways that violate the image), then capacities and the exercise of those capacities play an essential role in determining whether the potential inherent in the image of God is realized or not. In this sense, one can say, as John Paul does, that a murderer does not lose his dignity in this sense of his ontological gift of humanity by murdering, yet still maintain that the act of murder very much thwarts the *realization* of the individual's gift of humanity in attaining its full potential. Although John Paul does not explicitly define dignity in this way, I believe there are strong grounds for interpreting his conception of dignity—and the Catholic social thought tradition's conception of dignity more broadly—as having these two interrelated but distinct components—one given, one attained. While a full defense of this claim requires substantial additional argumentation, it at least helps indicate why John Paul might not be contradicting himself on this point.

God, John Paul argues, values every person as a person independently of their capacities, and, therefore, so must we: "[The] deepest element of God's commandment to protect human life is the *requirement to show reverence and love* for every person and the life of every person."[38]

This emphasis on the intrinsic, God-given value of all human life, in turn, explains why John Paul frequently describes dignity as "inviolable" and "indestructible." Although located in humans, human dignity is grounded in God, and so out of the reach of human attempts to harm or destroy. As he writes, "It is therefore urgently necessary… to rediscover those essential and innate human and moral values which flow from the very truth of the human being and express and safeguard the dignity of the person: values which *no individual, no majority, and no state can ever create, modify or destroy*, but must only acknowledge, respect and promote."[39] Insofar as dignity instantiates a divine truth about who human beings are—created in God's image and redeemed by Christ—there is nothing that the created world can do, as the passage says, to "create," "modify," or "destroy" that truth. Human beings are intrinsically and objectively valuable because God values every human being *no matter what* humans (or anything else in the created world) do or fail to do.

Dignity thus can be recognized or fail to be recognized by other individuals, societies, cultures, states, etc. But whether or not it is recognized has no effect on the integrity of the dignity itself. Indeed, God's constitutive, creative, and redemptive relationship with every individual creates worth that is, properly understood, "indestructible." Using the Book of Exodus to describe the effect that God's love has on human beings, John Paul explains, "Freedom from slavery meant the gift of an identity, the recognition of an indestructible dignity and

---

[38] John Paul II, *The Gospel of Life*, 69, document's emphasis. The distinction between "human life" and "human dignity" is a basic yet crucial distinction in John Paul's conception of dignity. At times, he appears to employ the terms "human life" and "human dignity" as synonyms, as, for example, when he states, "The present encyclical…is therefore meant to be a precise and vigorous reaffirmation of the value of human life and its inviolability" (John Paul II, *The Gospel of Life*, 17). Yet he also writes, "Certainly *the life of the body in its earthly state is not an absolute good* for the believer, especially as he may be asked to give up his life for a greater good" (John Paul II, *The Gospel of Life*, 17, document's emphasis). Acting in conformity with the Gospel of Life, in other words, may call one to sacrifice her biological life, which would not harm one's dignity but, to the contrary, be in accordance with one's dignity and even help bring it to its moral fulfillment. Human dignity thus includes human life, but it is not reducible to human life. This distinction also draws on the distinction between human dignity being both transcendent and temporal and, consequently, both vulnerable and invulnerable (see footnote 37 above).

[39] John Paul II, *The Gospel of Life*, 116, emphasis added.

the beginning of a new history in which the discovery of God and discovery of self go hand in hand."[40] Indeed, this human "identity" as intrinsically and indestructibly valuable is rooted so firmly in the individual that even those who commit grave moral offenses retain their equal worth, a claim that explains why John Paul can affirm, "*Not even a murderer loses his personal dignity,* and God himself pledges to guarantee this."[41] This invulnerability of human dignity to human action, or anything else in the created world, ultimately results from the invulnerability of its divine source. "Human life," John Paul concludes, "is thus given a sacred and inviolable character which reflects the inviolability of the Creator himself."[42]

CONCLUSION

While the validity or truth-status of John Paul II's conception of human worth remains a crucial question—one that I deliberately beg in this context—his theistic definition of dignity nevertheless provides a conceptually coherent foundation for his affirmation that all human beings have equal worth. Recall, as argued above, that the condition for the possibility of "universality" and "equality," from a conceptual perspective, is invulnerability to the possibility of extirpation, harm, and/or enhancement. In recognizing God as transcendent and, therefore, inviolable, and, furthermore, by describing this inviolable being as establishing an inviolable relationship with every human individual, John Paul can say that his account of dignity is universal and equal without inconsistency. Given that human worth is grounded in the non-contingent, there is nothing that we, the contingent, can do to eradicate, harm, or, even enhance it. And this invulnerable worth, John

---

[40] John Paul II, *The Gospel of Life*, 55.

[41] John Paul II, *The Gospel of* Life 24, document's emphasis.

[42] John Paul II, *The Gospel of* Life, 88. Although John Paul uses the term "inviolable" to describe dignity here, I have chosen to use the term "invulnerable" throughout the article to describe the same characteristic. This is not accidental. In one sense, the terms could be understood as being interchangeable: if something cannot be "violated" then it is, in a decisive way, invulnerable to harm. However, drawing on the term's Latin roots, I want to emphasize that dignity must be conceived as something that literally cannot be "wounded" in order to be defined as universally equal. I believe "invulnerability" captures this conceptual necessity more effectively than "inviolability."

That is not to say, however, that dignity must *only* be defined as invulnerable. Although defending this claim falls outside the scope of this article, I believe there is a way to coherently define dignity as vulnerable to harm (thus necessitating that it be protected and allowed to flourish) without sacrificing its invulnerability, and, hence, universal equality. To do so, one can, I believe, define dignity as both a static ontological quality in all human beings (invulnerable) and also as a potential to be realized (vulnerable). See footnote 37 above.

Paul makes clear, extends to all, regardless of each individual's distinct set of capacities.

It is crucial to note, however, that John Paul does not establish his conception of universally equal dignity independently of human capabilities. To act freely and with purpose, to be able to engage in practical and speculative reasoning, to immerse oneself in one's own imagination and the imaginations of others, to form families, to *love* God and others—these and other capabilities form a fundamental part of our moral identity as bearers of the image of God. But, in the end, they in no way constitute the sum total of our moral identity. In other words, it is not what we do that morally defines our worth as human beings. It is *who we are*: beings created in the image of God and redeemed on the Cross. And, unlike Gewirth and Nussbaum, John Paul can coherently say that that value-conferring fact applies to all humans everywhere all the time in absolute equality. It is a dignity of no exceptions.

This theistic vision of human worth, in the end, raises important and challenging theological, anthropological, and epistemological questions. Given the argument here, one could ask: Is it only the Christian—or Catholic—conception of the divine that can account for universally equal human dignity? How are we to conceive of the image of God in relation to human worth more specifically, especially in light of the Catholic and Christian recognition of human sin? How is this God who gives worth to be known? Does universal human dignity ultimately depend on a faith claim that, in turn, is ultimately reducible to a blind affirmation of religious authority? If so, how might these epistemological restrictions affect the status of dignity's universality and equality? Also, if human dignity is ultimately invulnerable to harm, does that ultimately render it a morally inert principle? Why, for example, have rights to protect dignity if it does not need protection? These are crucial questions that a deeper examination of a theistic account of human dignity would have to answer (and which I have sought to address elsewhere[43]).

Yet the central issue animating this article still remains: What is the condition for the possibility of coherently describing human dignity as universally equal? The answer, it appears, ultimately points to the Transcendent. If we wish to define human worth as truly universal

---

[43] For further discussion see Matthew Petrusek, "Catholic Social Ethics and the (In)vulnerability of Human Dignity" (Dissertation, University of Chicago, 2013).

and truly equal, we must somehow locate its ground beyond humanity and outside the reach of human hands.[44] ▮

---

[44] As a parting note, it is important to stress that theism as it relates to human dignity can potentially accommodate a great diversity of conceptions of the divine, including those (depending on their precise theological interpretation) generally attributed to the three Abrahamic faiths. In other words, while great and irreducible conceptual differences exist between Yahweh, Allah, and the Father, Son and Holy Spirit, insofar as each tradition's interpretation of God includes the recognition of God's non-contingency, agency, and value-conferring relationship with humans, there is no reason, from a conceptual perspective, why any one of these theistic conceptions could not provide a coherent foundation for universally equal human dignity—"coherent" in the sense of being able to account for dignity's universality and equality. And so, potentially, with any other conception of the divine in any other religious tradition: as long as it attributes non-contingency and some kind of agency to God, and can describe how God employs God's agency to endow all human beings with equal worth, there is no reason why *many* different conceptions of the divine could not coherently support the claim "human beings have universally equal dignity." This is not to say that any and every such account would be true; it is to say that every and any such account could, from a conceptual perspective, potentially be *coherent*.

Journal of Moral Theology, Vol. 5, No. 1 (2016): 65-85

A Case Study of Scholasticism: Peter Abelard and Peter Lombard on Penance

Lucas Briola

ULRICH LEINSLE BEGINS his *Introduction to Scholastic Theology* with an attempt to define scholasticism over the course of fifteen pages, only coming to conclude that "an unequivocal definition of 'Scholasticism' does not seem possible."[1] This lack of clarity has a simple explanation. Though sometimes seen as a smooth monolithic structure unaffected by the confines of time, medieval scholasticism can be more appropriately imaged as an ongoing debate spanning centuries, a debate that would greatly affect the future of Christian theology. The increasing desire to rationally articulate the faith alongside the ongoing development of sacramental traditions meant that attempts to express theologies of the sacraments provided some of the most heated and nuanced scholastic debates. Penance was no exception, reaching a developmental turning-point in the twelfth-century, particularly when considered by two of the most prominent theologians and "pioneers of sacramental theology" of the time—Peter Abelard and Peter Lombard. [2]

Because an adequate theology of the sacrament was only beginning to be formulated during this time, a study of this time period elucidates some interesting and important points for an adequate notion of penance. Additionally, medieval scholastic theology cannot be understood apart from its context, inarguably affected and conditioned by other historical and cultural currents. Taking this broader theo-cultural milieu into account, this essay deals with two key scholastic debates over penance. First, I will locate Abelard and Lombard as contritionalists—those who assert that God's forgiveness occurs at contrition rather than confession—and consequently consider their respective views on the necessity of confession. Second, since both acknowledge that God's forgiveness comes at contrition rather than confession, I will examine how this position changes the role of priests for the two thinkers, as priests are now considered judges or doctors who need to

---

[1] Ulrich G. Leinsle, *Introduction to Scholastic Theology*, trans. Michael J. Miller (Washington, D.C.: Catholic University of America Press, 2010), 16.
[2] Paul Anciaux, *La théologie du sacrement de pénitence au XIIᵉ siècle* (Louvain: É. Nauwelaerts, 1949), vii.

develop suitable tools for these roles. The guiding idea of both sections is simple—Abelard and Lombard put forth theologies that overcome any overly routinized understandings of penance, placing personal responsibility on both penitent and confessor.

THE TWELFTH CENTURY
INTERIORITY, CONTRITION, AND CONFESSION

The twelfth century marked an important but often unnoticed turning point in the history of Western Civilization, an incipient humanistic turn towards the subject that would eventually blossom in the Renaissance. [3] Suddenly, interiority—whether motivations or emotions—took on increased significance. Historical treatments of the time have revealed this trend. Colin Morris wrote an entire book arguing that the period from 1050-1200 "discovered the individual," a time which featured "a concern with self-discovery; an interest in the relations between people, and in the role of the individual within society; and an assessment of people by their inner intentions rather than by their external acts."[4]

Writers have rightly nuanced this historiographic approach away from overly individualistic conceptions, however. Caroline Walker Bynum has argued that rather than discovering the individual at the expense of a wider community and external acts, the period "was characterized by the discovery of the group and the 'outer man' as well as by the discovery of the inner landscape and of the self."[5] Discovering the "self" provided a more holistic approach that had "a quite particular sense of the relationship between inner and outer, between motive and model."[6] Writers such as Philip of Harvengt and Hugh of St. Vic-

---

[3] See M.-D. Chenu, "Nature and Man: The Renaissance of the Twelfth Century," in *Nature, Man, and Society in the Twelfth Century: Essays on New Theological Perspectives in the Latin West*, ed. and trans. Jerome Taylor and Lester K. Little (Chicago: The University of Chicago Press, 1979), 1-48.

[4] Colin Morris, *The Discovery of the Individual 1050-1200* (London: SPCK, 1972), 158. See also Robert W. Hanning, *The Individual in Twelfth-Century Romance* (New Haven, CT: Yale University Press, 1977), 1: "Recent research into various aspects of twelfth century European culture convinces me that one of the central motivating forces of the twelfth-century Renaissance was a new desire on the part of literate men and women to understand themselves as single, unique persons—as what we would call *individuals*. This impulse to understand operated in three distinguishable but not totally distinct areas: the individual in relation to his own makeup and character, the individual in relation to his social and institutional environment, and the individual in relation to his God."

[5] Caroline Walker Bynum, "Did the Twelfth Century Discover the Individual?," *Journal of Ecclesiastical History* 31, no. 1 (Jan. 1980): 3.

[6] Bynum, "Did the Twelfth Century Discover the Individual?," 5.

tor evinced "that, in reform and moral improvement, exterior and interior will and should go together."[7] Self-change could likewise only be brought on by others, whether in discovering suitable models to imitate or through one's communal surroundings.[8]

According to Jacques Le Goff, the interplay between these individual and communal elements would also play a significant theological role in the surging importance of purgatory in the twelfth century.[9] Though this increasingly central notion in the spiritual lives of Christians "strengthened family, corporate, and fraternal ties, Purgatory, caught up in a personalization of spiritual life, actually fostered individualism. It focused attention on individual death and the judgment that followed."[10] The moral self-improvement in the afterlife could only mean an increased spiritual and moral probing of the self in this life, albeit an examination that could not remain at interiority alone. Unsurprisingly, because of the substantial overlap between the two, shifts in purgatorial understandings would mean shifts in understanding and performing penitential practices during the twelfth century.

Indeed, penance and confession gradually moved away from being communal and public to being more individual and private in the Early Middle Ages, and by the twelfth century, private confession had become the norm rather than the exception. As scholastic theology began to emerge, producing synthetic accounts of Christian doctrine and developing a more robust sacramental theology, questions arose over these newer penitential developments. One major question concerned the locus of forgiveness. While all accepted the tripartite division of contrition, confession, and satisfaction, theologians debated over when exactly God forgave sins. Two theological camps emerged. Confessionalists—canonists like Gratian—contended that forgiveness only occurred with the confession of sins and the absolution by a priest. Others, like Peter Abelard and Peter Lombard, were considered contritionalists.[11] These theologians insisted that forgiveness occurred early, at the penitent's moment of sorrow. How and why Abelard and

---

[7] Bynum, "Did the Twelfth Century Discover the Individual?," 11. Also see 12: "That is what a saint *is*: one in whom extraordinary life (without) reflects extraordinary virtue and grace (within)."

[8] Bynum, "Did the Twelfth Century Discover the Individual?," 16.

[9] Jacques Le Goff, *The Birth of Purgatory*, trans. Arthur Goldhammer (Chicago: The University of Chicago Press, 1984), 3-6. Le Goff diligently traces the vestiges of purgatory over time but places special emphasis on its eventual "spatialization" between 1150-1200, identifying this span as the time of purgatory's birth. See 5: "Until the end of the twelfth century the noun *purgatorium* did not exist: *the* Purgatory had not yet been born."

[10] Le Goff, *Purgatory,* 233.

[11] For a detailed and comprehensive overview of the contours of this debate see Anciaux, "Le probleme de la necessite de la confession," in *La théologie du sacrement de pénitence au XIIe siècle*: 164-274.

Lombard argued these positions shows their underlying concerns for authenticity as well as the strong ties between interior contrition and exterior confession.[12]

PETER ABELARD ON CONFESSION AND CONTRITION

Peter Abelard, living from 1079 to 1142, has captured the public imagination more than any other twelfth-century figure. Indeed, Abelard can be seen as an encapsulation of the age, and it is precisely his paradigmatic representation of the century that 'discovered the self' which makes him so popular. Movies have depicted the romantic forays of Abelard and Heloise, a spectacle referenced in literary works from such writers as Alexander Pope to Mark Twain to Etienne Gilson and even in music by Cole Porter. This intense interest in Abelard's controversial and turbulent personal life is not accidental, as the seminal thinker provides a unique and fairly unprecedented glimpse into his own life, both through his correspondence with Heloise and his autobiographical *Historia Calamitatum*.

This strong sense of interiority goes beyond mere self-description though, affecting the entirety of his theological and philosophical work, especially his ethics. Abelard constructs his ethical framework in two works: his *Dialogus inter Philosophum, Judaeum, et Christianum* and *Scito Te Ipsum*, also known as his *Ethica*. The latter, the focus of this study, is aptly named *Know Thyself* for two reasons. First, as already discussed, the title corresponds well with the century's *zeitgeist*, turning toward the inner person. Second, in the work, Abelard concerns himself with what Marilyn McCord Adams has termed the "locus of imputability," that is, where moral judgments are made.[13] Unsurprisingly, Abelard offers a heavily internal and intentional ethics focused on "consent." This focus on interiority shapes Abelard's understanding of penance, placing the locus of reconciliation at the level of genuine contrition. Importantly though, Abelard still upholds the necessity of confession. Abelard's text merits closer attention.

Abelard begins his *Ethics* by offering his definition of sin: a "consent to what is inappropriate."[14] He arrives at this conclusion in part through a *reductio* argument, refusing to place sin in a bad will or an

---

[12] See Bernhard Poschmann, *Penance and the Anointing of the Sick*, trans. Francis Courtney (New York: Herder and Herder, 1964), 138-145, and James Dallen, *The Reconciling Community: The Rite of Penance* (New York: Pueblo Publishing Company, 1986), 140-148.

[13] Marilyn McCord Adams, introduction to *Ethical Writings*, by Peter Abelard, trans. Paul V. Spade (Indianapolis: Hackett Publishing Company, 1995), xix.

[14] Peter Abelard, "Ethics" in *Ethical Writings*, trans. Paul V. Spade (Indianapolis: Hackett Publishing Company, 1995), par. 7. Throughout the paper, I have used Spade's translation and his paragraph numbers. Latin references are taken from D.E. Luscombe's edition (New York: Oxford University Press, 1971).

act.[15] He first dismantles the argument that sin is located in a bad will.[16] More interestingly, however, in contrast to the penitential manuals before him, Abelard meticulously argues that sin is not in action, which "doesn't add anything to the merit, whether it springs from good or bad willing."[17] He continues, "In fact, deeds… are equally common to reprobates and to the elect, are in themselves all indifferent."[18] Abelard instead locates sin at one's interior consent, "when we don't draw back from committing [the sin] and are wholly ready to carry it out should the opportunity arise."[19] Interior consent to sin, rather than exterior, ostensibly sinful actions, constitutes sin.

Similarly, the effect of intention on sin plays an important role in the first half of Abelard's *Ethics*. As he writes, "For God doesn't think about the things that are done but rather in what mind they are done. The merit or praiseworthiness of the doer doesn't consist in the deed but the intention… [God] judges the mind itself in its intention's purpose, not in the result of the outward deed."[20] Regardless of the rightness or wrongness of an act, goodness or sinfulness resides at one's intentions. Abelard so vehemently defends this thesis that he takes it to the furthest point he thinks possible. Concerning the persecutors of Christ and the martyrs who felt that they were doing the will of God, "we certainly can't say they were sinning. No one's ignorance is a sin."[21] Abelard does not stop here, as these persecutors "would have even sinned more seriously through fault if they had spared them contrary to conscience."[22] Truly, acts are indifferent! In Abelard's ethical framework, interior conscience and intention take precedence even in the most extreme cases. In short, interiority guides Abelard's ethics.

This stress on interiority provides an important context for the second half of his *Ethics*, which deals with penance. As mentioned earlier, when exactly forgiveness occurred—whether in confession or contrition—preoccupied the minds of many early medieval theologians and Abelard was no exception.[23] He begins the second half of his *Ethics*

---

[15] Abelard, *Ethics*, 67.

[16] See Abelard, *Ethics*, 9-15.

[17] Abelard, *Ethics*, 25.

[18] Abelard, *Ethics*, 90. Also see 6: "For whatever is common to good and bad people equally is irrelevant to virtue or vice."

[19] Abelard, *Ethics*, 29.

[20] Abelard, *Ethics*, 57 and 90.

[21] Abelard, *Ethics*, 110.

[22] Abelard, *Ethics*, 131.

[23] Peter Abelard, *Sic et Non: A Critical Edition*, ed. Blanche B. Boyer and Richard McKeon (Chicago: The University of Chicago Press, 1977), 510: "*Quod sine confessione non dimttantur peccata et contra.*"

by acknowledging its three movements: penitence (contrition), confession, and satisfaction.[24]

Where, then, between these former two does reconciliation occur? Unsurprisingly, considering that interiority guides Abelard's thought, the French thinker argues that the locus of forgiveness is contrition, not confession. As he puts it:

> Now sin—scorn for God or consent to evil—doesn't persist together with this groaning and contrition of heart (*contritione cordis*) we call true penitence. For God's charity, which inspires this groaning, is incompatible with any fault. In this groaning we are at once reconciled with God and obtain forgiveness for the preceding sin.[25]

True penance occurs in one's inner life, *contritione cordis*.[26] Not only this, but contrition must be prompted by the right motivations. God's charity and love, not fear, should stir this inner sorrow, "moved to remorse not so much by fear of the penalties as by love for [God]."[27] Abelard sets high expectations for proper interior dispositions—sorrow out of love, not guilt—for Christian contrition. Abelard's stress on the sincerity of interiority parallels his larger ethical project.

But what, then, is the role of confessing sins? Based on what has been written thus far, it would seem that confession becomes superfluous for Abelard. He even writes, "There are people who think only God should be confessed to.... But I don't see what confession is worth before a God who knows all things, or what allowance the tongue gains for us."[28] Yet, instead of dismissing confession, Abelard somehow maintains the need for this external action.

He lists three practical advantages of confession. Confessing sins to confessors means more prayers from them. The humbling required in telling sins to another serves as part of the satisfaction. Likewise, in confessing sins, the confessor, and not the biased self, determines

---

[24] Abelard, *Ethics*, 150. "*Tria itaque sunt in reconciliatio peccatoris ad Deum, penitentia scilicet, confessio, satisfactio.*" (Luscombe ed., 32).

[25] Abelard, *Ethics*, 165.

[26] Abelard, *Ethics*, 151: "The mind's sorrow over what it has failed in is properly called penitence, namely when it troubles someone that he's gone out of bounds in some way."

[27] Abelard, *Ethics*, 164. Also see 168: "So wherever there is true penitence—that is coming only from the love of God—there remains no scorn for God..."
This theme is also important in his *Exposition of the Epistle to the Romans*: "Wherefore, our redemption through Christ's suffering is that deeper affection in us which not only frees us from slavery to sin, but also wins for us the true liberty of sons of God, so that we do all things out of love rather than fear—love to him who has shown us such grace that no greater can be found." In *A Scholastic Miscellany: Anselm to Ockham*, ed. Eugene R. Fairweather (New York: The Macmillan Company, 1970), 284.

[28] Abelard, *Ethics*, 183.

proper satisfaction, and accordingly penitents can rest more securely that they are properly atoning for their sins.[29]

Abelard goes beyond mere usefulness though, as he posits that Satan himself makes penitents "embarrassed that the deed ... should be known by humans."[30] He writes "But if someone wants medication for a wound, then no matter how disgusting the wound is, no matter how much it stinks, *it has to be disclosed* to the doctor so that the appropriate cure is used."[31] Confession, similarly, is mandatory.

Despite this, Abelard goes to great lengths to show that confession can still be omitted. He focuses on Peter's denial of Jesus as one example where confession was and should have been omitted since more benefit than harm came from it. Once again, Abelard stresses proper motivations behind Peter's omission. It would not have been right if done to maintain his reputation. Abelard notes that instead, Peter did it not for his own sake but with foresight for the sake of the church— had others known that its head was "so quick to deny and so faint-hearted," the church could have easily floundered in its infant stages.[32] Abelard broadens this Petrine prudence to all.[33] Nevertheless, though Peter did not *have* to confess sins, he could have confessed on account of the prayer support that he would have received—again, Abelard reiterates the usefulness over necessity of confession.[34] The thinker also adds that confession can be omitted if the priest is incompetent, further explored in the second half of this essay.

Abelard leaves his readers with a convoluted, if not contradictory, picture of confession's necessity, at least on the surface. Forgiveness and reconciliation occur at the level of inner contrition. Confession is at least useful, and eventually Abelard posits its necessity. At the same time, Abelard asserts that there are times when confession can be omitted. Does this all result in an incoherent treatment of confession? Marcia Colish thinks so:

> Despite the clarity and force of his contritionalist claims, Abelard wants to argue that confession is still necessary, even though the penitent's sin has already been forgiven before he speaks to the priest.... Abelard is aware of the difficulties he imposes on himself in seeking

---

[29] Abelard, *Ethics*, 184.

[30] Abelard, *Ethics*, 185.

[31] Abelard, *Ethics*, 185 (emphasis added). "[S]ed *qui plagae querit medicamentum, quantumcumque ipsa sordeat, quantumcumque oleat, medico reuelanda est ut competens adhibeatur curatio.*" (Luscombe ed., 100).

[32] Abelard, *Ethics*, 187.

[33] Abelard, *Ethics*, 186-189. "By this kind of foresight many other people could also delay confession or do completely without it without sin, if they believed it would be more harmful than beneficial."

[34] Abelard, *Ethics*, 190.

to make confession mandatory, and he makes heavy weather of his argument here, jumping from one idea to another in a kind of scatter-gun effort to distract the reader from the logical insufficiency of any of the claims he makes.[35]

A more coherent picture, however, can be gleaned. Though admittedly speculative, perhaps the distinction can be made in light of how the confession is made. In this view, an arbitrary act of confession in itself separated from contrition is not necessary. Genuine contrition, a preoccupation of Abelard, is necessary, and this interior feeling most frequently results in exterior acts like confession.[36] In this sense, confession *is* necessary, confession arising from genuine contrition borne out of a love for God that demands doing anything for God. Accordingly, the penitent wants to reap all the benefits possible from the useful features confession offers. If a person forgoes confession, then perhaps contrition was not out of love for God, a false contrition Abelard warns against.

Nevertheless, though unique, the Petrine exception remains. Willemien Otten offers a provocative and helpful reading of Abelard's use of St. Peter here.[37] She appropriately situates Abelard in his monastic setting and focuses her attention on Abelard's citation of Ambrose regarding Peter:

> I do not find what he said; I do find that he wept. I read about his tears; I do not read about atonement. The tears wash away the misdeed that it is a disgrace to confess out loud, and the weeping takes care of the forgiveness and shame. The tears speak without terror about the fault. They confess without detriment to the feeling of shame.[38]

Peter's tears, borne out of genuine sorrow, contrition, and love for Christ, serve as his confession. Here, Peter's contrition and external

---

[35] Marcia L. Colish, *Peter Lombard*, vol. 2 (New York: E.J. Brill, 1994), 596.
[36] Susan R. Kramer writes "But if Abelard delineates a secret and private part of the self, he also makes clear in his theory of penance that this secret self must be exposed in order to be judged and punished by others. Abelard's contritionism was highly influential, but the criticisms and refinements of Abelard's penitential theory betray not only a new interest in the inner self and its relation to God, but also a new concern with exposing that inner life to human judgment and control." In "'We Speak to God with our Thoughts': Abelard and the Implications of Private Communication with God," *Church History* 69, no. 1 (March 2000): 39.
[37] Willemien Otten, "In Conscience's Court: Abelard's Ethics as a Science of the Self," in *Virtue and Ethics in the Twelfth Century*, ed. István P. Bejczy and Richard G. Newhauser (Boston: Brill Academic Publishing, 2005), 53-74.
[38] Abelard, *Ethics*, 186.

tears serve as one continuous, quasi-sacramental act, much like external confession should follow from contrition.[39] However, in Peter's case, "By artificially isolating guilt from love, formalized confession would somehow stand in the way of the soul who, by humbling himself, is trying to make satisfaction to God directly."[40] Abelard, a monk, would have been familiar with the monastic *officium flendi*.[41] As a monastic reformer, the genuineness of Peter's tears help Abelard's larger project: "While he thereby seems to reinvigorate the concept of monastic life, including the office of weeping, he wants to dispense at the same time with the wear of its ritualized quality. In this regard Abelard's interest in the tears of Peter betraying Christ is quite revealing."[42] Just like above, where an arbitrary confession is not necessary, genuine weeping out of sorrow is more valuable than formalized acts of sorrow that can easily become trite and inauthentic.

Thus, Abelard's projects, whether in monastic reform or writing on penance, are inseparable—proper and authentic interior motivations trump formalized and ritualized external actions that have the potential of becoming mere routine. These types of actions are not necessary, particularly since the locus of reconciliation occurs at contrition for Abelard. Nevertheless, it is the authenticity of this contrition that so often produces exterior acts such as confession, resulting in one continuous movement between contrition and confession. In this sense, confession is necessary. Instead of forwarding an inconsistent theology of penance, Abelard provides a nuanced approach that emphasizes interior authenticity.

PETER LOMBARD ON CONTRITION AND CONFESSION

Peter Lombard, living from approximately 1105 to 1164, likewise was a key figure of the twelfth century, though for different reasons. While lacking the intrigue and escapades of Abelard, Lombard instead made his mark by producing the most influential theological textbook

---

[39] Otten, "In Conscience's Court," 65: "In this position the sacramental dimension, the depth of moral insight, and the attention for individual conscience and conduct all play their part...I have chosen to label this view a kind of poetico-monastic exemplarism." For the role of tears in medieval penance, see David N. Power, "Contrition with Tears: Motivation for Repentance," in *Church and Theology: Essays in Memory of Carl J. Peter*, ed. Peter C. Phan (Washington, D.C.: Catholic University Press, 1995), 215-40.

[40] Otten, "In Conscience's Court," 66-7.

[41] "Meanwhile it may be worth remembering that being tormented by a divided self was part of the monastic profession just as it was the monk's duty to lament the sinful state of the human condition regardless of the specifics of his own sinful behavior: the so-called *officium flendi*, the office of weeping." M.B. Pranger, "Bernard of Clairvaux: Work and Self," in *The Cambridge Companion to The Cistercian Order*, ed. Mette Birkedal Bruun (New York: Cambridge University Press, 2013), 190.

[42] Otten, "In Conscience's Court," 72.

for the medieval period, his masterpiece *Sententiarum Quatuor Libri*, the *Sentences*. Synthesizing and resolving disputes between conflicting historical authorities on a broad scope of topics, Lombard's work proved to be indispensable for the ongoing development of scholastic theology. Beyond this impact though, arguably Lombard's greatest legacy comes from the sacramental theology he bequeathed, particularly in response to the gradual growth of Catharism. Unsurprisingly, the "Master of the Sentences" tackled the contrition-confession question, reaching similar conclusions as Abelard although in a slightly different way. If authentic interiority producing authentic acts can be said to guide Abelard's treatment of the contrition-confession question, then sacramentality can be said to guide Lombard's analysis of the same question.

Lombard's fourth book of the *Sentences*, *De Doctrina Signorum*, deals with sacraments. In the very first question, he defines a sacrament as "a sign of the grace of God and the form of invisible grace, inasmuch as it bears the likeness of the grace and is its cause. Thus, the sacraments were instituted for the sake not only of signifying but of sanctifying."[43] Crucial here is the relationship between the *sacramentum tantum* (rite only) and the inner reality, *res* (thing). Beyond merely signifying or resembling inner grace, the external rite itself "contain[s] and convey[s] that inner reality."[44] In other words, the two—*res* and *sacramentum*, interior and exterior—are distinct but ultimately inseparable, forming one reality. Externals convey internals. This understanding is crucial for fully grasping Lombard's theology of penance.

In his first distinction regarding penance, Peter hints at the contrition-confession question. Already he acknowledges the difference between inner and outer penance:

> [B]ut penance is called both a sacrament and a virtue of the mind. For there is an inner penance, and an outward one. The exterior one is the sacrament; the interior one is the virtue of the mind and each of these is a cause of justification and salvation. But whether every outward penance is a sacrament and, if not everyone, then which is to be recognized by this name, we shall investigate later.[45]

---

[43] Peter Lombard, *The Sentences*, trans. Giulio Silano (Toronto: Pontifical Institute of Medieval Studies, 2010), IV, d. 1, c. 4, a.2.
[44] Thomas M. Finn, "The Sacramental World in the Sentences of Peter Lombard," *Theological Studies* 69 (2008): 568. See also Damien van den Eynde, *Les définitions des sacrements pendant la première période de la théologie scolastique (1050-1240)* (Rome: Antonianum, 1950), 40-46.
[45] Lombard, *Sent.* IV, d. 14, c. 1, a.1.

Shortly thereafter, Lombard offers a definition of penance similar to Abelard's, emphasizing interior contrition. Penance is "a virtue by which we bewail and hate, with purpose of amendment, the evils we have committed, and we will not to commit again the things we have bewailed. And so true penance is to sorrow in one's soul and to hate vices."[46] Rather than deriving from an external act, this penance comes from sorrow, compunction, and a resolve not to sin again—in other words, contrition.

Yet, Lombard only explicitly explores the question in Distinctions XVI and XVII. Referencing John Chrysostom and Augustine, he delineates the three traditional components of penance: "compunction of heart, confession of the mouth, satisfaction in deed (*compunctio cordis, confessio oris, satisfactio operis*)."[47] Soon after, he considers whether sin can be forgiven through only contrition without satisfaction and confession and from this whether at times one can confess to God without a priest and whether confession can be made to another layperson.[48] Lombard is well aware of the difficulties of these questions, "For in these matters even the learned are found to answer differently, because the doctors appear to have transmitted views regarding them which are various and almost contradictory."[49]

After considering some of these opinions, like Abelard, Lombard places the locus of reconciliation at contrition, asserting:

> Surely… sins are blotted out by contrition and humility of heart, even without confession by the mouth and payment of outward punishment. For from the moment when one proposes, with compunction of mind, that one will confess, God remits; because there is present confession of the heart, although not of the mouth, by which the soul is cleansed inwardly from the spot and contagion of the sin committed, and the debt of eternal death is released.[50]

At this point, Marcia Colish, who earlier criticized Abelard's unwillingness to take his contritionism further, lauds Lombard as "a staunch contritionist, and as the only supporter of that side of the debate in the mid-twelfth century who refuses to shrink from the logic of its claims, who goes on to develop a coherent and non-contradictory theory of the relations between contrition and the other two traditional elements

---

[46] Lombard, *Sent.* IV, d. 14, c. 3, a.1.
[47] Lombard, *Sent.* IV, d. 16, c. 1, a.1.
[48] Lombard, *Sent.* IV, d. 17, c. 1, a.1.
[49] Lombard, *Sent.* IV, d. 17, c. 1, a.2.
[50] Lombard, *Sent.* IV, d. 17, c. 1, a.11.

in the penitential rite... [offering] arguments that are relatively extreme in their defense."[51] Colish ultimately concludes that given Lombard's contritionalist position, confession, while useful, is no longer necessary, "willing to regard confession and satisfaction as optional."[52]

Against this, however, while maintaining that forgiveness and reconciliation do occur at contrition for Lombard, Phillip Rosemann directly challenges Colish's position that confession no longer becomes necessary for the medieval thinker. This challenge arises from what Rosemann correctly identifies as a centerpiece of Lombard's understanding of penance; namely, that exterior acts arise from true interior contrition. As he writes:

> It seems to me that Professor Colish is exaggerating the decisiveness of the Lombard's stance on these matters, indeed to the point of misrepresenting his position. For Colish downplays a crucial aspect of Peter's theory: the penitent's intention or desire (*votum*) to complete his or her contrition, or inner penance, with the requisite outer acts, and to do so as soon as possible.[53]

---

[51] Colish, *Lombard*, 602-3. On 603, she writes: "Can sins be remitted without confession and without satisfaction? Can one confess just to God, purely by one's contrition of heart, without a priest as accessory? Can one confess to a lay person? Peter plans to answer each of these questions with a resounding 'yes'."

[52] Colish, *Lombard*, 603-4: "Peter's own chosen solution is that the remission of sin is a gift of God that is given in the contrition stage of penance...If the penitent has time, he should also confess to a priest, although the sin has already been remitted. Peter presents this issue as if penitents are people with such busy schedules that, for perfectly legitimate reasons, they may be unable to go to confession.... In any event, Peter emphasizes, while it is a good idea, confession is not necessary, 'since the sin has already been forgiven in contrition'."

She continues on 608: "Of all the masters on the contritionalist side of the debate, the Lombard is the only one who is truly and wholly faithful to the logic of that position, to the point of being willing to regard confession and satisfaction as optional, to abridge dramatically the power of the keys in penance, and to exempt penitents, whose spiritual welfare comes first, for this is the reason why the sacrament was instituted, from having to subject themselves to the ministrations of indiscreet priests, encouraging them instead to seek the counsel they need wherever they may find it....Peter's systematic and consistent defense of contritionism, along with the corollaries of that stance, which he does not hesitate to draw, put Peter in a rather more exposed position. It was one that lay well within the orthodox consensus of his own day, to be sure, but it came close to locating itself on the radical fringe just inside the limits of that orthodox consensus. Peter Lombard is the only contemporary contritionist able to offer as strong, as well-reasoned, and as well-documented a case on behalf of its cause as Gratian was able to offer on behalf of confessionism."

[53] Philipp W. Rosemann, *Peter Lombard* (New York: Oxford University Press, 2004), 163.

A few texts from the *Sentences* confirm this interpretation that authentic interior sorrow produces corresponding exterior acts of contrition—confession. Hence, confession is necessary.

Still, as a pastor, Lombard does offer flexibility when one is unable to confess but still has a desire to do so.[54] These exceptions, however, do not make confession on a whole optional, as Colish asserts. For Lombard, just the opposite is true; confession is necessary precisely because the contrite want to confess: "For just as inward penance is enjoined upon us, so also are outward satisfaction and confession by the mouth, if they are possible and so he is not truly penitent, who does not have the intention to confess."[55] Much like Abelard, Lombard views confession as useful—as a humbling satisfaction and as a way to receive penance from another. He writes:

> And so, if it is asked for what is confession necessary, since the sin is already blotted out in contrition, we say: because it is a kind of punishment for the sin, as is satisfaction in deed. Also, through confession the priest understands what judgment he is to give as to the crime. Through it, too, the sinner is made humbler and more careful.[56]

Here, Lombard unequivocally states the necessity of confession. Though the locus of reconciliation is still interior contrition, for Lombard, true contrition wants to reap the benefits and humbling of confession, and "true penance includes the intention to submit oneself to each divine rule."[57] Understood this way, confession becomes necessary.

Perhaps the best way to articulate the role of confession in Lombard's reckoning of penance can be found in his sacramental theology, discussed earlier. Here, *res* and *sacramentum* form one seamless reality. Externals convey inner realities, going beyond merely signifying to actually sanctifying.[58] The parallels to confession are clear here: inner feelings produce exterior actions, true contrition produces confession. Unlike other sacraments, Lombard only examines the *res* and *sacramentum* of penance at the end of his considerations.[59] Positing

---

[54] Lombard, *Sent.* IV, d. 17, c. 3, a. 8. "[I]t is indubitably shown that it is necessary to offer confession first to God, and then to the priest, if the opportunity for this exists; nor is there any other way to come to the gate of paradise."

[55] Lombard, *Sent.* IV, d. 17, c. 1, a.13.

[56] Lombard, *Sent.* IV, d. 17, c. 5, a.1.

[57] Anciaux, *Sacrement de pénitence,* 230: "*La vraie penitence comprend l'intention de se soumettre à toutes les prescriptions divines.*"

[58] As Karl Rahner would say, grace has an "incarnational tendency." See his "Personal and Sacramental Piety," *Theological Investigations* (vol. 2), trans. K.-H. Kruger (New York: Crossroad Publishing, 1990), 119.

[59] Colish, *Lombard*, 600: "One striking and unusual feature of Peter's handling of penance is that he offers his fullest definition of the *sacramentum* and *res sacramenti*

that inward and outward penance constitutes one sacrament, he concludes: "For inward penance is both the thing of the sacrament, that is, of outward penance, and the sacrament of the remission of sin, which it both signifies and brings about. Outward penance is also a sign of both inward penance and the remission of sins."[60] Though forgiveness occurs at contrition, this inward penance cannot be separated from outward penance, confession, which signifies true contrition. Or, as Rosemann succinctly concludes, "Genuine remorse is keen to show itself in external acts."[61]

Bynum's interpretation of the twelfth century, reinforced by Le Goff's work, confirms this trend. By correcting overly individualistic descriptions of the century's renaissance, they illustrate the interplay between the individual and the outside world, particularly in external actions. This nuanced approach provides a more adequate framework for understanding how contritionalists like Abelard and Lombard could maintain the necessity of confession. Abelard's emphasis on genuine interiority and Lombard's sacramentality allowed them both to assert this necessity out of a conviction that a prior authentic interiority drives resultant exterior actions.[62] For both, confessing sins is not considered an act to be done perfunctorily, but rather a result of genuine contrition.

THE ROLE OF PRIESTS AND CONFESSION
IN THE TWELFTH CENTURY

Abelard and Lombard's contritionalist positions affect the role of the priest; if confession is necessary because of its usefulness, it must actually be useful. Rather than simply reciting a perfunctory formula,

---

at the end of his treatise on the subject, rather than at the beginning...Peter adopts this strategy because he seeks to present the definitions with which he concludes as following logically from the analysis and argumentation that precede them."

[60] Lombard, *Sent.* IV, d. 22, c. 2, a.5.

[61] Rosemann, *Lombard*, 164: "These three texts can hardly be interpreted as ringing endorsements of contritionism. Again and again, they emphasize the unity of the three aspects of penance: contrition of heart, external manifestation of that contrition (shown in a confession made to a priest, together with works of expiation), and remission of sins. Peter's argument for the necessity of outer penance seems to be based upon commonsense pastoral experience. Genuine remorse is keen to show itself in external acts. A true penitent will be eager to consult a priest on the appropriate satisfaction required to atone for his or her misdeeds; to undo the damage, as it were. A truly remorseful person, moreover, will not be reluctant to humble him- or herself by accepting the priest's judgment."

[62] See Robert Hancock and Robert Williams, "The Scholastic Debate on the Essential Moment of Forgiveness," *Resonance* 1 (1965), 66. "Even though reconciliation with the Church had by this time lost its sacramental significance, Peter Lombard held the opinion of Abelard in essence concerning confession, i.e., that confession will inevitably follow contrition, but that it (confession) is only the payment of eternal penalty."

the priest is tasked with discerning the authenticity of contrition and assigning proper satisfaction. The competency and ability of the priest is now considered.

This too can be situated in historical, cultural, and theological developments of the time. Stemming particularly from the Investiture Controversy and the ensuing Gregorian Reforms of the late eleventh century, church life was gradually becoming increasingly clerical as the papacy asserted power above and distinct from secular leaders. Higher moral, quasi-monastic standards and increasingly exclusive sacred powers set priests apart from other Christians. The personal authenticity so important in Abelard and Lombard's work would require priestly competencies that actually corresponded to these lofty ideals. So too did the complexification of sin—taking into account consent, will, and act and delineating between venial and mortal—and the connected increase of purgatory's prominence in the twelfth-century Christian imagination greatly magnify the importance of priestly responsibilities in the confessional.[63] Satisfaction properly done in this life would mean mitigation of punishment in the next; thus, the assignment of satisfaction became an especially vital priestly role. How exactly Abelard and Lombard integrated these clerical considerations into their penitential accounts is the next concern of this essay.

ABELARD ON THE ROLE OF THE PRIEST IN CONFESSION

On multiple occasions in his treatment of penance, Peter Abelard criticizes and rues the incompetency of priests of his time, especially as confessors. Since God forgives at compunction, Abelard allows for a person to forgo confession if it does more harm than good. Gossiping priests disclosing confessions, for instance, can be an occasion for sin as penitents only become more absorbed in anger than before they went to confess sins. In other words, incompetent priests can lead to even more sinning. He writes:

> Just as many people become incompetent doctors (*medici*) whom it is dangerous or useless for the sick to be sent to, so too with the Church's prelates. There are many who are neither religious nor discreet, and who are furthermore quick to divulge the sins of those who confess to them, with the result that confessing to them appears not only useless but even destructive (*perniciosum*)… Since they also frivolously disclose the confessions they receive, as we said, they move penitents to outrage, and those who ought to have cured sins bring about new

---

[63] Le Goff, *Purgatory*, 233.

wounds of sins and scare the people who hear about it away from confession.[64]

Comparing the confessor to a doctor is telling. Doctors can make diseases worse by misdiagnosing or not taking the disease seriously enough. While doctors themselves cannot heal diseases (only medicine or other means can), they do play an important role in assigning the proper means to facilitate cures. Not received passively, competency to diagnose effectively comes from training, experience, and even natural ability.

Because competency plays such a large role for Abelard, he raises a few more points. Monks desiring better confessors than assigned, though they should first consult their superiors, can ultimately go against their superiors' restrictions if they truly feel the need for a better confessor. For "it is better to pick a leader who sees than it is to follow someone over the cliff by mistake who has been assigned to him by mistake."[65] Nevertheless, Abelard distinguishes between a confessor's conduct and his effective teaching. As long as a hypocritical confessor does not lead the penitent to more sin, his advice and judgment and the act of confession itself should still be valued.[66] Thus, a priest's ability as a confessor is most important, even more so than his conduct.

Abelard's acknowledgement of incapable priests affects his treatment of the *claves* of binding and loosing in Matthew 16:19, a question that preoccupied many of the early scholastics. Like the incompetent confessors, Abelard now considers the "many bishops who have neither religion nor discernment even though they have episcopal power."[67] He acknowledges that, though Christ gave discernment and holiness to the apostles, this endowment does not necessarily apply to their successors.[68] Borrowing heavily from Jerome's interpretation of the Matthean passage, Abelard affirms that a bishop does not bind or loose people himself; rather, he knows "who is to be bound or who is

---

[64] Abelard, *Ethics*, 191. See 192: "Sometimes too, in revealing sins out of either rage or frivolousness, they seriously scandalize the Church and put those who have confessed into great perils."

[65] Abelard, *Ethics*, 193. See 192: "Hence people are in no way to be blamed who have decided to avoid their superiors because of these improprieties, and pick other people whom they believe are more appropriate in such cases. *Instead they are more to be commended for going off to a more skillful doctor." [Emphasis added]*

[66] Abelard, *Ethics*, 196: "Therefore, such people's judgment isn't to be scorned—that is people who preach well but live badly, who educate by word but don't edify by their example. They show the way they are unwilling to follow."

[67] Abelard, *Ethics*, 205.

[68] Abelard, *Ethics*, 206.

to be released once he has heard their various sins in his official capacity."[69] In other words, binding and loosing is not an eclectic episcopal power that determines eschatological placements, but one of recognition and discernment; the ability and conduct of the bishops becomes important.[70] Again, responsibility is placed on the cleric here—the keys require properly discerning who is and who is not forgiven by God.

Since the keys are primarily about discerning God's judgment and will, this places episcopal power below God's. While this may sound like an obvious point, it has important implications, especially when paired with incompetent clerics; namely, that there can be a discrepancy between ecclesiastical judgment and God's. Abelard begins by referencing Gregory, "ecclesiastical power is unable to do any binding or releasing if it departs from justice's fairness and doesn't conform to divine judgment…it is obvious that the bishops' judgment is worthless if it departs from divine fairness, wanting to deal death to or enliven those they cannot."[71] Ecclesiastical judgment, from macro-matters like excommunication to micro-matters in the private confessional, is held to a standard extant beyond itself. God's judgment takes precedence over the judgment of priests and bishops, sometimes even contradicting it.[72] Unbecoming clerics who, mired in sin or engrossed in worldly occupations, make judgments to satisfy personal vendettas prove that this can be the case. Carefully discerning God's judgment becomes the task of clerics when it comes to binding and loosing sins.

If Abelard stressed the proper interior motivations and sorrow in contrition for confessees, he now places the responsibility on confessors and the entire hierarchical church. By comparing the role of confessors to doctors and noting that there can be a gap between ecclesiastical and divine judgment, clerics are held to a high standard. Now,

---

[69] Abelard, *Ethics*, 208. See 209, where Abelard extends this to beyond bishops. "[W]e understand this binding or absolving as the judging just mentioned, which was granted generally to all, so that they have the power to judge who is to be bound or absolved by God and to discriminate between the clean and unclean."

[70] In Abelard, *Ethics*, 210, Abelard quotes Origen, who emphasizes the conditionality of Matt 16:19: "[I]t is ridiculous for us to say that one who is bound with the shackles of his sins, who drags his sins behind him like a long cord, and who continually drags his iniquities around like a calf's leash has this kind of power solely because he is called a 'bishop', so that those released by him on earth are released in heaven, or those bound on earth are bound in heaven."

[71] Abelard, *Ethics*, 214, 218.

[72] Abelard, *Ethics*, 220: "When someone who gets into an excommunication he didn't earn is kept out of the Church, so that association with the faithful isn't granted to him, he is indeed bound unjustly. But God tears apart these shackles of anathema, because he voids the pastor's judgment so that it doesn't cut off from grace the person whom the pastor separated from the Church."

they are tasked with diagnosing correctly and scrutinizing properly the will of God beyond their own wills.

LOMBARD ON THE ROLE OF PRIESTS IN CONFESSION

Peter Lombard likewise provides an involved account of the priest's role in confession and the keys of Matthew 16:19, reaching conclusions similar to Abelard. While the image of a doctor was dominant for Abelard, the image of a judge is Lombard's primary metaphor. He begins Distinction XVIII by questioning what exactly the role of the priest is in confession: "[I]f the sin is entirely remitted by God through contrition of the heart and from the moment when the penitent has the intention of confessing, what is afterwards remitted to him by the priest?"[73] Lombard notes that God, not the priest, saves sinners from eternal punishment.[74] At the same time, he wants to maintain that priests can still remit and retain sins "in another" way.[75] The author of the *Sentences* diligently explores exactly what this other way is.

Like Abelard, Lombard begins his discussion by referencing Jerome's interpretation of Matthew 16:19. Jerome refers readers to Leviticus 14:2, where priests themselves do not cure lepers but "merely discern which are clean·and which unclean."[76] Lombard concludes from this "that God does not follow the Church's judgment, for sometimes the latter judges through deception and ignorance but God always judges according to the truth."[77] Just as Abelard admits, there can be discrepancies between ecclesial and divine judgment, and the former does not dictate the latter. Remission and retention of sins only occurs when priests reflect God's own judgment.

Clerical binding and loosing occurs in the imposition of satisfaction on penitents as well. Crucially, priests do not impose penitential satisfaction on just anybody, only those "whom the priest adjudges to be truly penitent; if he does not impose it on someone, he thereby indicates that the sin has been retained by God."[78] The priest is tasked with judging true sorrow and contrition; the priest must be competently prudent in detecting this authenticity. Lombard still maintains the priority of God's judgment. Since the discernment of the priest is a natural phenomenon, it can be mistaken. Indeed, "sometimes they

---

[73] Lombard, *Sent.* IV, d. 18, c. 1, a. 1.
[74] Lombard, *Sent.* IV, d. 18, c. 4, a. 7. He concludes "By these and other testimonies, it is taught that God alone by himself remits sins; and just as he remits them from some, so also he retains the sins of others."
[75] Lombard, *Sent.* IV, d. 18, c. 5.
[76] Lombard, *Sent.* IV, d. 18, c. 6, a. 2.
[77] Lombard, *Sent.* IV, d. 18, c. 6, a. 3.
[78] Lombard, *Sent.* IV, d. 18, c. 6, a. 5.

show as loosed or bound those who are not such before God."[79] Ultimately, God alone remits sins, and clerics only recognize this, parsing out appropriate satisfaction.[80] It is the cleric's duty to align his judgment with God's.

From this conclusion, Lombard turns in Distinction XIX to address the qualities of priests in the context of his discussion of the keys. He bifurcates the keys into the knowledge of discernment and the power of binding and loosing. The former, for Lombard, is not given automatically at ordination since "it does not seem that all, or only, priests have these keys, because several have the knowledge of discernment before ordination, many lack it after consecration."[81] Abilities to discern are not passively received at ordination, but rather are found in natural and developed capacities. Lombard does maintain, however, that the key of binding and loosing is given to all priests. He again nuances this position with the proper personal conduct of priests, as they do not have this power "rightly and worthily, unless they preserve the manner of life and teaching of the Apostles."[82] Nevertheless, priests can still exercise this power despite their unworthiness, since God can work through unworthy ministers.

At this point, a tension begins to emerge in Lombard's understanding of priests between natural abilities for discernment on one hand and the power of God working through the minister on the other hand. Referencing Augustine's writings against the Donatists, Lombard maintains that "the order is not deprived of the power to confer grace because of the minister's unworthiness."[83] Similarly, Lombard argues that worthy priests confer the fullness of blessing and that unworthy priests do not harm their subjects' reception of grace. Following Abelard in Augustine's anti-Donatist footsteps, he maintains that one should still follow the good advice of a bad priest.

To compensate for these deficiencies, Lombard ends Distinction XIX with an epideictic description of the ideal "ecclesiastical judge," taken from Pseudo-Augustine's *De Vera et Falsa Poenitentia*. Confessors are to be conscientious, becoming aware and taking care of their own sins. Likewise, they are to possess a good will and have a sweet disposition. They should be good questioners, taking into account all circumstances of a sin.[84] Though Lombard sums it up in only

---

[79] Lombard, *Sent.* IV, d. 18, c. 7, a. 1.
[80] Rosemann, *Lombard*, 165, writes "Just as genuine compunction seeks to externalize itself, in order to make a positive difference in the world of the now repentant sinner, so God's forgiveness has its external counterpart in the judgment of the priest."
[81] Lombard, *Sent.* IV, d. 19, c. 1, a. 3.
[82] Lombard, *Sent.* IV, d. 19, c. 1, a. 8.
[83] Lombard, *Sent.* IV, d. 19, c. 2, a. 1.
[84] Lombard, *Sent.* IV, d. 19, c. 4, a. 1.

two words—"discreet and just"—his high expectations for confessors, as judges, are clear.

Like Abelard then, Lombard places high responsibility on priests alongside penitents. For both, since forgiveness occurs at contrition, the priest is tasked to evaluate contrition and sins, assigning satisfaction accordingly. At the same time, both thinkers lament the ubiquity of incompetent priests of the age and so acknowledge that divine and ecclesiastical judgment can sometimes be two different things. To prevent this divergence from happening, Abelard and Lombard both stress proper conduct and the cultivation of confessional skills. These tools come neither passively nor naturally; priests must be active and diligent in pursuing these ideals.

Abelard and Lombard use two different metaphors for the confessor—doctor and judge respectively. Lombard's metaphor of a judge portrays sin more as an offense against God, while Abelard's metaphor sees sin more as a disease to be cured by mercy. Perhaps Lombard's juridical emphasis comes from his deeper integration of purgatory in his theological system.[85] The "penitential bookkeeping" that came with the stronger awareness of purgatory required as much in the twelfth century.[86] Meanwhile, Abelard's stress on love and mercy throughout his larger theological project is more prone to see the confessor as a doctor. For both though, situated in the midst of an increasingly cultic notion of priesthood prompted by the Gregorian reforms, the ability to forgive sins and assign satisfactions does not necessarily come just through *sacra potestas* given at ordination. Their images instead require abilities that need developing, and this cultivation is the responsibility of the confessor. Indeed, the Spirit works through, though is not identified with, human processes.[87]

CONCLUSION

This essay has attempted to examine and compare two features of Peter Abelard and Peter Lombard's theologies of penance. First, both were contritionalists who maintained confession's necessity. Here, authentic interiority guided Abelard while sacramentality guided Lombard. Both accentuated the need for a genuine contrition that prompted

---

[85] See Lombard, *Sent.* IV, d. 21, c. 45.
[86] Le Goff, *Purgatory*, 152.
[87] In explaining the interplay of the Holy Spirit and human processes, Richard McCormick warns against two extremes. One explains the Spirit's assistance as dispensing with human processes while the other reduces this assistance to human processes. Though McCormick is principally concerned with the magisterium and infallibility, the same categories and need for middle ground can be applied to confession. See Richard A. McCormick, *Notes on Moral Theology: 1965 Through 1980* (Washington, D.C.: University Press of America, 1981), 260-265.

the subject to confess sins orally. A theme of the twelfth century, interiority was to produce corresponding exterior acts. Second, both saw the priest's fundamental role in confession as a doctor or judge. A priest's ability and aptitude to diagnose and judge was crucial, particularly given the increased importance of purgatory in the twelfth century. Together, these points meant that both confessees and confessors were held to a high standard.

Abelard and Lombard thus offer a theology that demolishes any overly formalistic, ritualistic, and stale practices of penance. Penance is not a perfunctory duty to be performed; rather, penitents need to scour their own intentions and conscience, seeking true remorse for sins. Priests cannot formulaically or absent-mindedly absolve sins; they need to carefully listen to oral confessions, assigning satisfaction borne out of wisdom, experience, and mercy that reflects God's own. When viewed this way, the sacrament takes on a new serious, discerning, and even dramatic character. While overemphasizing this character could lead to over-scrupulosity and guilt, ultimately these theologies can and should lead to more fruitful practices and experiences of penance and, with those, experiences of God's merciful love. ∎

An Analysis of GSUSA's Policy of Serving Transgender Youth: Implications for Catholic Practice

John S. Grabowski and Christopher K. Gross

R ECENTLY THE GIRL SCOUTS OF AMERICA (GSUSA) announced a new policy allowing transgender youth to participate in their troops, though the specifics and implementation of this new policy has been left to the judgment of individual local troops.[1] Given the historic affiliation of Girl Scouts with
Catholic schools and parishes in the United States, this change raised
questions as to how to respond to this new policy. Some wondered
whether Catholic parishes and schools could continue to sponsor such
troops without raising the specter of scandal or involving themselves
in some unacceptable form of cooperation with evil.

---

[1] This policy seems to stem from the decision in October 2011 of a Colorado troop to
admit a transgender youth who had previously been denied admission. This sparked
an effort on the part of a California teen and others in January 2012 to organize a
boycott of Girl Scout cookies. See Katia Hetter, "Girl Scouts accepts Transgender Kid,
Provokes Cookie Boycott," *CNN* (January 13, 2012), www.cnn.com/2012/01/13/liv-
ing/girl-scout-boycott/.
The current policy of the Girl Scouts of the United States of America (GSUSA) on
transgender youth is as follows:
Q: What is Girl Scouts' position on serving transgender youth?
A: Girl Scouts is proud to be the premiere leadership organization for girls in the
country. Placement of transgender youth is handled on a case-by-case basis, with the
welfare and best interests of the child and the members of the troop/group in question
a top priority. That said, if the child is recognized by the family and school/community
as a girl and lives culturally as a girl, then Girl Scouts is an organization that can serve
her in a setting that is both emotionally and physically safe.
Q: How does Girl Scouts' position on serving transgender youth apply to situations
involving camping or volunteers?
A: These situations are rare and are considered individually with the best interests of
all families in mind. Should any girl requiring special accommodations wish to camp,
GSUSA recommends that the local council makes similar accommodation that
schools across the country follow in regard to changing, sleeping arrangements, and
other travel-related activities. With respect to volunteers, Girl Scouts welcomes both
male and female adult volunteers and has developed appropriate safeguards regarding
roles and responsibilities to ensure that girls receive the proper supervision and support.
Policy available at www.girlscouts.org/program/gs_central/mpmf/faqs.asp#a1.

The reflections which follow aim to provide a brief overview of the transgender phenomenon as understood within contemporary culture, clinical practice, and Catholic teaching on sexuality in order to formulate an ethical and pastoral response to the GSUSA policy from the standpoint of Catholic practice. It is the contention of this analysis that while the designation of children as belonging to the "transgender" category is misguided and often reflects a failure on the part of adults to responsibly care for them or even use them for political purposes, the policy of GSUSA on this issue by itself does not warrant Catholic parishes or schools cutting ties with the organization. Any cooperation in evil on the part of the sponsoring parish should be understood as at most constituting some form of remote mediated material cooperation.

This essay will proceed by first providing an overview of the evolving and contested transgender category as a descriptor of the sexual identity of human persons. It will then briefly discuss equally controversial clinical perspectives on this reality. The third section of the paper will consider recent Catholic teaching and theological reflection on the status of sexual difference. The final section will draw these strands together in an ethical analysis of the specific case at hand—the situation of Catholic parishes and schools who sponsor Girl Scout troops.

WHAT IS "TRANSGENDER"?

The intellectual roots of the identification of certain groups of people as "transgender" lie at least in part in second wave feminism's separation of "sex" and "gender." In this view "sex" is the (quite minimal) biological difference between men and women, while "gender" is the social and cultural construction of the meaning of these differences. The connection between the two realities is understood to be partial and often arbitrary. Under the influence of process ontology and postmodern thinking, many feminist thinkers, academics, and scientists influenced by them have come to view the meaning of "gender" and even "sex" as products of culture or of individual choice and self-articulation.[2]

Current cultural definitions of the phenomenon, though themselves in flux, often tend to focus on people whose self-concept or identity does not conform to accepted gender roles but moves between them;

---

[2] Thus, feminist philosopher Judith Butler sees "gender" and "sex" as constraints on individual personhood. See her *Undoing Gender* (Oxford: Routledge, 2004). For a critical overview and analysis of feminist thought regarding human nature and sexual difference from a Catholic "new feminist" perspective, see Michele Schumacher, "The Nature of Nature in Feminism Old and New: From Dualism to Complementary Unity," in *Women in Christ: Toward a New Feminism*, ed. Michele Schumacher (Grand Rapids: Eerdmans, 2004), 17-51.

people who feel that their biological sexual configuration does not correspond to their inner reality; or the rejection of the gender identity assigned to one at birth. In her book, *Transgender History*, Susan Stryker summarizes the concept of transgender by defining it as *"the movement across a socially imposed boundary away from an unchosen starting place."*[3]

Luke Woodward, for example, was born a woman and began to experience same-sex attraction early in her life.[4] Even though Luke identified as a lesbian, over time, she began to question whether she was actually a woman.[5] During a studying abroad year in Cuba, Luke notes that people "were genuinely shocked when I said I was a woman. It was disorienting and scary. And I had to really think about it: am I a woman?" Luke became exceedingly uncomfortable with her biological sex, and she notes that she spent a great deal of effort trying "to pass as male." Eventually, Luke decided to have a double mastectomy in order have her physical appearance match the gender with which she identified.

Jamison Green's story is similar to Luke's, but Jamison felt the disconnect between his biological sex and the gender with which he identified at a much earlier age. In her book, *Becoming a Visible Man*, Jamison describes the frustration and oppression that she felt as her parents made her dress like a girl. She writes:

> To me, on the other hand, the easier course would have been for them to acknowledge the boy they were trying to suppress and let me wear the clothing in which I felt right. Instinctively, I knew the discrepancy would not be so glaring. But although I could not resist "proper" attire, I could not find the words to say that I felt like a boy.[6]

---

[3] Susan Stryker, *Transgender History* (Berkeley, CA: Seal Press, 2008), 1. Emphasis in original. Transgender persons should not be confused with transvestites. In the latter group, individuals cross-dress but only episodically, and that behavior brings about erotic pleasure. Unlike transvestites, transgender persons live with the daily, persistent feeling that their physical bodies do not match their interior selves, e.g., interiorly a woman may feel like a man, even though she has a female body. For more on this distinction, see Colette Chiland, *Transsexualism: Illusion and Reality*, trans. Philip Slotkin (Middletown, CT: Weslyean University Press, 2003), 12-16.

[4] Throughout this article, we have chosen to use the pronoun that corresponds to the biological sex of the transgender person and not the pronoun which matches the chosen "gender" of the individual.

[5] Luke's story is captured by Fred Bernstein in his article "On Campus, Rethinking Biology 101," which originally appeared in the *New York Times* (March 7, 2004): Style, 1-6. The article is available at: http://fredbernstein.com/articles/display.asp?id=59. The quotations here are Luke's own words. For a more substantial and detailed description of the experiences of a transgender person, see Jamison Green, *Becoming a Visible Man* (Nashville, TN: Vanderbilt University Press, 2004).

[6] Green, *Becoming a Visible Man*, 10-11.

Transsexuals often seek a variety of treatments in order to overcome the disconnect that they experience with their physical sex. On the one hand, despite the risks, expense, and pain of surgery, like Woodward and Green, many transsexuals opt for sexual reassignment surgery in order to correct what they frequently refer to as a "mistake of nature."[7] On the other hand, some transsexuals choose hormone therapy or no medical intervention at all.[8] However, it should be noted that transsexuals often resist psychotherapy, because they are convinced that they are in the wrong body. Therefore, when they do seek treatment, frequently it is in the form of some type of medical intervention that will bring about changes in their physical bodies.[9]

CLINICAL PERSPECTIVES

Clinical psychology recognizes the existence of disorders that affect one's self-identification as male or female, and among those disorders is gender identity disorder (or GID—which has now come to be called "gender dysphoria").[10] Thus, the older *Diagnostic and Sta-*

---

[7] Chiland, *Transsexualism*, 2. Woodward's surgery was partial sexual reassignment surgery, because her genitalia were not altered. Green, conversely, opted for complete sexual reassignment surgery, which included a bilateral mastectomy as well as a metoidioplasty (114). For a fuller explanation of transgender surgeries, see Benedict M. Guevin's article, "Sex Reassignment Surgery for Transsexuals: An Ethical Conundrum?" *National Catholic Bioethics Quarterly* 5, no. 4 (Winter 2005): 728-29.

[8] Gayle Salamon, *Assuming a Body: Transgender and Rhetorics of Materiality* (New York: Columbia University Press, 2010), 84.

[9] Joanne Meyerowitz, "A'Fierce and Demanding' Drive," in *The Transgender Studies Reader,* eds. Susan Stryker and Stephen Whittle (New York: Routledge, 2006), 368. Guevin makes this same point in his article "Sex Reassignment," 727.

[10] While the diagnosis of gender identity disorder was included in the fourth edition of the *Diagnostic and Statistical Manual of Mental Disorders* (DSM), the American Psychiatric Association renamed the disorder in the fifth edition of the manual that was published in 2013. Gender identity disorder was replaced with gender dysphoria. While this change may appear to be minor, it is actually a very significant. First, it is a serious step toward the normalization of the transgender phenomenon both among psychiatrists and in American culture. Second, it provides a glimpse into how many psychiatrists think that the disorder should be treated in children, adolescents, and adults. In an informational bulletin about the switch, the APA explains, "DSM-5 aims to avoid stigma and ensure clinical care for individuals who see and feel themselves to be a different gender than their assigned gender. It replaces the diagnostic name 'gender identity disorder' with 'gender dysphoria' as well as makes other important clarifications in the criteria. It is important to note that gender nonconformity is not itself a mental disorder. The critical element of gender dysphoria is the presence of clinically significant distress associated with the condition."
There was actually a substantial push to remove gender identity disorder from the DSM-5 completely rather than merely renaming it. Even though many in the APA supported that move, there was a concern among the Gender Identity Disorders Work Group that removing the condition as a psychiatric condition would prevent people

tistical Manual of Mental Disorders of the American Psychiatric Association (DSM IV TR) describes GID as a strong and persistent cross-gender identification with at least four of the following marks:

- A repeated stated desire to be of the opposite sex
- In boys a preference for cross-dressing or simulating female attire and, in girls, wearing stereotypical masculine clothing with a rejection of feminine clothing such as skirts
- A strong and persistent preferences for cross-sex role in play
- A strong preference for playmates of the opposite sex
- Intense desire to participate in games and pastimes of the opposite sex.

As Dr. Richard P. Fitzgibbons notes, "in adolescents and adults, the disturbance is manifested by symptoms such as a stated desire to be the other sex, frequent passing as the other sex, desire to live or be treated as the other sex, or the conviction that he or she has the typical feelings and reactions of the other sex."[11] Children who have this disorder are often ostracized by their peers or targeted for bullying, and many suffer from low self-esteem or depression. Such children are often at higher risk for alcohol and drug use, prostitution, and homosexual activity, and their condition may manifest itself in other disorders in adulthood as in the case of individuals who live as transvestites or transsexuals or those who develop Body Dysmorphic Disorder.[12]

---

with GID from getting insurance coverage for all treatment options, including counseling, hormone therapy, and sexual reassignment surgery. See the informational bulletin on gender dysphoria at www.dsm5.org/documents/gender%20dysphoria%20fact%20sheet.pdf.

We have chosen to use "gender identity disorder" rather than "gender dysphoria" throughout this paper, because we believe that renaming the condition "gender dysphoria" minimizes the condition and the suffering of the person who experiences it. In the aforementioned bulletin, the APA suggests that gender dysphoria focuses more on the distress caused by the condition rather than the condition itself. Our focus here is both on how to treat the condition as well as the distress that it causes the individual. Furthermore, the change also seems to be based as much or more on political as scientific considerations.

[11] See Richard P. Fitzgibbons, "Gender Identity Disorder" on his website Marital Healing available at http://maritalhealing.com/conflicts/genderidentitydisorder.php.

[12] See Fitzgibbons, "Gender Identity Disorder." Ashley, DeBlois, and O'Rourke also see transvestitism as a separate reality and probably a form of fetishism. See Benedict Ashley, O.P., Jean DeBlois, C.S.J., and Kevin O'Rourke, O.P., *Healthcare Ethics: A Catholic Theological Analysis*, 5th ed. (Washington, D.C.: Georgetown University Press, 2006), 109. Their discussion focuses on what they term "transsexualism" or gender dysphoria. Its characteristics include: a "sense of discomfort and inappropriateness about one's anatomical sex"; the "wish to be rid of one's own genitals and to live as a member of the other sex"; "the disturbance has been continuous (not limited to periods of stress) for at least two years"; the "absence of physical intersex or genetic abnormality"; and the condition is "not caused by another mental disorder such as

The development of such disorders is not necessarily caused by or related to physical conditions which result in an ambiguous manifestation of physical sex—ambiguous genitalia, hormonal imbalances which affect secondary sex characteristics in the body, or genetic abnormalities. These conditions—today often referred to as a person being "intersexed"—sometimes result in one being "assigned" a sexual identity at birth or in early childhood by parents in consultation with doctors. But many such persons develop an ego-syntonic view of their given (or assigned) sexual identity and do not develop symptoms of GID.[13]

While each case of GID in children is somewhat unique, there are essentially two different models for treatment.[14] On the one hand, some mental health professionals and LGBT advocates embrace the accommodation model and advocate the "de-medicalization" of GID. They argue that it should not be regarded as a disorder but simply as a feature of human sexual diversity.[15] Proponents of this approach point to the de-medicalization of homosexuality by the APA in 1973 and insist that, like homosexuality, transgenderism should no longer be viewed as a mental disorder.[16] Alice Dreger points out that according

---

schizophrenia" (109). While the conditions are expressed somewhat differently, especially in regard to their duration, they closely resemble those of GID described above.

[13] However, cases of intersexed persons are complicated by the fact that many "gender rights" activists have used these conditions to advance a particular social and political agenda. Thus, some point to the fact of the intersexed condition to argue against the hegemony of male-female sexual dimorphism in the sciences and even in theology. For example, Patricia Beattie Jung and Anna Marie Vigen argue that there are some 5.5 million intersexed persons in the world today and that this fact calls into question the sexual dimorphism upon which Catholic teaching rests. See their "Introduction" to the volume which they coedited, *God, Science, Sex, Gender: An Interdisciplinary Approach to Christian Ethics,* eds. Patricia Beattie Jung and Anna Marie Vigen (Chicago: University of Illinois Press, 2010), 7-8. Many of the essays in this volume (most of which come from a series of symposia at Loyola University in Chicago in 2007) seek to advance a similar argument through various disciplines (science—particularly evolutionary biology—philosophy, theology, ethics, and literature).

[14] Alice Dreger, "Gender Identity Disorder in Childhood: Inconclusive Advice to Parents," *Hastings Center Report* 39, no. 1 (2009): 26-9. In what follows, we borrow the names that Dreger assigns to these models.

[15] The recent revisions to the *DSM* exemplify this position. See footnote 10. For more on this position, see also Alice Dreger, "How and Why to Take 'Gender Identity Disorder' out of the DSM," *Bioethics Forum* (June 22, 2009), www.thehastingscenter.org/Bioethicsforum/Post.aspx?id=3602.

[16] On the APA decision, see Ashley, DeBlois, and O'Rourke, *Healthcare Ethics,* 67-8. Oftentimes an effort is made to distinguish "transgender" from issues of sexual orientation, but this is not wholly successful as transgender persons and sexual orientation are often lumped together in advocacy for Lesbian, Gay, Bisexual, and Transgender (LGBT) issues. Recognition of the rights and needs of transgender persons is therefore often part of a larger effort to accommodate and promote sexual diversity against the perceived oppressive hegemony of the heterosexual norm within society

to the accommodation model, the problem is with our intolerant, close-minded culture and not with the transgender child. Thus, the role of medicine is not to resolve the child's GID but to provide him or her with the necessary hormones, surgeries and psychological support to deal with a hostile world.[17]

On the other hand, juxtaposed to the accommodation model, the therapeutic model recognizes GID as a psychological condition and treats it as such. The therapeutic approach maintains that the child's desire to grow up as the opposite sex represents a problematic fantasy that can be made to dissipate with proper treatment in many cases.[18] Dr. Kenneth Zucker, who is the Psychologist in Chief and Head of Gender Identity Services in the Child, Youth, and Family Program at the Centre for Addiction and Mental Health in Toronto, rejects the notion that GID can simply be attributed to biology. Instead, he argues that there are a myriad of factors contributing to GID, including family dynamics.[19] Thus, for Zucker, the key to treatment is to find and address the underlying causes of the condition. Comparing ethnic identity disorder to GID, Zucker asks, "If a 5-year-old black kid came into the clinic and said he wanted to be white, would we endorse that? I don't think so. What we would want to do is to say, 'What's going on with this kid that's making him feel that it would be better to be white?'"[20] Similarly, Zucker maintains that the best way to treat GID is find and fix the psychological root of the problem rather than merely accepting the condition and offering hormone therapy or sexual reassignment surgery as the solution.[21]

---

and the Church. For example the "Yogyakarta Principles" adopted by a meeting at Gadjah Madah University on Java in November 2006, purports to be an application of international human rights law to LGBT issues. See the English summary and overview provided at www.yogyakartaprinciples.org/principles_en.htm. In point of fact, these principles are often used to assess the "friendliness" of various groups and organizations to LGBT causes and to advance this agenda under the banner of human rights and international law. See Jane Adolphe, "'New Rights' in Public International Family Law?: What International Law Actually Says." *Ave Maria Law Review* 10, no. 1 (2011): 149-68; and *eadem*, "Gender Wars at the U.N." *Ave Maria Law Review* 11, no. 1 (2012): 1-31.

[17] Dreger, "Gender Identity Disorder," 27.
[18] Dreger, "Gender Identity Disorder," 26.
[19] Kenneth Zucker and Susan Bradley, "Re: Children with Gender Nonconformity," *Journal of the American Academy of Child and Adolescent Psychiatry* 42, no. 3 (2003): 267.
[20] Qtd. in Hanna Rosin, "A Boy's Life," in *The Atlantic* (November 2008), www.theatlantic.com/magazine/archive/2008/11/a-boys-life/307059/.
[21] It must be noted that Zucker and Bradley seem to believe that there are cases among adolescents where hormone therapy and surgical sex-reassignment may be the best approach. See their letter "Re: Children with Gender Nonconformity," 267. While they suggest that these options are needed in only a rare number of cases, we reject these as ethical treatment options for reasons that we outline in the next two sections.

Echoing Zucker, Fitzgibbons argues:

A loving and compassionate approach to these troubled children is not
to support their difficulty in accepting the goodness of their masculinity or femininity, which is being advocated in the media and by many
health professionals who lack expertise in GID, but to offer them and
their parents the highly effective treatment which is available.[22]

He goes on to specify some of the forms which such treatment can
take.

For boys it might include the following:
- Increasing quality time for bonding with the father
- Increasing affirmation of the son's masculine gifts by the father
- Participating in and support for the son's creative efforts by the
  father
- Encouraging same sex friendships and diminishing time with op-
  posite sex friends
- Coaching the son in the development of athletic confidence and
  skills if possible
- Slowly diminishing play with opposite sex toys
- Encouraging the boy to be thankful for his special male gifts
- Slowly leading the boy into team play if the athletic abilities and
  interest improve
- Working at forgiving boys who may have hurt him
- Communicating with other parents whose children have been
  treated successfully for GID and who have come to appreciate
  and to embrace the goodness of their masculinity and femininity
- Addressing the emotional conflicts in a mother who wants her
  son to be a girl
- In those with faith, encouraging thankfulness for one's special
  God-given masculine gifts.

For girls struggling with GID the treatment is similar yet distinct:
- Encouraging the daughter to appreciate the goodness and beauty
  of her femininity, including her body
- Encouraging same sex friendships and activities
- Increasing the mother-child quality time
- Encouraging parental praise of their daughter
- Working with the daughter to forgive peers who have hurt her
- Encouraging pursuit of a balance in athletic activities
- Addressing conflicts in parents who want her to be a boy
- In those with faith, encouraging thankfulness for one's special
  God-given femininity.[23]

---

[22] Fitzgibbons, "Gender Identity Disorder."
[23] Fitzgibbons, "Gender Identity Disorder." See also the analysis provided by the
NARTH Scientific Advisory Committee, "Gender Identity Disorders in Childhood

The therapeutic model has been highly effective in treating children suffering from GID, particularly those who began treatment prior to adolescence. Writing about their experience with the therapeutic model, Zucker and Susan Bradley, in their book *Gender Identity Disorder and Psychosexual Problems in Children and Adolescents*, remark:

> It has been our experience that a sizable number of children and their families achieve a great deal of change. In these cases, the gender identity disorder resolves fully, and nothing in the children's behavior or fantasy suggests that gender identity issues remain problematic. In a smaller number of cases, there is minimal or no evidence of change in the children's cross-gender identification and other behavioral difficulties. All things considered, however, we take the position that in such cases a clinician should be optimistic, not nihilistic, about the possibility of helping the children to become more secure in their gender identity.[24]

Despite their successes, Zucker and others who use the therapeutic model often are heavily criticized by activists in the transgender community and proponents of the accommodation model. They view the therapeutic model as highly repressive and an affront to greater acceptance of the LGBT community.[25] Sadly, in their opposition, activists frequently lump the disparate issues of adolescents and pre-adolescents with GID together with highly contested and politicized issues involving LGBT adults.

One unfortunate result of the politicization of these issues is that children who suffer from GID are sometimes employed to advance a particular agenda and are used to leverage greater acceptance of "sexual diversity" (variously understood) in schools and youth organizations. For example, Helen Carroll, who serves as the sports director at the National Center for Lesbian Rights, wrote a model policy for school systems, struggling to deal with the question of whether children with GID can play on teams of the opposite sex. While the number of students nationally who request this accommodation is very low, Carroll and other activists are happy that at least a few "transgender" kids are pushing school districts to have these conversations. Carroll

---

And Adolescence: A Critical Inquiry And Review Of The Kenneth Zucker Research," (March 2007), www.narth.com/docs/GIDReviewKenZucker.pdf.

[24] Kenneth Zucker and Susan Bradley, *Gender Identity Disorder and Psychosexual Problems in Children and Adolescents* (New York and London: The Guilford Press, 1995), 282.

[25] See for example, Simon Pickston-Taylor, "Children with Gender Nonconformity," *Journal of the American Academy of Child and Adolescent Psychiatry* 42, no. 3 (2003): 266.

notes, "Generally, our society is becoming more accepting in its understanding of gender identity and what that means, and we've been very lucky that in the last few years this cadre of young kids has started identifying themselves as trans from a young age. It's really pushing folks to really grapple with and understand what it means."[26] Unfortunately, oftentimes in these heated public debates, the suffering of the children with GID seems to be overlooked by activists, and as Carroll's quotation intimates, the children become a means of pushing people toward greater acceptance of the LGBT population.

The advocacy of LGBT activists on behalf of children with GID raises still more complex issues of the relationship between gender identity, sexual attraction, and what some refer to as "sexual orientation."[27] It is safe to say that that these concepts in themselves as well as the relationships among them are complex and contested. It is beyond the scope of this paper to attempt to adjudicate these debates. In regard to the last of these concepts, a few basic observations are in order. First, there is not now, and there never has been one universally agreed upon definition of "sexual orientation."[28] Second, even those who tend to speak in terms of sexual orientation rather than attraction

---

[26] Sandhya Somashekhar, "A question for schools: Which teams should transgender students play on?," *Washington Post* (October 2, 2014), www.washingtonpost.com/politics/a-question-for-schools-which-sports-teams-should-transgender-students-play-on/2014/10/02/d3f33b06-49c7-11e4-b72e-d60a9229cc10_story.html.

[27] For an outstanding analysis of the complex interplay of gender identity and sexual orientation in the psychological care of persons struggling with same sex attraction (SSA), see Philip Sutton, "Who Am I: Psychological Issues in Gender Identity and Same Sex Attraction," in *Fertility and Gender: Issues in Reproductive and Sexual Ethics*, ed. Helen Watt (Anscombe Bioethics Centre: Oxford, 2011), 70-98.

[28] Michael Hannon notes that the very concept of "sexual orientation" –whether homosexual or heterosexual—is a very recent modern invention. He writes, "Contrary to our cultural preconceptions and the lies of what has come to be called 'orientation essentialism', 'straight' and 'gay' are not ageless absolutes. Sexual orientation is a conceptual scheme with a history and a dark one at that ...Over the course of several centuries, the West had progressively abandoned Christianity's marital architecture for human sexuality. Then, about one hundred and fifty years ago, it began to replace that longstanding teleological tradition with a brand new creation: the absolutist but absurd taxonomy of sexual orientations. Heterosexuality was made to serve as this fanciful framework's regulating ideal, preserving the social prohibitions against sodomy and other sexual debaucheries without requiring recourse to the procreative nature of human sexuality." See "Against Heterosexuality," *First Things* 241 (2014): 27-34. His historical claim here builds on the work of Michel Foucault who argued that the 19th century took a category of forbidden acts (i.e., sodomy) and turned it into "an interior androgyny a hermaphroditism of the soul" and a "new specification of individuals" See *The History of Sexuality* Vol. 1: *An Introduction,* trans. Robert Hurley (New York: Vintage Books, 1978), 42-43. The result was that what had been treated as matter for confession was now turned into a medical pathology (cf. 67).

admit to some degree of plasticity in the concept.[29] Third, the relation-ship between these realities in adults is different from that of adoles-cents whose brains (and self-concepts) are undergoing significant de-velopment as a result bodily biochemical and neurological changes and even more than in pre-adolescent children.[30]

Our focus here is on adolescent and pre-adolescent children with GID and their treatment options. In the following section, we will ex-plain how the therapeutic model described above is in many ways con-gruent with recent Catholic teaching on sexuality.[31]

CATHOLIC TEACHING ON SEXUAL DIFFERENCE

In the face of growing modern confusion about sex differences caused in differing ways by second wave feminism and the resulting dissociation of sex and gender, the sexual revolution powered by oral contraception, and its own internal theological disagreement, the

---

[29] Thus, the widely used scale developed by Kinsey and his associates in 1948 envi-sions sexual orientation as a 7 point scale with 0 being an exclusively heterosexual person and 6 being exclusively homosexual with many gradations (representing most of the adult population) in between. The Klein Sexual Orientation Grid (KSOG) takes this further, factoring in sexual desire and arguing that orientation can and does change over time. See Fritz Klein, *The Bisexual Option* (New York: Arbor House, 1978). Many recent studies document the fluidity of sexual orientation and attraction among persons and groups. See, for example, J.D. Weinrich and Fritz Klein, "Bi-gay, bi-straight, and bi-bi: Three bisexual subgroups identified using cluster analysis of the Klein sexual orientation grid," *Journal of Bisexuality* 2, no. 4 (2002): 109–139; O.F. Kernberg, "Unresolved issues in the psychoanalytic theory of homosexuality and bi-sexuality," *Journal of Gay and Lesbian Psychotherapy* 6, no. 1 (2002): 9–27. Neil and Brian Whitehead, *My Genes Made Me Do it: A Scientific Look at Sexual* Orientation, 3rd ed. (October 2013), www.mygenes.co.nz/download.htm.
This idea of the malleability of sexual orientation/attraction is taken to another level by groups and therapeutic approaches which argue for the possibility of change. For an overview of such "reparative" therapies, see Joseph Nicolosi, *Shame and Attach-ment Loss: The Practical Work of Reparative Therapy* (Downers Grove,IL: IVP Ac-ademic, 2009). See also the report by the National Association for the Research and Therapy of Homosexuality (NARTH) "What Research Shows: NARTH's response to the APA Claims on Homosexuality," *Journal of Human Sexuality* 1 (2009): 1-121. For contrary read of the data and a critical evaluation of these therapeutic approaches and their impact see the American Psychological Association (APA) report *Appropri-ate Therapeutic Responses to Sexual Orientation* (Washington D.C.: APA, 2009), 1-130.
[30] For a helpful (and generally non-politicized) overview of the impact of adolescence on brain development, see Luann Brizendine, *The Female Brain* (New York: Broad-way Books, 2006), 31-56; and *eadem, The Male Brain* (New York: Random House, 2010), 30-53.
[31] The APA report argues that there is no conclusive evidence to show that such ther-apies directed at children have the ability to change later adult sexual orientation. It further cautions that they could increase self-stigma and stress in children but offers no evidence to support this concern. See *Appropriate Therapeutic Responses to Sex-ual* Orientation, 4.

Church has repeatedly affirmed the goodness and profound signifi-cance of sexual difference.[32] Created together in the image of God (cf. Gen. 1:27), men and women are both fundamentally equal their hu-manity and irreducibly different as embodied persons. Church teach-ing has often described this equality in difference through the language of "complementarity." Thus the *Catechism of the Catholic Church* states:

> Man and woman were made "for each other"—not that God made them half-made and incomplete: he created them to be a communion of persons, in which each can be "helpmate" to the other, for they are equal as persons ("bone of my bones...") and complementary as mas-culine and feminine.[33]

Thus man and woman together are in the image of God whom Reve-lation discloses to us as a communion of Person's in His inner Trini-tarian life.[34]

Saint Pope John Paul II used much of his magisterium to deepen the Church's understanding of the importance and anthropological depth of sexual difference. Addressing the Church in the wake of the 1980 Synod on Family, he taught in *Familiaris consortio:* "In creating the human race 'male and female' God gave man and woman an equal personal dignity, endowing them with the inalienable rights and re-sponsibilities proper to the human person."[35] Yet within this equal dig-nity exists a profound personal difference. In his catecheses on the body, he used the language of the "originality" of men and women as persons to mediate this reality:

---

[32] By internal disagreement we refer particularly to the bitter controversy and theo-logical dissent which wracked the Church after Pope Paul VI's encyclical letter *Hu-manae vitae* (1968). This contentious debate started with the issue of birth control but quickly spread to other issues of sexual ethics. In this same period, the Church has been further polarized by ongoing arguments in favor of the ordination of women which have not been entirely quelled by authoritative statements by the Church's teaching office in *Inter insignores* (1976) and *Ordinatio sacerdotalis* (1994).

[33] *CCC*, 372. The citation is from the Second Edition. Libreira Editrice Vaticana. Eng-lish translation by the USCC. (Washington: USCC, 1997), 95.

[34] This does not mean that God is male or female. As a divine and spiritual being, God transcends the distinctions of biological sex. However, both Scripture and the Church's tradition have analogously applied qualities of human masculinity and fem-ininity to God *simpliciter* or to the Persons of the Trinity. See *CCC*, 370 and John Paul II, Apostolic Letter, *Mulieris dignitatem*, no. 8.

[35] See Apostolic Exhortation, *Familiaris consortio*, no. 22. The citation is from *The Role of the Christian Family in the Modern World*. Vatican trans. (Boston: Daughters of St. Paul, 1981), 39.

98   *John Grabowski and Christopher Gross*

The knowledge of man passes through masculinity and femininity, which are, as it were, two incarnations of the same metaphysical solitude before God and the world—*two reciprocally completing ways of "being a body" and at the same time of being human*—as two complementary dimensions of self-knowledge and self-determination and, at the same time, *two complementary ways of being conscious of the meaning of the body.*[36]

The bodily differences of men and women point to two unique personal ways of existing as a person within a common human nature. As the late pope says: "Their unity *denotes* above all *the identity of human nature; duality on the other hand, shows what, on the basis of this identity, constitutes the masculinity and femininity* of created man."[37] Yet these differences are themselves a summons to the self-gift of love in the communion of persons—a reality that John Paul II frequently described as "the spousal meaning of the body."[38] The same focus on the mutual relation and irreducible difference of men and women as persons within a shared human nature can be found in his 1988 Apostolic Letter *Mulieris dignitatem* and was at the basis of his call for women to more fully explicate their unique gifts in a "new feminism" in his 1995 Encyclical Letter, *Evangelium vitae.*[39]

---

[36] The citation is from *Man and Woman He Created Them: A Theology of the Body*, trans. Michael Waldstein (Boston: Pauline, 2006), 10:1, 166. Emphasis in original.
[37] John Paul II, *Man and Woman* 9:1, 161. Emphasis in original. This distinction between person and nature as a key to understanding sexual difference has been highlighted in recent Catholic theological reflection on sexual difference. Hence Walter Kasper speaks of male and female as the "two equally valuable but different expressions of the one nature of humanity." See "The Position of Women as a Problem of Theological Anthropology," trans. John Saward, in *The Church and Women: A Compendium*, Helmut Moll, ed. (San Francisco: Ignatius, 1988), 58-59. Michele Schumacher speaks of "one nature in two modes" see "The Nature of Nature in Feminism," 38-41. Put more sharply, one might speak of sexual difference as accidental on the level of nature but essential to existing human persons. Cf. John S. Grabowski, "The Status of the Sexual Good as a Direction for Moral Theology," *Heythrop Journal* 35 (1994), 15-34.
[38] Waldstein in the index to *Man and Woman* (pp. 682-83) notes that the term is an important and wide-ranging one in the ToB catecheses, appearing some 117 times. For an overview of the range of meaning of the term as employed in these catecheses see Earl Muller, S.J., "The Nuptial Meaning of the Body," in *John Paul II on the Body: Human, Eucharistic, Ecclesial*. Festschrift for Avery Cardinal Dulles, S.J. ed. John McDermott, S.J. and John Galvin, S.J. (Philadelphia: Saint Joseph's University Press, 2008), 87-120.
[39] On these points see *Mulieris dignitatem*, nos. 7, 10, and *Evangelium vitae*, no. 99 respectively.

Pope Benedict XVI continued and even deepened some of these same emphases found in the teaching of his predecessor.[40] In his first encyclical letter *Deus caritas est*, he pointed to the love of man and woman as the key to understanding the mystery of God's love for us:

> Corresponding to the image of a monotheistic God is monogamous marriage. Marriage based on exclusive and definitive love becomes the icon of the relationship between God and his people and vice versa. God's way of loving becomes the measure of human love.[41]

It is in this way that we can understand that authentic human love, particularly sexual love, is simultaneously *eros* (passionate desire for union) and *agape* (sacrificial self-gift for the other) as we see these same qualities displayed in God's love for his people particularly as expressed in Christ's incarnation, life, death, and resurrection and continued Eucharistic presence in the Church.[42]

In his 2012 Christmas address to the Roman Curia, Pope Benedict described the false and misleading nature of the separation of "gender" and "sex" in modernity which ends up undermining the very concept of human nature. Because of their profundity and importance for the subject at hand, his remarks deserve to be quoted at length:

> The Chief Rabbi of France, Gilles Bernheim, has shown in a very detailed and profoundly moving study that the attack we are currently experiencing on the true structure of the family, made up of father, mother, and child, goes much deeper. While up to now we regarded a false understanding of the nature of human freedom as one cause of the crisis of the family, it is now becoming clear that the very notion of being—of what being human really means—is being called into question. He quotes the famous saying of Simone de Beauvoir: "one is not born a woman, one becomes so" (*on ne naît pas femme, on le devient*). These words lay the foundation for what is put forward today under the term "gender" as a new philosophy of sexuality. According

---

[40] Following John Paul II and Benedict XVI, Pope Francis has continued to emphasize the importance, significance, and beauty of complementarity. See the "Address of His Holiness Pope Francis to Participants in the International Colloquium on the Complementarity Between Man and Woman Sponsored by the Congregation for the Doctrine of the Faith" (November 17, 2014), available at: https://w2.vatican.va/content/francesco/en/speeches/2014/november/documents/papa-francesco_20141117_congregazione-dottrina-fede.html. See also his weekly general audience on Marriage of April 29, 2015 available at: https://w2.vatican.va/content/francesco/en/audiences/2015/documents/papa-francesco20150429udienza-generale.html. In his 2013 Apostolic exhortation, *Evangelii gaudium* Pope Francis speaks of a need for a greater recognition of "the feminine genius" in society (see no. 103).

[41] Benedict XVI, *Deus caritas est*, no. 11. The citation is from the Liberia Editrice Vaticana edition (Vatican City: Liberia Editrice Vaticana, 2006), 29.

[42] See *Deus caritas est*, nos. 9-10, 12.

to this philosophy, sex is no longer a given element of nature, that man has to accept and personally make sense of: it is a social role that we choose for ourselves, while in the past it was chosen for us by society. The profound falsehood of this theory and of the anthropological revolution contained within it is obvious. People dispute the idea that they have a nature, given by their bodily identity, that serves as a defining element of the human being. They deny their nature and decide that it is not something previously given to them, but that they make it for themselves. According to the biblical creation account, being created by God as male and female pertains to the essence of the human creature. This duality is an essential aspect of what being human is all about, as ordained by God. This very duality as something previously given is what is now disputed. The words of the creation account: "male and female he created them" (*Gen* 1:27) no longer apply. No, what applies now is this: it was not God who created them male and female—hitherto society did this, now we decide for ourselves. Man and woman as created realities, as the nature of the human being, no longer exist. Man calls his nature into question. From now on he is merely spirit and will. The manipulation of nature, which we deplore today where our environment is concerned, now becomes man's fundamental choice where he himself is concerned. From now on there is only the abstract human being, who chooses for himself what his nature is to be. Man and woman in their created state as complementary versions of what it means to be human are disputed. But if there is no pre-ordained duality of man and woman in creation, then neither is the family any longer a reality established by creation.[43]

For the Holy Father, the separation of "gender" from "sex" begun in second wave feminism is a "profound falsehood"—a denial of our bodily identity as male and female and their complementary duality and hence a denial of our created nature as human beings.[44] Humanity

---

[43] Pope Benedict XVI, "Address of His Holiness Benedict XVI on the Occasion of Christmas Greetings to the Roman Curia" (December 21, 2012), www.vatican.va/holy_father/benedict_xvi/speeches/2012/december/documents/hf_ben-xvi_spe_20121221_auguri-curia_en.html. In these reflections, one can clearly see the intersection between the thought of John Paul II and Benedict XVI. One could say that in these remarks he lays the historical and epistemological foundations for the need for something like his predecessor's articulation of "the spousal meaning of the body." Both popes stress how sexual difference is a gift, while focusing on different aspects of that gift. Recall that for John Paul II, sexual difference is a call to a self-gift of love in the communion of persons. Conversely, here Benedict emphasizes the importance of accepting the gift of sexual difference—our maleness and femaleness—that comes from the Creator. Taken together, their thoughts form a kind of continuum, where sexual difference is received as a gift and then it summons one to make a gift of self in one's vocation.

[44] Pope Francis also has expressed similar concerns over "gender ideology." For example, see his "Address of His Holiness Pope Francis to the Bishops of the Episcopal

is reduced to self-creating spirit whose bodily reality and sexual make up is comprised by an assertion of will. Such a false understanding of the human person constitutes one of the heresies which besets our times.[45] It is also a view common among some contemporary gender rights activists whereby all manner of self-articulations as a sexual (or asexual) beings are celebrated as part of human diversity.

ETHICAL ANALYSIS

The Church's teaching summarized above sheds light on ethically appropriate means of treating and caring for individuals who must contend with the psychological challenges of conditions such as GID or ambiguous physical sex.

Even though adults who are not ego-syntonic with their own physical sex are able to give informed consent in regard to their care, both Catholic moral theologians and clinicians have rightly questioned the ethical propriety of using so-called sexual reassignment procedures as a means of treatment in these cases. For example, John Hopkins, which was once a leading center for sexual reassignment surgery, decided to stop prescribing this type of surgery in the late 1970s at the urging of Dr. Paul McHugh, the psychiatrist-in-chief at Hopkins at the time.[46] Based on the research of Jon Meyer, who followed-up with adults who had received the surgery, McHugh discovered that patients "were no better in their psychological integration or any easier to live with [after their surgery]." He writes, "With these facts in hand I concluded that Hopkins was fundamentally cooperating with a mental illness. We psychiatrists, I thought, would do better to concentrate on trying to fix their minds and not their genitalia."[47]

Conference of Puerto Rico on Their '*Ad Limina*' Visit" (June 8, 2015), http://w2.vatican.va/content/francesco/en/speeches/2015/june/documents/papa-francesco_20150608_adlimina-porto-rico.html. In his 2015 Encyclical Letter *Laudato si,* he speaks of the importance of accepting one's body including one's masculinity or femininity as gifts (see no. 155). For their part, Catholic new feminists reacting to de Beauvoir and her impact on modern thought argue for the need to reunite these realities. See Beatriz Vollmer Coles, "New Feminism: A Sex-Gender Reunion," in *Women in Christ,* 52-66.

[45] Perhaps a sign of such times can be found in the recent decision by Facebook to gives users some 50 different options for their gender self-identification. On this see Aimee Lee Ball, "Who Are You on Facebook Now? Facebook Customizes Gender with 50 Different Choices," *The New York Times* (April 4, 2014), www.nytimes.com/2014/04/06/fashion/facebook-customizes-gender-with-50-different-choices.html?_r=0.

[46] Paul McHugh, "Surgical Sex," *First Things* 147 (2004), 34-8.

[47] McHugh, "Surgical Sex." Similarly, Colin Ross notes that if sexual reassignment surgery is offered as a viable treatment option, then gender identity disorder is the only diagnostic category where the psychiatrist agrees with the with the patient's de-

As McHugh suggests, even though many transsexuals see surgery as the solution to their dissatisfaction with their biological sex, unfortunately it actually does not solve their problem. While surgery and/or hormone therapy may make the person's body appear to be the opposite sex, in reality, these procedures fail to actually change a person's physiological sex and therefore offer no true benefit. Ultimately, these procedures prioritize the individual's subjective experience of him/herself over objective reality, and they simply enable the transsexual person to live a lie while also failing to address the underlying psychological issues.[48]

From the perspective of Catholic theology, all creation is a gift from God, including our bodies. As a gift from God, our bodies must be valued and respected, particularly in medical decisions. As Pope Pius XII explains, "Because he [the patient] is a user and not a proprietor, he [the patient] does not have unlimited power to destroy or mutilate his body and its functions."[49] However, as the Pope goes on to note, under the principle of totality, "the patient can allow individual parts to be destroyed or mutilated when and to the extent necessary for the good of his being as a whole."[50]

Unfortunately, sexual reassignment surgery ignores the goodness of the body and is completely contrary to the principle of totality. The surgery is unnecessary. It permanently mutilates healthy sexual organs while offering no physical benefit to the patient. Such mutilation sadly leaves the person unable to bear children as a member of their cosmetically reassigned sex. In light of the Church's teaching described above, hormone therapy, including medications that delay or inhibit puberty, and sexual reassignment surgery can be understood as a tragic rejection of the gift of one's own sexual constitution and a misguided attempt to re-make oneself in pursuit of happiness or psychological relief.[51] Therefore, Catholic doctors and theologians have consistently recommended psychotherapeutic means of treatment and pastoral care

lusion. See his article, "Ethics of Gender Identity Disorder," *Ethical Human Psychology and Psychiatry* 11, no. 3 (2009): 165-170. For more on this particular point, see p. 167.

[48] William E. May echoes this point in his article "Sex Reassignment Surgery," *Ethics & Medics* 13, no. 11 (1988): 1-2.

[49] Pope Pius XII, "The Moral Limits of Medical Research and Treatment" (September 14, 1952), no. 12, www.ewtn.com/library/PAPALDOC/P12PSYCH.HTM.

[50] Pope Pius XII, "The Moral Limits of Medical Research and Treatment," no. 13. Here he is specifically referring to the well-being of physical body.

[51] Obviously, one's culpability for making such a choice can be mitigated by factors such as psychological distress or confusion about the meaning of sexuality.

which have actually been proven to be more effective at alleviating psychological distress in such persons.[52]

These procedures can be distinguished from surgical intervention or hormonal and other therapy aimed at clarifying the physical expression of one's sex when it is ambiguous. When a child is born who is intersexed in some fashion, the parents may have to choose, in consultation with their doctors, the gender in which to raise the child. [53] Usually the decision has been made on the basis of a judgment about which sex the child would be best able to function, frequently resulting in such children being raised as girls.[54] Yet there is emerging evidence that many children raised in a manner different than their genetically given sex, may come to resent this decision made on their behalf after they reach puberty. As a result, parents must exercise great care in making such decisions. Such persons upon reaching adulthood or mature adolescents with the consent of their parents (and after adequate counseling), might rightly elect to undergo surgical or medical treatments aimed at clarifying the gender that is determined to be the most appropriate for him or her. [55]

What about the case of an adolescent or pre-adolescent child who is not intersexed, but nonetheless manifests symptoms of a condition such as GID? In light of both the clinical information considered above and the perspective afforded by the Church's teaching, the best option to care for such children is offer them effective psychological therapy aimed at helping them to accept and affirm the bodily expression of their sex as an integral part of their personal identity.[56] Given that parents can be a factor in children's non-acceptance of their sexual identity, such therapy should generally include parents as well as the affected child.

Unfortunately, there are parents or adult guardians of children who, for a variety of reasons, are unwilling to seek such therapeutic assistance for children suffering from conditions such as GID. In some cases, they may themselves be ambivalent about their child's physical sex, wishing that the child had been born other than he or she is or

---

[52] See Ashley, DeBlois, and O'Rourke, *Healthcare Ethics*, 110-12; and Richard Ritzgibbons MD, Philip Sutton PhD, and Dale O'Leary, "The Psychopathology of 'Sex Reassignment Surgery': Assessing its Medical, Psychological and Ethical Appropriateness," *National Catholic Bioethics Quarterly* 9, no. 1 (Spring 2009): 97-125.

[53] "Gender" is used here in the older sense as a synonym for sex difference.

[54] Ashley, DeBlois, and O'Rourke note that this practice has generally been approved by Catholic moralists. See *Healthcare Ethics*, 112.

[55] This is the position of Ashley, DeBlois,and O'Rourke. See *Healthcare Ethics*, 112-13.

[56] If such surgery is not a wise ethical choice for adults with GID who are capable of giving informed consent, then this is even more certain for children and adolescents whose self-concept and sexual identity is still in a process of development.

exacerbating the child's struggle with GID while mistakenly thinking that they are being supportive. As Fitzgibbons argues, this can be a factor in a child's development of this disorder. In other cases the parents or guardians might be unwilling to seek therapy on other grounds (e.g., fear, ignorance, or poverty). If this is a deliberate choice on the part of the parents or guardians, it is an unfortunate one as it subjects children to a great deal of psychological stress and interpersonal problems which might have been alleviated with appropriate psychological intervention. Such parents or guardians are guilty of failing to act in the best interests of the children entrusted to their care.[57]

But more troubling still is the case of parents or guardians who, for whatever reason, find their child's gender non-conformity as something to be publically identified (perhaps even celebrated) and which must be accommodated by the wider community. In some cases such parents find willing accomplices in school officials and community leaders who use the psychological struggles of these children to advance the cause of "gender rights" or "sexual diversity" in the groups and institutions with which they are affiliated. In these instances, a particular ideological agenda is being advanced at the expense of the psychological well-being of particular children. The children in this case are generally unwitting victims who are often being used in ways that they do not fully understand. The responsible adults around them who use them in this way are guilty of more than just a failure to act in the children's best interests; they are guilty of a kind of exploitation of these children for ideological or political purposes. They are also responsible for causing scandal within their communities by furthering the growing social confusion about the goodness and meaning of sexual difference highlighted by Pope Benedict XVI.[58]

APPLICATION TO GSUSA POLICY AND CATHOLIC PARISHES

Having identified the particular evil involved in "using" children described as "transgender" persons to promote sexual diversity and inclusiveness in school and community organizations, how does this bear upon the current policy of the Girl Scouts USA and the practice of Catholic parishes that sponsor troops?

It should be noticed that the GSUSA policy as formulated seems to be aimed at prudential judgment of cases—not at general advocacy for sexual inclusiveness or gender rights. The policy states: "Placement of transgender youth is handled on a case-by-case basis, with the welfare and best interests of the child and the members of the troop/group

---

[57] Though if they are constrained by factors such as ignorance or fear in this failure, then their culpability for such choices is correspondingly lessened.

[58] Again, factors such as ignorance can reduce one's moral culpability. Many crusaders for "gender rights" act out of sincerity and goodwill.

in question a top priority." It does not state that all groups must include such members. It makes the well-being of individual children and the harmony of individual troops the key concern for the policy.

In addition, the policy does not distinguish between physiological and psychological manifestations of sexual ambiguity—that is between intersexed children and those who suffer from psychological conditions such as GID. In the case of the former group, there really are children who have ambiguity in the physical expression of their sexuality. Such individuals should not be ostracized or shunned because of such a condition. There should indeed be, as the policy suggests, a "setting that is both emotionally and physically safe" for such children. In a Catholic scout troop, this presents a unique opportunity to practice hospitality and love of one's neighbor for a vulnerable peer. These cases are significantly different than those in which a child is physically a boy but is not ego-syntonic with this identity and wants (or has parents who want him) to be accepted and treated as a girl. This might prove to be disruptive to an individual troop, but the prudential tone of the policy mentioned above seems to leave some discretion to the leaders of individual troops in such matters.

Yet even in the case of children who are physiologically boys suffering from a condition such as GID and who want to take part in a group dedicated to the development of girls, it is not clear that this is inherently destructive. Historical and anthropological studies have shown that female sexual identity tends to be more stable than that of males and therefore less threatened by the presence of males in a female-oriented setting whereas the presence of a girl in a group of boys might well have much more profound impact on the activities and identity of that group.[59] Furthermore, in the case of children and families who are open to therapeutic help, it may provide some stimulus to seek it and actually help the confused child begin to work through his misidentification with the opposite sex. What the troop is doing in including a child like this is supporting a sexually confused child—rather than adding rejection to his psychological struggles—not advancing a larger agenda.

These considerations suggest that GSUSA and its fairly nuanced policy of openness to accommodating individual children who manifest different forms of a confused sexual identity should not necessarily be taken as advancing an agenda of sexual confusion under a banner of gender rights. The practice of the organization therefore need not be construed as any kind of formal cooperation with this evil,

---

[59] On this point, see the outstanding study of Walter Ong, S.J., *Fighting for Life: Contest, Sexuality, and Consciousness* (Ithaca: Cornell University, 1981; rpt. Eugene, OR: Wipf & Stock, 2011).

especially insofar as it is aimed at accommodating the needs of individual children and troops on a case by case basis. It is also clearly remote from the actual evils identified in the analysis above—the decision of parents or adult guardians of sexually confused children not to seek appropriate therapeutic assistance for them or, worse, for parents or others in positions of authority to "use" such children for ideological or political purposes. The GSUSA policy represents an effort to accommodate in individual cases decisions made by parents or guardians of children outside of the group.

The Catholic parish which chooses to sponsor such a troop devoted to the development of girls—even in light of the GSUSA policy—is more remote still from these evils. In light of this, there does not seem to be justification or any kind of moral necessity for Catholic parishes to cut ties with GSUSA or forbid the group to meet on Church property at this point.

Two caveats should be appended to the analysis above. First, concerning transgender youth, "GSUSA recommends that the local council makes similar accommodation that schools across the country follow in regard to changing, sleeping arrangements, and other travel-related activities."[60] Unfortunately, some school districts and states have adopted policies that permit transgender youth to choose the bathroom and locker rooms that they want to use based on the sex with which they identify.[61] Therefore, an adolescent boy (who views himself as a young girl) may use female restrooms and locker rooms.

This policy is troubling for a number of reasons. On the one hand, it seems replete with the potential for abuse, particularly by older students. For example, some school districts require very little evidence to support the student's asserted gender identity. In Massachusetts, for instance, a letter from a health care provider or a parent is not required for a student to be recognized as a different gender. The testimony of the transgender student's friends appears to be sufficient to enable him/her to use the facilities of the other sex. The policy states, "Confirmation of a student's asserted gender identity may include a letter from a parent, health care provider, school staff member familiar with the student (a teacher, guidance counselor, or school psychologist, among others), or other family members or friends."[62] School officials

---

[60] See footnote 1 for a link to the policy.

[61] Don Thompson, "Transgender Bathroom Rights Bill Passed By California Lawmakers," *HuffingtonPost.com* (July 3, 2013), www.huffingtonpost.com/2013/07/03/transgender-bathroom-rightsn3543601.

[62] Massachusetts Department of Elementary and Secondary Education, *Guidance for Massachusetts Public School Creating a Safe and Supportive School Environment: Nondiscrimination on the Basis of Gender Identity* (Malden, MA: 2013), 5. Available at www.doe.mass.edu/ssce/GenderIdentity.pdf. While acknowledging the possibility that a student may assert the opposite gender for an improper purpose, the document

do not even seem to require parental consent for the child to switch genders at school, because according to Massachusetts' policy, students may not feel comfortable expressing their transgender struggles with their parents and ultimately the decision rests with the student anyway.[63]

On the other hand, these policies leave little room for school administrators to make prudential judgments about particular cases and render them powerless to take into account the emotional, moral, and physical well-being of non-transgender youth. Because they are open to abuse by curious youth or sex offenders, these policies pose serious physical risk to other non-transgender students. In addition, while these policies respect and obviously preference the feelings of transgender youth, the emotional and moral impact that sharing bathrooms and locker rooms with the opposite sex will have on very young, impressionable non-transgender children is extremely unclear and should not be ignored.

Therefore, if GSUSA is recommending that local councils follow some school districts by adopting these types of policies concerning transgender youth, then our moral analysis of the GSUSA's policy would differ substantially. In order words, if GSUSA is suggesting that transgender youth be able to share bathing and sleeping facilities with young girls, then we would oppose their policy, because it would potentially endanger the physical, emotional, and moral well-being of the rest of the troop while also undermining parental authority and the ability of local leaders to decide what is in the best interest of their individual troops.

The second caveat to our moral analysis concerns the purported relationship between GSUSA and Planned Parenthood. There have for some time been accusations that GSUSA surreptitiously donates money to the International Planned Parenthood Federation and has supported some of that group's radical sexual education programs.[64] These accusations have had enough of an impact that the same Girl

also states, "In most situations, determining a student's gender identity is simple. A student who says she is a girl and wishes to be regarded that way throughout the school day and throughout every, or almost every, other area of her life, should be respected and treated like a girl. So too with a student who says he is a boy and wishes to be regarded that way throughout the school day and throughout every, or almost every, other area of his life. Such a student should be respected and treated like a boy" (4).
[63] Massachusetts Department of Elementary and Secondary Education, *Guidance for Massachusetts Public School Environment*, 6. This point was brought to our attention by Kirsten Andersen in her report "Massachusetts forces schools to let 'transgender' boys use girls' restrooms, lockers," *LifeSiteNews.com* (February 19, 2013), www.lifesitenews.com/news/massachusetts-forces-schools-to-let-39transgender39-boys-use-girls39-restro.
[64] See, for example, the information and accusations complied at the website Honest Girl Scouts. Available at www.honestgirlscouts.com/.

Scout website that articulates the policy on "transgender" youth includes a denial of any support for abortion as well as a denial of any relationship with Planned Parenthood.[65]

Should these public denials by GSUSA prove to be false and the accusations by their critics prove to be true, that would substantially alter the conclusions reached above. For then the policy on "transgender" youth would appear not to be a prudential approach to accommodate sexually confused young people on a case by case basis in an organization aimed at fostering the development of youth, but part of a larger and more systematic assault on traditional understandings of sexuality and the family by that organization. In such a case GSUSA would appear to be engaged in some sort of formal cooperation with the evil of "using" sexually confused children as part of an organizational effort to advance a destructive agenda and ideology. In such a case Catholic parishes might well want to discontinue their relationship to the Girl Scouts since it would be scandalous for them to support an organization dedicated to advancing the sexual confusion which is endemic to our time.[66]

---

[65] Responses to these accusations may be found at www.girlscouts.org/program/gs_central/mpmf/faqs.asp#a1. Below are the most relevant sections:

Q: What is Girl Scouts of the USA's position regarding human sexuality, birth control, and abortion?

A: Girl Scouts of the USA (GSUSA) does not take a position or develop materials on these issues. We feel our role is to help girls develop self-confidence and good decision-making skills that will help them make wise choices in all areas of their lives. Parents or guardians make all decisions regarding program participation that may be of a sensitive nature. Consistent with that belief, GSUSA directs councils, including volunteer leaders, to get written parental permission for any locally planned program that could be considered sensitive.

Q: Does GSUSA have a relationship with Planned Parenthood?

A: No, Girl Scouts of the USA does not have a relationship or partnership with Planned Parenthood.

Q: Did GSUSA distribute a Planned Parenthood brochure at a United Nations event?

A: No, we did not. In 2010, GSUSA took part in the 54th Commission on the Status of Women at the United Nations. Our participation in that conference was the subject of numerous Internet stories and blogs that were factually inaccurate and troubling. Girl Scouts had no knowledge of the brochure in question and played no role in distributing it.

[66] For more information on the relationship of GSUSA to the World Association of Girl Guides and Girl Scouts (WAGGGS), to sex ed programs including those of IPPF, to local troops, and to Catholic groups and parishes which sponsor them see the reportage of the dialogue between the USCCB's Committee on Laity, Marriage, Family and Youth and representatives of GSUSA entitled "Questions and Answers About Girl Scouts of the USA (GSUSA) and About Catholic Scouting" available on the USCCB website at www.usccb.org/beliefs-and-teachings/who-we-teach/youth/catholic-scouting-questions.cfm.

CONCLUSION

In our brave new world of gender reinvention and confusion, riven by ideological wars over sexual identity, rights, and desires, it is little wonder that some children find themselves confused about their own identities. After all, many adults show themselves to be confused as well by both their words and their deeds. Unfortunately, there are those who prey on such confusion in others and seek to use such children to advance a particular social and political agenda.

The fact that GSUSA allows individual troops to admit "transgender" young people to their ranks is not in itself objectionable. In many respects it is laudatory and could be prudently accepted and implemented by troops sponsored by Catholic organizations. A young person struggling with the burdens of ambiguous physical sexuality (i.e., an intersexed child) or psychological acceptance of their biological sex (i.e., GID) could certainly use a safe environment in which to foster friendships and develop interpersonal and leadership skills. At the same time, it is incumbent on the adults who care for these children to seek appropriate medical and psychological assistance for them in dealing with and, to the degree possible, working through these physical or mental challenges.

However, this analysis has also pointed out ways that such a policy could be misused to the detriment of these children. When responsible adults (parents, educators, administrators, politicians) affix labels such as "transgender" to confused and struggling children in order to use them as a wedge to advance a particular agenda of sexual rights or politics in an organization or community, this is a violation of the dignity of the children entrusted to their care. When such policies open the door to inappropriate access of older, more sexually aggressive, children to younger ones or to outright sexual abuse, they must be viewed as the threat which they are. And if it becomes clear that such policies are tied to a larger agenda hostile to the Church's vision of the dignity or the human person as male and female and the beauty of marital sex as ordered to both love and life, then Catholic groups would do well to specify the grounds of their opposition.

Surely hospitality and providing welcome to the vulnerable is an ethical responsibility incumbent upon followers of Jesus—but so is the protection of children from those who would use them for their own ends. The same Savior who said, "Let the children come to me, and do not prevent them; for the kingdom of heaven belongs to such as these" (Matt. 19:14b-d) also warned those who cause "little ones" who believe in him to sin of "millstones" (cf. Matt. 18:6).[67] Catholic

---

[67] The citations are from the NAB. It should be noted that the reference to "little ones who believe in me" in Matthew 18:6 and its parallels may well refer to the simple

groups who have a relationship with GSUSA therefore need to exercise prudence in their oversight of troops which they sponsor. ◼

---

faith of disciples within the Christian community. For our purposes, this does not significantly change the point or relevance of the warning.

Journal of Moral Theology, Vol. 5, No. 1 (2016): 111-128

"For He is our Peace"
Thomas Aquinas on Christ as Cause of
Peace in the City of Saints

Matthew A. Tapie

M OST SCHOLARS WHO HAVE COMMENTED upon Aquinas's
view of peace have done so in the context of discussing
his teaching that peace, defined as the "tranquility of order" (*tranquillitas ordinis*), is the aim of a just war.[1] Although "civic peace" falls short of the perfect peace that the saints will

---

[1] An abridged version of this essay appears in *Reading Scripture as a Political Act*
copyright © 2015 Fortress Press. In *Summa Theologiae* II-II 29.2, Aquinas adopts
Augustine's definition of peace as *tranquillitas ordinis*. English translations of the
Summa Theologiae are from the Benziger edition unless otherwise noted. Thomas
Aquinas, *Summa Theologica*, trans. Fathers of the English Dominican Province (New
York: Benziger, 1948). Avery Cardinal Dulles observes that, "political theorists have
frequently dealt with ...civic peace ...according to Saint Thomas." Avery Cardinal
Dulles, *A Church to Believe In: Discipleship and the Dynamics of Freedom* (New
York, NY: Crossroads Publishing, 1983), 149. Most scholarly comment upon Aqui-
nas's view of peace treats the concept in the context of his teaching on war in *ST* II-II
q. 40. John Finnis's treatment of peace is representative since he places emphasis on
the fact that Aquinas taught that genuine peace is not the absence of war but the
maintenance of the common good. John Finnis, "The Ethics of War and Peace in the
Catholic Natural Law Tradition," in *Christian Political Ethics*, The Ethikon Series in
Comparative Ethics (Princeton, N.J: Princeton University Press, 2008), 193. See also
Heinz-Gerhard Justenhoven and William Barbieri, eds. *From Just War to Modern
Peace Ethics* (Berlin: De Gruyter, 2012); Gregory M Reichberg, and others, "Thomas
Aquinas: Just War and Sins Against Peace," in *The Ethics of War: Classic and Con-
temporary Readings* (Oxford: Wiley-Blackwell, 2006), 169–98; Richard B. Miller,
"Aquinas and the Presumption against Killing and War," *Journal of Religion* 82, no.
2 (April 1, 2002): 173–204; James Turner Johnson, "Aquinas and Luther on War and
Peace," *Journal of Religious Ethics* 31, no. 1 (Spring 2003): 3–20. Aside from Mat-
thew Levering's indirect but helpful treatment of peace in Aquinas's *Commentary on
John* in Thomas G. Weinandy, John P. Yocum, and Daniel A. Keating, *Aquinas On
Scripture: An Introduction To His Biblical Commentaries* (London: T. & T. Clark
Publishers, 2005), the only scholars that directly address the subject are Francis E.
McMahon, "A Thomistic Analysis of Peace," *Thomist* 1, no. 3 (July 1939) 169–92;
and Edwin J. Buers, "Saint Thomas Aquinas and Peace," Catholic University of
America, M.A. Thesis 1934. R. A. Johnson advances the position that Aquinas's the-
ological method represents a "nonviolent" theological confrontation of the Cathars.
See Roger A. Johnson, *Peacemaking and Religious Violence: From Thomas Aquinas
to Thomas Jefferson* (Eugene, OR.: Pickwick Publications, 2009).

possess in heaven, such peace is a positive state of civil well-being, and not merely the absence of war.[2] Scholarly focus on this true-but-imperfect peace in the secondary literature creates the impression that peace in Aquinas mostly concerns the peace of the city of man, and has little to do with the church.

However, as Gregory M. Reichberg has shown, Aquinas's commentary on the Gospel of Matthew, especially his comment upon Matthew 5:39 ("But I say to you, do not resist and evil doer"), indicates a more complex picture, which Reichberg refers to as a "two stage theory."[3] Although the use of force is licit for the civil power (*respublica*), Reichberg shows that, for Aquinas, peacemaking is the appropriate response to evil for the "agency" of the church whose members' actions proceed directly from charity, and therefore "steadfastly... [avoid] any responsibility whatsoever for the shedding of blood."[4]

---

[2] Peace as "tranquility of order" is to be distinguished from evil peace (*ST* II-II q. 40, a. 1, ad. 3). The idea that peace is not simply the absence of war is not an original concept, since this line of thinking can be traced to the Stoics, Neo-Platonists, Aristotle, and Plato. James Turner Johnson, "Peace, War, and the Rejection of Violence in the Middle Ages," in *The Quest for Peace: Three Moral Traditions in Western Cultural History* (Princeton, N.J.: Princeton University Press, 1987), 68.

[3] Matt. 5:39 (NRSV). The idea of a dual agency in regard to evil should not be misunderstood as two separate spheres of activity, one secular and the other sacred. As Elizabeth Phillips points out, premodern authors "used the term 'secular' not to mean that which is not 'sacred', but to mean that which is temporal and not eternal." See her discussion of the relation of Aquinas's political theology to Augustine's in *Political Theology: A Guide for the Perplexed* (New York: T&T Clark, 2012), 26, 32–36.

[4] Gregory M. Reichberg, "Thomas Aquinas between Just War and Pacifism," *Journal of Religious Ethics* 38, no. 2 (June 1, 2010): 219–41. One of the merits of Reichberg's essay is that he demonstrates that Aquinas's comments concerning the permissibility of armed violence are scattered throughout the *Summa Theologiae* and biblical commentaries. After a thorough analysis of the texts, he concludes that the most focused attention to the "dual exigencies" of church (*ecclesia*) and state (*respublica*) appears in Aquinas's commentary on Matthew. Just war and nonviolence are " ...represent ways of dealing with evil, the first by active resistance especially on behalf of the innocent under attack, the second by the voluntary acceptance of harm, assumed out of love for the spiritual good of the attacker. The first pertains first and foremost to the kingdoms (*respublicae*) of this world ...[and] the second pertains to a kingdom that transcends this world, the Church (*ecclesia*), led by Christ, who directs actions of all its members to the goal of eternal life ...the unity of the Church is constituted by the bond of charity; hence, only what proceeds directly from charity, as poured into human hearts by the Holy Spirit, is properly speaking 'of the Church'. Acts of violence, even licit violence, as with just war, cannot be attributed to the Church as such." Reichberg, "Thomas Aquinas," 238–9. Reichberg admits that Aquinas's approval of knightly religious orders (made up of lay brothers) sits in tension with this interpretation, but argues Aquinas viewed such measures as a provisional exception to the general rule that warfare pertains to the civil power, whereas the church, *per se*, "steadfastly avoids any responsibility whatsoever for the shedding of blood." Reichberg, "Thomas Aquinas," 235.

Based on a thorough examination of relevant texts in the *Summa The-ologiae* and commentary on Matthew, Reichberg argues that, for Aquinas, the church "has a natural affinity, with respect to its own proper order of activity, with a nonviolent, 'redemptive' response to evil."[5]

This essay takes Reichberg's treatment of war and peace in Aquinas as a point of departure and explores the concept of an ecclesial "affinity" for peace in two of Aquinas's commentaries that contain teaching on peace as it relates to the church: the commentary on the Gospel of John, and the commentary on Paul's letter to the Ephesians.[6] I examine these commentaries in order to address a specific problem. Though Christians enjoy the civic peace often highlighted in discussions of "true-but-imperfect" peace in Aquinas, it is not clear in what sense the church has been given the particular peace that Christ said he gave to the disciples in John 14:27 ("my peace I give you."), and referenced in the Rite of Peace in the Roman Catholic Liturgy of the Eucharist. Since any peace we have in this life is subject to disturbance and conflict how can we say we have received Christ's own peace? Is there a sense in which the church, which is obviously imperfect, possesses Christ's own peace now?

In what follows, I argue that in addition to the frequently discussed idea of a true-but-imperfect civic peace in Aquinas, there exists a true-

---

[5] Reichberg does not think this affinity for nonviolence can be limited to priests and bishops: "Aquinas typically frames this response by reference to the expectations incumbent upon ordained priests, since, on the sacramental rationale ...they especially represent Christ within the Church. Yet this call to nonviolence, as embodied in the 'counsels of perfection', was not understood by him to be a prerogative of priests alone, for he was well aware of the numerous female and lay martyrs. As a consequence, the distinction between nonviolence and just war does not neatly parallel the related distinction between clergy and laity." Reichberg, "Thomas Aquinas, 235."

[6] I am indebted to Kevin Hughes, Gregory Reichberg, and William Mattison for their comments on earlier drafts of this essay. All citations of Aquinas's commentaries are from the Latin/English Aquinas Institute for the Study of Sacred Doctrine edition, which is based on Fabian Larcher's translation of the Marietti edition of the commentaries. See St. Thomas Aquinas, *Commentary on the Letters of Saint Paul to the Galatians and Ephesians* vol. 39 (Lander, Wyoming: Aquinas Institute for the Study of Sacred Doctrine, 2012); *Commentary on the Gospel of John, Chapters 9–21*, vol. 36 (Lander, Wyoming: Aquinas Institute for the Study of Sacred Doctrine, 2013). In order to simplify citation and reference, citations consist of the abbreviated Latin titles for the commentaries (*In Ioannem* and *Ad Ephesios*). Citations also employ the Marietti edition's numbers for chapter and lecture, which are commonly used when citing the commentaries. According to the Aquinas Institute editors, Aquinas appears to be familiar with more than one translation of scripture, often quotes from memory and paraphrases. The closest available version of scripture to Aquinas's text is the Clementine Vulgate of 1598, and the closest translation of the Clementine Vulgate in English is the Douay-Rheims version. Therefore scripture citations, aside from the above reference to the NRSV, are of the Douay-Rheims.

but-imperfect ecclesial peace that, despite being subject to disturb-ances, can be described as "of Christ." Christ's gift of peace in John 14:27, for Aquinas, refers not only to the perfect state to be enjoyed in heaven but also to a true-but-imperfect ecclesial peace possessed by the saints now. Furthermore, because Aquinas understands virtuous activity as constitutive of happiness, Christ's gift of peace to the church is not merely a state of affairs. The preservation of peace is also a human activity. I argue that Aquinas understands the faithful to be called by God to preserve Christ's ecclesial gift of peace through the development of what might be called four peacemaking virtues: humility, meekness, patience, and mercy.[7]

Below, I present this Christological peace in Aquinas in four steps. First, I show how this peace compliments Aquinas's thought in the *Summa Theologiae*, by briefly outlining the four categories of peace discussed in II-II q. 29. Second, I focus attention on the "multivoiced literal sense" of Aquinas's interpretation of scripture[8] in order to show that Aquinas employs the same literal meaning of John 14:27, "my peace I give you." to explain the meaning of Paul's words about Christ in Ephesians 2:14. Aquinas understands "For he is our peace," to refer not to the perfect peace to be enjoyed in heaven but to a form of im-perfect ecclesial peace had by the saints on earth. Third, I explain the sense in which this peace can be described as being "of" or "from" Christ by identifying what Aquinas understands as the cause, purpose, and bond of the peace of the saints. Lastly, I show how this true-but-imperfect state of ecclesial peace includes the activity of preserving peace through the cultivation of four virtues that Aquinas says prevent peace from disappearing among members.

---

[7] I am not claiming that peace is a virtue. Aquinas clearly teaches otherwise in *ST* II-II 29, a. 4. However, peace is an activity. In particular, it is an act of charity. When it is combined with other forms of virtuous activity (humility, meekness, and patience) it preserves the ecclesial state of peace that is the body of Christ. The overlooked ecclesiological dimension of true-but-imperfect ecclesial peace in Aquinas's thought might serve as a resource for contemporary calls for a Catholic peace theology and ethics of peacemaking. See Scott Appleby, Robert J. Schreiter, and Gerard Powers, eds. *Peacebuilding: Catholic Theology, Ethics, and Praxis* (Orbis Books, 2010); and Robert John Araujo's discussion of contemporary Catholic thought on these themes in *Religion, War, and Ethics: A Sourcebook of Textual Traditions*, ed. Gregory M. Reichberg and Henrik Syse (Cambridge University Press, 2014).
[8] The idea that the literal sense can refer to a number of realities. Stephen E. Fowl, "Thomas Aquinas and the Multifaceted Literal Sense of Scripture," Paper presented at the SBL Annual Meeting, Christian Theology and the Bible Section: The Literal Sense of Scripture According to Various Interpreters, Chicago, November 17, 2012. Fowl goes into greater detail concerning the multivoiced or multifaceted literal sense of scripture in his essay, "The Importance of a Multivoiced Literal Sense of Scripture: The Example of Thomas Aquinas," in *Reading Scripture with the Church: Toward a Hermeneutic for Theological Interpretation*, ed. A. K. M. Adam et al. (Baker Aca-demic, 2006), 35–50.

A brief comment on Aquinas's approach to scripture might help the reader to appreciate Aquinas's interpretation of peace in the biblical commentaries. That Aquinas was a theologian deeply shaped by reading scripture is evidenced in his upbringing in liturgical and biblical-patristic culture[9]; his training in the monastic tradition of *lectio divina*; his attraction to the Order of Preachers; and his discussion of scripture in the "inaugural sermons" (presented at the ceremony for his installment as *magister in sacra pagina* or master of the sacred page) at the university of Paris, not to mention the requirements of the office of *magister* itself.[10]

Perhaps the clearest indication that Aquinas was a theologian of scripture is the frequent use of the Word of God in the *Summa Theologiae*[11] as highest authority (a commonplace practice in the scholastic hierarchy of sources),[12] and the fact that Aquinas wrote commentaries on five Old Testament books (Psalms, Job, Isaiah, Jeremiah, and Lamentations); two commentaries on the Gospels (Matthew and John); and all of the Pauline letters.[13]

For Aquinas, the literal sense (*sensus litteralis*) of the biblical text was the basis for all theology.[14] The literal sense (to be distinguished

---

[9] Fergus Kerr, "Thomas Aquinas," in *The Medieval Theologians: An Introduction to Theology in the Medieval Period*, ed. G. R. Evans, 1st ed. (Wiley-Blackwell, 2001), 201–220.

[10] The office of the *magister in sacra pagina* in the twelfth-century consisted of a threefold function: *legere* (to read scripture and comment verse by verse); *disputare* (to teach through objections and responses on a given theme); and *praedicare* (to preach). Jean-Pierre Torrell, *Saint Thomas Aquinas, Vol. 1. The Person and His Work*, Revised (Washington, D.C.: The Catholic University of America Press, 2005), 54. The inaugural sermons can be found in *Thomas Aquinas: Selected Writings*, ed. and trans. Ralph McInerny (Penguin Classics, 1999), 3–17.

[11] Pim Valkenberg, *Words of the Living God: Place and Function of Holy Scripture in the Theology of St. Thomas Aquinas*, Thomas Instituut te Utrecht, v. 6 (Leuven: Peeters, 2000), 207.

[12] Servais-Théodore Pinckaers, "The Sources of the Ethics of St. Thomas Aquinas," in Stephen J. Pope, ed., *The Ethics of Aquinas* (Washington, D.C.: Georgetown University Press, 2002), 19.

[13] Eleonore Stump, "Biblical Commentary and Philosophy," in *The Cambridge Companion to Aquinas*, eds. Norman Kretzmann and Eleonore Stump (Cambridge: Cambridge University Press, 1993), 252–268. Aquinas's "biblical commentaries" are actually lectures designed for the medieval classroom. The lectures would be taken down by a cleric who Aquinas thought would be capable of the work. Aquinas is thought to have lectured on Paul's letters twice, 1265–68 and 1272/3. The lecture on John is dated around 1270–2. Christopher T. Baglow, *"Modus Et Forma": A New Approach to the Exegesis of Saint Thomas Aquinas with an Application to the Lectura Super Epistolam Ad Ephesios*, Analecta Biblica 149 (Roma: Pontificio Istituto biblico, 2002), 120; 165.; See Thomas Weinandy et. al., *Preface*, "*Aquinas on Doctrine*, x.

[14] Fowl points out that although this was not unique, Aquinas was "in a decided minority in his day." Fowl, "Thomas Aquinas and the Multifaceted Literal Sense of Scripture." See also Mark Johnson, "Another Look at St. Thomas and the Plurality of

from the *sensus spiritualis* or spiritual sense) refers to concepts in scripture that have some referent in reality. "To know the literal sense is to know the reality intended by the author and signified by those words."[15] The literal sense is "the first important level of signification" since it is the basis for any spiritual interpretation of the text.[16]

What is important for my purpose here is to point out that Aquinas thought the literal sense of scripture could refer to a number of realities. As Stephen Fowl observes, "any particular passage of scripture may legitimately support a diversity of interpretations, each of which counts as the literal sense of that passage."[17] What Fowl calls the "multivoiced literal sense" of scripture is evident in how Aquinas interprets Christ's words, "my peace I give you." since this verse becomes the interpretive key for his reading of Paul's words about Christ as peace of the church in Ephesians 2:14: "For he is our peace."

In the next section, I discuss Aquinas's view of peace in the *Summa Theologiae* and then summarize his interpretation of John 14:27, "Peace I leave with you; my peace I give you." in lecture 7 of his commentary on John. Following my discussion of Aquinas's reading of this verse, I focus on how Aquinas employs the same literal meaning of "peace" from the commentary on John to explain the meaning of Paul's phrase, "For he is our peace," in the Ephesians commentary.

FOUR TYPES OF PEACE IN THE *SUMMA THEOLOGIAE*

Before examining Aquinas's interpretation of peace in the commentary on John it is helpful to observe that in the *Summa Theologiae* II-II 29, Aquinas teaches that there exist four types of peace: 1) concord; 2) apparent or false peace; 3) true but imperfect peace; and 4) perfect peace. "Concord" is simple agreement among the wills of various persons concerning one thing. However, when concord is focused

---

the Literal Sense of Scripture," *Medieval Philosophy and Theology* 2 (1992): 118–42. For Aquinas's comments on hermeneutics see Ia 1 a. 10 ad. 2; *Quaestiones de quodlibet*, 7.6.1–3, 145–48; *Super epistolam ad Galatas lectura*, 4.7; *Quaestiones disputatae de potentia*, 4.1. Busa, *Sancti Thomae Aquinatis Opera Omnia*.

[15] John Boyle, "St. Thomas Aquinas and Sacred Scripture," Aquinas Lecture, presented at the Notre Dame Seminary, New Orleans, April 8, 2011). This "reality" could include history, etiology, and analogy. When this first level of reference is employed to point to another level of meaning it pertains to the spiritual.

[16] The spiritual sense is organized into three variations informed by three periods of salvation history: Old Testament figures of Christ; moral action of Christians (based on action of Christ); and the anagogic meaning as foreshadowing future glory. "All three spiritual meanings interpret the objects of a certain status in salvation history as a sign of a subsequent status ..." Boyle, "St. Thomas." Aquinas does not always provide a spiritual interpretation of a verse of scripture. See Thomas Rik Van Nieuwenhove and Joseph Wawrykow, *The Theology Of Thomas Aquinas* (University of Notre Dame Press, 2005), 393–4.

[17] Fowl, "Thomas Aquinas and the Multifaceted Literal Sense of Scripture," 2.

on evil as its object, such concord is only apparent peace or what Aquinas calls the "peace of the wicked."[18] Peace includes the simple agreement on something (concord) but adds to it. For Aquinas, there is a difference between true and false peace: "There can be no true peace except where the appetite is directed to what is truly good...Hence true peace is only in good men and about good things. The peace of the wicked is not a true peace but a semblance thereof."[19] It is well known that Aquinas considers the civic peace sought in a just war as a good but imperfect peace: "Those who wage war justly aim at peace, and so they are not opposed to peace, except to the evil peace."[20] Yet Aquinas also explains that truly good peace is when the "chief movement of the soul finds rest in God."[21] True peace can therefore be had in two ways. It can be possessed imperfectly and perfectly. In the vulnerable condition of faith, peace in this life is always possessed imperfectly since there are certain things within and without which disturb peace. In the invulnerable condition of the beatific vision (seeing God face to face), good peace is possessed perfectly.[22]

CHRIST'S PEACE IN AQUINAS'S *COMMENTARY ON JOHN*

In the commentary on John, Aquinas follows Augustine's interpretation of John 14:27, "Peace I leave with you; my peace I give you." when he explains that the two references to the term peace may communicate a twofold meaning. In this verse, "peace" can mean true-but-imperfect peace enjoyed on earth as well as perfect peace enjoyed in heaven. This twofold meaning of peace mirrors Aquinas's treatment of the term in *ST* II-II, q. 29. In the commentary on John, Aquinas says Christ's words, "Peace I leave with you," refers to true-but-imperfect peace, whereas, Christ's words, "my peace I give you" refers to the perfect peace of the invulnerable condition.

"Peace I Leave with You"
Our Present and Imperfect Peace in this Life

The first form of peace—the peace Christ *leaves* with the disciples here on earth—brings order to "three things," which he says must "be put in order within us" (the intellect, will, and sensitive appetite).[23] The peace that Christ leaves with the disciples effects a "calmness of mind." This calmness of mind consists of the following: 1) a reason

---

[18] An example of apparent peace might be concord among thieves concerning a plan to rob a particular house.
[19] *ST* II-II q. 29, a. 2.
[20] *ST* II-II q. 40, a. 1, ad. 3.
[21] *ST* II-II q. 29, a. 2, ad. 4. Aquinas also states that without sanctifying grace, peace is not real but merely apparent. *ST* II-II 29, a. 3, ad. 1.
[22] *ST* II-II q. 29, a. 2, ad. 4.
[23] *In Ioan.* 14.7.1962.

liberated from disordered affections; 2) a tranquility of soul, which is defined as not being harassed by emotional states; 3) a simplicity of heart, which refers to the will entirely set toward God and neighbor. It is important to recognize that this first form of peace ("peace I leave with you"), which orders the interior disposition of the person, is a peace that is had now, in this present life.[24]

However, there is a downside to this peace. Because it is a peace that is had in this world it is also subject to disturbance. Therefore, following Augustine, Aquinas reasons that since this peace—although it is true peace had now—is an imperfect peace, and therefore *cannot* be described as the peace that belongs to Christ. This first description of the peace Christ left us in this world emphasizes that true-but-imperfect peace is *not* Christ's but ours. The peace that belongs *to* Christ (perfect peace) is not yet a peace that the saints share.

"My Peace I Give You"
Our Future, Perfect Peace in the Heavenly Jerusalem
Next, Aquinas comments upon Christ's words, "my peace I give you." and explains that this phrase refers to the perfect peace possessed by Christ. Nevertheless, Christ's own peace is, again, not ours in this world because Christ's peace is undisturbed and "has always been perfect." Indeed, how could any peace that belongs to Christ be imperfect? Christ always had this second kind of peace because he was "always without conflict." Therefore, when Christ says *"my peace I give you."* he refers to the perfect peace to be obtained in our "native land," the heavenly Jerusalem.

"My Peace I Give You"
Christ as Author of the Present Peace of the Saints in this Life
However, Aquinas seems to think this interpretation of "my peace I give you." is lacking an important distinction.[25] Aquinas writes, "Since whether in this world or in our native land, all the peace possessed by the saints comes to them through Christ …why does our Lord, when speaking of the peace of the saints in this life not say, my peace I give to you, instead of reserving this for the peace of our native land?"[26] Here, Aquinas is concerned to articulate how the peace of the

---

[24] It is this form of peace as ordering of intellect and will that McMahon identified as "from Christ" in his discussion of peace in charity in "A Thomistic Analysis of Peace," 186–7.
[25] Aquinas seems to be taking up Augustine's speculations about the "my" of Christ's gift of peace. Aquinas cites Augustine's comment on verse 27 of John 14, which he includes in the *Catena Aurea*. Thomas Aquinas, *Catena Aurea: Commentary on the Four Gospels Collected Out of the Works of the Fathers* (Southampton, England: Saint Augustine Press, 1997).
[26] *In Ioan.* 14.7.1963.

"church militant" or saints *in this life* (*pace sanctorum in via*) can be described as a peace that is *also of Christ* despite our imperfect condition. The difficulty is that it seems Christ's peace cannot be the peace the saints possess now because their present peace can be disturbed. How can a disturbed peace, which the church clearly experiences in schism and conflict, also be described as Christ's peace? Is there any sense in which the peace of the saints is a sharing in the peace that belongs to Christ? Matthew Levering summarizes the problem as follows: "[I]s it not theologically erroneous to suggest that 'my peace [I give you]' refers solely to perfect peace of heaven, since any peace that followers of Jesus enjoy on earth also comes from Jesus and is a real sharing in his peace?"[27]

Aquinas does not reject the first interpretation of "my peace I give you." (perfect peace enjoyed by the saints) but he does add a distinction which provides an important shade of meaning to the literal sense of Christ's words since the distinction makes theological room for speaking about how the pilgrim church truly shares in Christ's peace in the present.

Aquinas explains that the *present peace* of the saints can indeed be described as "of Christ" in the sense that Christ is the author (*auctoris*) or originator of this peace: "We should say that each peace, of the present and of the future, is that of Christ. But our present peace is Christ's because he is only its author."[28]

Although we do not hold Christ's peace in the same way Christ himself possesses peace, the peace that the church has now is still a peace that is of Christ.[29] The present peace of the saints—despite its imperfect condition—is also Christ's peace because, it is a peace authored by Christ.[30] It is in this sense that the peace of Christ can also be described as belonging to the church now. Here, Aquinas's move deepens the notion that the church, although it exists under the two

---

[27] Michael Dauphinais and Matthew Levering, *Reading John With St. Thomas Aquinas: Theological Exegesis and Speculative Theology* (Washington, D.C.: Catholic University of America Press, 2010), 116.

[28] *In Ioan.* 14.7.1963. Aquinas actually explains that there are *two* ways in which Christ's own peace is present in the lives of the saints here and now. First, there is peace that is authored by Christ and had now by Christians; second, there is peace that is authored by Christ and had now by Christians as well as peace of Christ in future glory (this second is essentially a restatement of his first interpretation of ". . . my Peace I Give you" as the future peace of the saints. I list only the first to simplify the presentation.

[29] *In Ioan.* 14.7.1963.

[30] Aquinas also explains that the present peace of the saints is different from the peace of the world in that the peace of the world is a "pretended peace" since it is only on the outside. "The peace of Christ," writes Aquinas, "is true, because it is both on the outside and the inside." The peace of Christ brings tranquility both within and without. *In Ioan.* 14.7.1963.

conditions of faith (now) and beatific vision (future) is one church. The church that hopes to share Christ's perfect peace is also the church established by Christ's gift of peace.

In the commentary on Ephesians, Aquinas deploys this second interpretation of "my peace I give you." (as present peace which Christ causes among the saints) in order to articulate a rich ecclesial vision of Paul's phrase in Ephesians 2:14, "For he is our peace." It should become clear that a communal or ecclesial concept of true-but-imperfect peace emerges in these two commentaries and compliments Aquinas's concise categories of peace in the *Summa Theologiae*.

THE CAUSE, PURPOSE, AND BOND OF THE PEACE OF THE CITY OF THE SAINTS IN THE COMMENTARY ON EPHESIANS

In the second chapter of his commentary on Ephesians, Aquinas comments upon the blessings of Christ. Included among the blessings is the truth that the Gentiles have been "converged with the Jewish people" and were reconciled to God."[31] It is in this context of his discussion of Christ's reconciliation of Gentiles and Jews that Aquinas draws upon his second interpretation of "my peace I give you." which emphasizes Christ as author or cause of peace. Indeed, when Aquinas interprets Paul's words in Ephesians 2:14, "For he is our peace, who has made both one," his commentary includes discussion of what might be called the "cause, purpose, and bond of the saints," and consists of the following: 1) Christ as cause of the present peace of the saints; 2) the purpose of the present peace of the saints as the unification of two peoples into "one body," which Aquinas says, is peace; 3) how this ecclesial peace is preserved among the faithful.

Christ as Cause of the Peace of the Saints

Aquinas identifies Christ as cause of the convergence between Gentiles and Jews. He states that this convergence is precisely what Paul refers to when he says, in Ephesians 2:14, "For he is our peace, who has made both one." Aquinas explains Paul's reason for saying this:

> Christ is the cause of this drawing together, [and] for [this] reason he affirms *for he is our peace, who has made both one.* This is an emphatic way of speaking to better express the reality, as though he said: rightly do I say that you are drawn near each other, but this occurs

---

[31] Aquinas, *Ad Ephesios* 2.5.111. As Christopher Baglow has observed, for Aquinas, the relationship between Jewish and Gentile Christians becomes the major theme of chapter two and serves as a concrete pole that bounds his exposition of the entire epistle. Baglow, 165.

through Christ since *he is himself our peace*, that is, he is the cause of our peace.

Immediately after his explanation of "for he is our peace," Aquinas cites John 14:27, "my peace I give you." He explains further that, "It is useful to adopt this way of speaking, when the totality of the effect depends on its cause."[32] As he did in the commentary on John, Aquinas identifies Christ as cause of the peace that belongs to the church now, in the era of grace. Drawing together Jews and Gentiles in one body is an effect caused solely by Christ.

Reconciliation of Jews and Gentiles in One Body
as the Purpose of the Peace of the Saints
However, the material in Ephesians concerning how the blessing of Christ affects the church (Eph. 1–2) allows Aquinas to elaborate upon how and why Christ has caused peace for the church. Aquinas comments that Paul makes the purpose of this convergence between Jews and Gentiles clear when he says, "that he might make the two in himself into one new man, making peace."[33] The end (*finis*) of the convergence effected by Christ is that the "two peoples would be formed into one people."[34] Commenting upon Paul's metaphor for the convergence of Jews and Gentiles as a structure being built into a holy temple (Eph 2:21) with Christ as the cornerstone, Aquinas says Christ is called a cornerstone on account of the convergence of both Jews and Gentiles, whom he refers to as "two walls" joined to a corner.[35] "As two walls are joined at the corner," he writes, "so in Christ the Jewish and pagan peoples are united."[36] Aquinas therefore understands the present peace of the saints as Christ's creation of a new social situation of Jews and Gentiles united into the temple of Christ's body.

The ecclesial unity of these two peoples united in one body is peace because Christ "killed hostility" between them and between these people and God: first, "[Christ] killed the hostility that had arisen through

---

[32] *Ad Eph.* 2.5.111. The manner of the convergence includes Christ's fulfillment and destruction of the ceremonial law, a source of enmity between the two peoples. The theological difficulty surrounding this issue of a destruction of the ceremonial law is discussed at length in Matthew Tapie, *Aquinas on Israel and the Church: A Study of the Question of Supersessionism in the Theology of Thomas Aquinas* (Eugene, Oregon: Pickwick, 2014).
[33] *Ad. Eph.* 2.5.111.
[34] *Ad. Eph.* 2.5.116.
[35] *Ad Eph.* 2.6.131. That Aquinas assumes Paul's building metaphor as contained within the literal sense of scripture is clear when he pauses to explain that the building metaphor can also be understood allegorically.
[36] *Ad Eph.* 2.6.129.

the law between the Jews and the gentiles" by fulfilling the Old Testament symbols, and, second, he "killed in himself" the hostility that existed between God and men through sin. The purpose of the convergence is Christ's reconciliation of humankind and God. It is for this reason that Paul states, "that he might reconcile us both… in one body of the Church."[37] Christ made both peoples into one body by "joining into unity both the Jews who worshiped the true God and the gentiles who were alienated from God's cult."[38]

In addition to Aquinas citing John 14:27, "my peace I give you." to explicate Eph. 2:14, there is a second key intertextual connection where Christ as literal cause of the peace of the church is referenced. Immediately after commenting on "he hath made both one …" (Eph. 2:14) Aquinas cites John 10:16: "And other sheep I have, that are not of this fold; them also I must bring. And they shall hear my voice; and there shall be one fold and one shepherd." This connection runs both ways between the commentaries, since the commentary on John also contains a citation of Ephesians 2:14. In Lecture 4 of Ch. 10 of the commentary on John, Aquinas draws upon Ephesians 2:14 to explain Christ's teaching that he is the good shepherd who lays down his life for the sheep and gathers them into his fold: "I am the good shepherd; I know my own and my own know me, as the Father knows me and I know the Father; and I lay down my life for the sheep. And I have other sheep that are not of this fold; I must bring them also, and they will heed my voice. So there shall be one flock, one shepherd." Aquinas understands Christ's first reference to the sheep that he gathers into his fold to refer to the Jews, "who regarded themselves as God's sheep—'We thy people, the flock of thy pasture' (Ps. 79:13)." He explains that the Jews were kept as his sheep by the precepts of the Old Law: "For as sheep are enclosed in a fold, so the Jews were enclosed within the precepts of the Law."[39] This "enclosure" in worship of the God of Israel is explained as the second of a twofold *ratio* of the ceremonial law in the *Summa Theologiae*. The first, and primary *ratio* of these precepts was to prefigure Christ.[40]

Aquinas says that Christ could have said that he laid down his life for them alone. But he does not. Christ has come not only to gather the Jews but also the Gentiles: "Our Lord adds that it is not only for them, but for others too." When Christ says, "I have other sheep," Aquinas explains that he is referring to "the Gentiles, that are not of this fold, i.e., of the family of the flesh of Israel… other sheep, I say, that is, the Gentiles, I have from my Father through an eternal predestination."

---

[37] *Ad Eph.* 2.5.118.
[38] *Ad Eph.* 2.5.111.
[39] *In Ioan.* 10.4.1417.
[40] *ST* I-II q. 102, a. 5.

The Jews and Gentiles are likened to two flocks that Christ gathers together to bring into grace when they heed Christ's voice in three ways.[41] Aquinas understands each of these three ways are "necessary for righteousness": Jews and Gentiles heed Christ's voice when they are 1) obedient to the commandments of God; 2) unified in charity as one flock; and 3) unified in faith in one shepherd. It is the second way of heeding Christ's voice (union in charity as one flock), which Aquinas thinks Paul refers to in Ephesians when he writes that, "he is our peace." Aquinas attaches Ephesians 2:14 to his description of the unity of charity between these two peoples that Christ teaches them, when he says, "So there shall be one flock." Therefore, the two peoples being brought under Christ into one flock is the way in which the peace of the saints is also Christ's peace. Aquinas then writes (in the commentary on John), "For he is our peace, who has made us both one" (Eph. 2:14)."[42]

That Aquinas thinks the preservation of peace among Jews and Gentiles requires the virtuous activity of the faithful is evident when he explains Paul's use of the phrase "one body." By this phrase, Paul means, "be united in the bond of peace that you may be one body." It is to his view of this vital virtuous activity that we now turn.

The Virtues that Preserve the Peace of the City of Saints

When Aquinas moves on to comment upon what is often referred to as the "ethical material" in Ephesians (Ch. 4–6), and especially Paul's words that the Ephesians ought to "walk worthy of the vocation to which [they] were called" (Eph. 4:1–2), he describes their vocation, and he does so using the political terms borrowed from Ephesians 2: "[Y]ou should be attentive to the dignity to which you are summoned, and you ought to behave in a way conformable to it ... you are called to be fellow citizens with the saints (Eph. 2:19)."[43]

This civic language is prompted by Paul's words that Gentiles are no longer "aliens" to the "commonwealth of Israel" (Eph. 2:12) and are now "citizens with the saints" (Eph. 2:19). Aquinas explains that here, the Apostle draws a conclusion concerning the present state of the church. In Aquinas's view, Paul's description of the community of the faithful as fellow citizens is described by Augustine in the *City of God*: "two loves have formed two cities. For the love of God, even to the contempt of self, namely, of the man loving builds the heavenly

---

[41] *In Ioan.* 10.4.1418.
[42] *In Ioan.* 10.4.1419. See also Aquinas's two interpretations of Matt. 20:1–16 in David C. Steinmetz, "The Superiority of Pre-Critical Exegesis," in *The Theological Reading of Scripture: Classic and Contemporary Readings*, ed. Steven Fowl (Oxford: Blackwell, 1997), 32–33.
[43] *Ad Eph.* 4.1.190.

city of Jerusalem. But the love of self, even to the contempt of God, builds the city of Babylon." After citing these famous words from Augustine, Aquinas writes, "Everyone, then, either is a citizen with the saints if he loves God to the contempt of self... or, if he loves himself even to the contempt of God, he is a citizen of Babylon."[44] This society of saints is therefore not only established by Christ's gift of peace but its members are animated by the activity of the theological virtues. Indeed, for Aquinas, the community of the faithful *is* a city (*civitas*) because its members possess the infused virtues: "If the [community of the faithful is] considered in themselves, it is a city since they have in common with one another the particular acts of faith, hope and charity. In this way, the community is a civil one."[45]

The citizens of this body of peace are expected to behave in a manner worthy of God's calling to maintain "unity of the Spirit in the bond of peace."[46] Seeking to explicate Paul's words in Ephesians 4: 2 ("With all humility, mildness, with patience, supporting one another in charity ..."), Aquinas explains that, "Four virtues must be cultivated" in order to preserve the peace of the city: humility, meekness, patience, and charity.[47] Cultivation of these four virtues preserves the present peace of the city of the saints against four vices that cause "dissension," "disturbances," and "turmoil." Without the cultivation of these virtues, peace "disappears" from the society. Aquinas then comments on each of the four virtues that must be cultivated as well as the corresponding vices to be shunned.[48]

First, the city of the saints must guard against pride, the queen of all vices, because it "causes dissension among members of the body."[49] Aquinas understands pride as "the disordered desire for exaltation.[50] "When one arrogant person decides to rule others, while the other proud individuals do not want to submit, dissension arises in the society and peace disappears."[51] In order to eliminate this obstacle to ecclesial peace, the city of the saints must cultivate the virtue of humility, which Aquinas identifies elsewhere as mutual submission to one another out of reverence for God.[52]

---

[44] *Ad Eph.* 2.6.125.
[45] *Ad Eph.* 2.6.126.
[46] There is also a thematic correlation in the commentary between 2.5.121, which discusses the cause and form of peace, and the explication of "careful to keep the unity of the Spirit in the bond of peace," in 4.1.187.
[47] *Ad Eph.* 4.1.191.
[48] *Ad Eph.* 4.1.191.
[49] *ST* II-II q. 162, a. 8.
[50] *ST* II-II q. 62, a. 1, ad. 2.
[51] *Ad Eph.* 4.1.193.
[52] *ST* II-II q. 161, a. 1, ad. 1; a. 3; a. 5 ad. 1; q. 162, a. 6. Aquinas considers humility as one of the potential parts of the virtue of temperance.

In addition to pride, anger (defined as the desire to punish or to have revenge) is a threat to maintaining peace of the church.[53] "An angry person is inclined to inflict injury, whether verbal or physical, from which disturbances occur."[54] Anger, explains Aquinas, is the result of sorrow, which scripture also refers to as bitterness. At the root of this bitterness is memory of how others have harmed us—all bitterness arises from "the memory of past injuries"[55] and produces "a craving for revenge." However, Aquinas interprets Paul's words, "Be angry: and do not sin. Do not let the sun go down upon your anger." as indicating a good and bad form of anger.[56] Aquinas thinks righteous anger is imperative based on Paul's statement, "Be angry." For Aquinas, it is imperative that one should be angry at their own sin as well as the sin of others. Anger is evil when, contrary to justice, it strives for revenge. Regarding the bad form of anger, it may arise in a person but it should not be acted upon: "should it happen that anger wells up within you—which is human—do not sin. You must not be led on to act upon it." Aquinas says "do not persist in anger, but cast it off before sunset; for although the first impulses of temper are excusable, due to human frailty, it is illicit to dwell on them."[57] In order for the church to "discard" this bad form of anger, the cultivation of the virtue of meekness is required.[58] Meekness suppresses the passion for revenge.[59] Meekness helps remove anger in two ways: it enables the person to retain control over rational powers and therefore assists in the capacity to speak the truth to others.[60] Aquinas says that cultivating the virtue of meekness among the faithful "softens arguments and preserves peace."[61]

Impatience is the third obstacle to preserving the peace of the church. Occasionally, explains Aquinas, some who possesses the first two virtues (humility and meekness) and "refrain from causing trouble nevertheless will not endure patiently the real or attempted wrongs done to himself."[62] Aquinas is aware that pride or anger in some can cause hardship for others—even those who possess humility and meekness. Such hardship can give rise to sorrow, anger, and hatred,

---

[53] Anger is not evil when it promotes justice. It can be evil in excess or deficiency. *ST* II-II q. 158, a. 2.
[54] *ST* II-II q. 158, a. 2.
[55] *Ad. Eph.* 4.10264.
[56] *Ad. Eph.* 4.8.250. The good form of anger seeks a just vindication.
[57] *Ad. Eph.* 4.8.250.
[58] Aquinas considers meekness as a potential part of the virtue of temperance.
[59] *ST* II-II q. 157, a. 1; a. 3; a. 4, ad. 3.
[60] *ST* II-II q. 157, a. 4, ad. 3.
[61] *Ad Eph.* 4.1.191.
[62] *Ad Eph.* 4.1.191

among the members of the church.[63] For this reason, Aquinas says the body must guard against these potential disturbances by cultivating the virtue of patience.[64] Patience is not simply endurance of hardship but is, on Aquinas's account, caused by charity, which proceeds from the love of God above all things.[65] "Now the fact that a man prefers the good of grace to all natural goods, the loss of which may cause sorrow, is to be referred to charity, which loves God above all things."[66] The virtue that the citizens of the faithful must possess in order to endure the hardship of their fellow citizen's real or attempted wrongs is possible only if the faithful cultivate patience by cherishing the good of grace over natural goods. Therefore, Aquinas thinks the peace of the church can be preserved only when its citizens love God above material things.[67]

"Inordinate zeal" is the fourth vice that threatens peace. Such zeal causes members to pass judgment on "the faults of others" or "whatever they see, not waiting for the proper time and place."[68] Zealous judgment of others' failures is the opposite of "bearing with one another in charity" (Eph. 4:2). Aquinas is not discouraging judgment of others' faults along the lines of the contemporary idea that one ought not judge another person's deeds. Rather, charity requires judgment but with the aim of correction. The proper way to bear the failures of others is by means of "fraternal correction," which is chiefly an act of the virtue of charity[69] aimed at the correction of the wrongdoer.[70] Correction of others is part of what it means to "bear with the weak."[71] However, to discern whether and how correction takes place requires prudence: "When someone falls," writes Aquinas, "he should not be

---

[63] *ST* II-II q. 136, a. 2, ad. 1.

[64] *ST* II-II q. 136. Aquinas considers patience as a part of the virtue of fortitude.

[65] *ST* II-II q. 136, a. 3, ad. 3.

[66] *ST* I-II q. 136, a. 3.

[67] Aquinas will say further on that the inordinate desire for material goods is a sin that causes corruption of members of the body. The degree to which the members of the faithful desire material goods in an inordinate way will directly impugn their capacity to patiently endure the hardship of living together as a community (because they have learned to desire not God above all things and the grace that God gives but other things).

[68] *Ad Eph.* 4.1.193. *Emended.*

[69] *ST* II-II q. 33, a. 1. It is secondarily an act of prudence, which executes and directs the action. *ST* II-II q. 33, a. 2, ad. 3.

[70] *ST* II-II q. 133. Eleonore Stump points out that, on Aquinas's terms, "there is no obligation to seek out wrongdoers in order to reprove them, or to spy on people in order to know what their wrong actions are." Eleonore Stump, *Aquinas* (New York: Routledge, 2005), 328.

[71] *ST* II-II q. 33, a. 3.

immediately corrected—unless it is the time and the place for it."[72] Indeed, Aquinas says that if there is no concern for the circumstances surrounding another person's moral failure, judging leads to turmoil. Moreover, Aquinas thinks the act of fraternal correction requires the virtue of mercy: "With mercy these should be waited for since 'charity bears all things' (1 Cor. 13:7)."[73] Therefore, patient endurance of the faults of others in the community is not enough to preserve peace in the body of Christ. Aquinas thinks the virtue of mercy is necessary to properly address those faults.[74]

In addition to the four virtues that preserve peace, Aquinas also addresses forms of spiritual corruption that can harm the peace of the church, including lying,[75] anger (mentioned two more times), and stealing.[76] Aquinas thinks that Paul's words "steal no more" are not simply about theft but about the "contaminating desire for transitory goods which he also refers to as the "inordinate desire for temporal goods."[77] He frequently warns against harmful language among Christians, which he calls, "wicked and injurious words."[78] Such language consists of false words by which a person says one thing but means another, and vain talk.[79] Such words "upset or sadden other men" and weaken the peace of the society of saints.

CONCLUSION

In this brief sketch of the peace of the saints in the Ephesians commentary, I have shown that Aquinas's multi-voiced literal sense of scripture allows him to overcome a difficulty concerning whether the pilgrim church has received Christ's gift of peace now, in the era grace. How can a peace that belongs to Christ also be described as a peace of the church if such a peace is subject to disturbance? Aquinas reflects

---

[72] Stump, *Aquinas*, 328. Aquinas's discussion of this act of charity includes important distinctions I lack the space to treat here. See Eleonore Stump's helpful treatment of fraternal correction.

[73] *ST* II-II q. 30. Aquinas thinks fraternal correction is one of the spiritual works of mercy. See *ST* II-II q. 33, a. 4.

[74] *Ad Eph.* 4.1.191.

[75] *Ad Eph.* 4.8.248. Aquinas says that lying corrupts a person's rational powers. This is why Paul says "putting away lying, speak the truth" (Eph. 4:25). Paul "bans lying because through this sin of the tongue (*peccatum oris*) the truth of reason is corrupted."

[76] He refers to these as personal "sins of disorder" and sins that consist in the "disorder of others." *Ad Eph.* 4.8.247.

[77] *Ad Eph.* 4.9.253.

[78] Aquinas's comments are based on several texts, including the following: "Let no evil speech proceed from your mouth . . ." (Eph. 4:29); "Let all bitterness and anger and indignation and clamor and blasphemy be put away from you, with all malice. And be kind to one another; merciful, forgiving one another… (Eph. 4:31–30).

[79] *Ad Eph.* 4.9.259.

upon this issue as he is commenting upon Christ's words, "my peace I give you." I have argued that Aquinas overcomes this difficulty by articulating what might be called a Christological and ecclesial peace. This true-but-imperfect ecclesial peace is present in Aquinas's description of the cause, purpose, and preservation of the present peace of the saints. Christ's gift of peace is the same reality that Paul refers to when he says, "For he is our peace." This reality is the church— Christ's uniting the "two walls of the temple," Jews and Gentiles, into one body, making peace. Aquinas also thinks God has given this society of saints a distinctive vocation to preserve unity "in the bond of peace" by cultivating the virtues of humility, meekness, patience, and mercy. The ecclesial peace that is Christ's gift to us is not only a state to be held now, albeit imperfectly. It is also an activity constitutive of the happiness of the faithful. Indeed, this Christological and ecclesial peace in Aquinas could be described as "civic" peace, though it is a civic peace sustained by the love of God above material things. **M**

Journal of Moral Theology, Vol. 5, No. 1 (2016): 129-143

Infused Virtue and "22-Carat" Morally Right Acts

Angela Knobel

ECENT DECADES HAVE WITNESSED a renewed interest in Aristotle's theory of the virtues. Contemporary Christian philosophers and theologians have embraced this interest, and for good reason: there is much in the Aristotelian theory of virtue that seems compatible with Christian notions of the good life.[1] But there are also some important discrepancies between Christian and Aristotelian understandings of the good life, discrepancies that carry over into their respective theories of virtue. In this paper I wish to examine one such discrepancy, namely the notion that the possession of Aristotelian virtue is a necessary prerequisite of exemplary moral action. While this notion follows naturally from an Aristotelian account of virtue, it is also, I will argue, something that contradicts the Christian view. Having established that the problem exists, I will propose a solution: contemporary Christian scholars need to re-appropriate some aspects of the traditional Christian notion of infused habits.

In order to make my case more clearly, I will focus on the account of a single contemporary Aristotelian ethicist, Rosalind Hursthouse. I have chosen Hursthouse not only because she is a clear representative of the contemporary Aristotelian account of virtue but because she both (a) argues that Aristotelian virtue is a precondition of exemplary moral action and (b) is demonstrably attentive to Christian concerns: she even speculates about how her account might accommodate important Christian examples.[2] I argue that although Hursthouse's insights about the components of exemplary moral action are correct,

---

[1] For a discussion of the fit between Christianity and virtue ethics, see Joseph Kotva, The Christian Case for Virtue Ethics, (Washington, D.C.: Georgetown University Press 1996). I will argue that the fit is less harmonious than Kotva believes.

[2] Hursthouse is not the only contemporary Aristotelian virtue ethicist who is attentive to Christian examples. But Hursthouse addresses these examples in the context of the claim I want to focus on, namely that one cannot act in a morally exemplary way unless one also possesses Aristotelian virtues. For a different example of a contemporary virtue ethicist who is attentive to specifically Christian examples, see Linda Zagzebski, *Virtues of the Mind* (Cambridge: Cambridge University Press 1999) and David Brown, "No Heaven without Purgatory," *Religious Studies* vol. 21, no. 4(1985):447-56.

her account cannot sufficiently accommodate the Christian view. In order to accommodate central Christian examples of exemplary moral action, Hursthouse needs recourse to an antique idea: the notion of "infused" habits.

Before turning to the body of this paper, I want to make a preliminary remark about terminology. Throughout this paper I will refer to the traditional Aristotelian account of virtue—the type of virtue that Hursthouse believes is a necessary precondition of genuinely moral motivation—as virtue.[3] I will take virtue to be defined as Hursthouse defines virtue at the outset of her book, namely as a deeply rooted (and difficult to change) character trait involving a disposition that reliably produces a certain kind of action and is accompanied not only by the relevant approvals, disapprovals and emotions but also by the ability to "read" a situation correctly: to understand what a situation requires and to respond appropriately.[4] Virtue is, in the typical case, only acquired gradually, through a prolonged process of habituation.[5]

VIRTUE AS A NECESSARY PRECONDITION FOR MORALLY EXEMPLARY ACTS

There is an important distinction to be made between an act that is more or less good and an act that does not in any way fall short of what a morally right act should be. The latter type of act, which Hursthouse eventually refers to as a "22-carat morally right act," will be an act where the agent "does the right thing because it is the right thing to do." This definition is more restrictive than it might initially sound. For it requires not merely that the agent recognize the "right thing" as right but also that the agent perform the act in the right way. Recognizing that one ought to (say) look out for the well-being of one's elderly relations is a step in the direction of moral goodness, for very selfish or vicious individuals are not even capable of having such recognitions. Actually taking measures to look after those relations is a still further step. But even this latter action, while good, may still lack something of full moral goodness. For if I turn out to have done my deed not just because I recognized it as right but also because I felt guilty or wanted to shame my less dutiful siblings or for any other less than exemplary reason, then my action will fall short of full moral goodness: it will be a morally right act but not a 22-carat morally right

---

[3] The "A" subscript is intended to capture the fact that the type of virtue under discussion is in keeping with the traditional Aristotelian understanding of virtue: it refers, at a minimum, to a habit an individual creates in herself via her own repeated good acts. Although this is assumed to be the case in most contemporary discussions of virtue, I am interested in retrieving a rather different understanding of virtue: i.e. an account under which good habits are bestowed directly by God.
[4] Rosalind Hursthouse, *Virtue Ethics* (Oxford: Oxford University Press, 1999):11-12.
[5] Hursthouse, *Virtue Ethics,* 157.

act. And Hursthouse insists that only those who possess virtue are capable of 22-carat morally right acts.

At first glance, the thesis that only those who possess virtue are capable of 22-carat morally right acts seems clearly false. For there seem to be countless examples where otherwise weak or vicious individuals do exemplary deeds. A timid grandmother fights off an assailant; a mean, selfish individual does something selfless; Ebenezer Scrooge wakes up on Christmas morning a changed man. Hursthouse argues that in each of these cases the individual in question will either (a) turn out to have virtue after all or (b) turn out not have actually performed a "22-carat" morally right act. In all, Hursthouse will acknowledge only one instance where an individual who clearly lacks virtue might perform a 22-carat morally right act: the sort of situation made possible by direct divine intervention. Even such instances, however, will not disprove her thesis, because what she believes direct divine intervention will supply is virtue. In what follows, I will examine Hursthouse's account of each possible counter-example. Although she omits an important class of examples, her insights are compelling.

Some exemplary deeds surprise us only because we (wrongly) assume that the agent lacks virtue. A timid grandmother saves children from a burning building or the reclusive neighborhood boogey man saves small children from an assailant. As Hursthouse rightly notes, the fact that we assume that such individuals lack virtue is no evidence that they do: such deeds most likely reflect already possessed character traits, traits they have heretofore simply not had the occasion to express. The fact that To Kill a Mockingbird's Boo Radley was a recluse and that the local children feared him is no indication that he actually lacked courage. What we really need to know in such cases, Hursthouse rightly points out, are his underlying attitudes. When Boo Radley read of attacks against small children in the newspaper, did he react with approval or disapproval? Was he horrified by injustice? If he had had children, would he have raised them to help those in need? As Hursthouse notes (albeit not with respect to this particular example), his reactions in these lesser instances are very likely of a piece with his heroic act. And if they are, then it cannot be correct to say that he acted "out" of character. What is more likely is that he had virtue all along. So we cannot point to these sorts of examples as evidence that those who lack virtue can perform 22-carat morally right acts. A true counter-example must involve an individual demonstrably lacking in virtue.

Hursthouse offers two examples of cases where individuals demonstrably lacking in virtue seem to perform 22-carat morally right acts. In the first sort of case, the individual briefly begins doing the right thing, and cites the right reasons for doing so, but then immediately returns to his or her previous behavior. She offers an example:

an otherwise selfish or fearful individual suddenly "gives with an open hand, spurns the offer of an unfair advantage, she speaks out boldly in defense of an unpopular colleague—and gives the appropriate X reasons."[6] But, "it turns out that... love or success has momentarily transformed her. And shortly afterwards, she lapses back into behaving as she did before."[7] Hursthouse, then, envisions a situation where an individual who is (say) prone to abusing her unpopular colleague very briefly stops doing so and then immediately resumes her previous behavior.

Even if such individuals briefly do the right thing and cite the appropriate reasons for doing so, Hursthouse denies that they will really turn out to have done the right thing because it is the right thing to do: "I want to say 'No', all the way through..., because I believe that when we talk of agents acting 'because they thought it was the right', 'from duty', etc. we are ascribing something to the agent that is clearly absent from all of the above cases."[8] What is it that is absent?

Hursthouse thinks that what 22-carat morally right acts have, and similarly what the acts described above lack, "has something to do with reliability or predictability in the loose sense."[9] If it is really true that an agent has done the right thing because it is right, then, Hursthouse argues, it must be the case that she will do the action more than once: "An agent of whom it can be truly said that she did what was V because she thought it was right, etc., on a particular occasion is, thereby, an agent who, by and large, will act in similar ways on similar occasions."[10] Someone who insists that they have done a right act 'because it was right' and who then immediately fails to perform similar acts when the situation requires cannot have had the appropriate motivation in the first place: "If we think someone did something 'because he thought it was right' and then find him failing to do the very same sort of thing the next day, for no better reason than (he says) he doesn't feel like it, we say he couldn't have done the first thing 'because he thought it was right'."[11]

Hursthouse argues that when we understand why otherwise weak and vicious individuals sometimes do good things, it becomes clear that they cannot be said to have done the good thing because it was the right thing to do. Weak and vicious people sometimes do good things, Hursthouse argues, because the value of the act—something they are

---

[6] Hursthouse, *Virtue Ethics,* 133.
[7] Hursthouse, *Virtue Ethics,* 133.
[8] Hursthouse, *Virtue Ethics*, 133.
[9] Hursthouse, *Virtue Ethics,* 134.
[10] Hursthouse, *Virtue Ethics,* 134.
[11] Hursthouse, *Virtue Ethics*, 134.

typically blind to—is "lit up" for them by a special feature of the situation. As such, the action does not reflect their deepest values and commitments, but rather a fleeting, temporary value: "The agent who surprises us by her virtuous actions when momentarily transformed by love or success seems to recognize the value of V actions only when it is, as it were, lit up for her by her love or success."[12] What, then, can justifiably be said to produce morally motivated acts? For Hursthouse, the answer is clear: virtue: "What it is that makes the agent who does what is V for X reasons on a particular occasion both actually and counterfactually reliable and predictable, if she is—what it is for her to be 'really committed to the value of her V act'—is that she acts 'from a fixed and permanent state', namely the virtue in question."[13]

The example described above is an instance where an individual is only temporarily motivated to do the right thing. Under the influence of love, our hypothetical individual temporarily sees that it is wrong to demean one's colleagues. But then, having fallen out of love, she once again becomes an enthusiastic participant, and resumes demeaning the very same colleague she (briefly) defended. I think Hursthouse is right to insist that in a case like this the individual never really "has" the motive to do the right thing. But I also wonder how realistic the example is. For although it is easy to think of examples where weak or vicious individuals are supposed to have done "the right thing for the right reason," their motives are typically not as fleeting as Hursthouse suggests.

Consider two fictional, but highly believable examples where otherwise weak or vicious individuals seem to do the right thing because it is the right thing to do. In The Game of Thrones, the amoral Jamie Lannister risks his life to save the ugly but virtuous Brienne of Tarth from the torture and defilement her captors have planned for her. Jamie is not particularly opposed to the torture and defilement of virtuous women, particularly ugly ones. But for some reason, he is moved to save Brienne. Similarly, the weak, dissipated Sydney Carton of A Tale of Two Cities loves a woman who does not love him in return. When her fiancé is sentenced to die, Carton switches places with him and dies in his stead. In neither case does the good act result in any sustained character change. Jamie Lannister does not, after returning to save Brienne, become a good man. Although Carton dies for his good deed, it is entirely reasonable to suppose that his good action was not accompanied by any sustained change in character: if his execution had been stayed at the last moment, Carton would in all likelihood have resumed his dissipate ways. So how are we to understand these

---

[12] Hursthouse, *Virtue Ethics,* 135.
[13] Hursthouse, *Virtue Ethics,* 136.

apparently good acts? Did Jamie Lannister and Sydney Carton do the right thing because it was the right thing to do?

Although Hursthouse certainly would not concede that Jamie and Sydney have performed 22-carat morally right acts, her initial analysis cannot be applied to them. For whatever other flaws Jamie and Sydney might have, their motives really do seem to be their own. Hursthouse argues that the vicious person's good act is not really his because he does not do such acts reliably. It is certainly true that Jamie Lannister's character cannot be reliably counted on to save virtuous women from defilement, any more than Sydney Carton can be reliably counted on to prefer another's good to his own. In that respect, Jamie's saving of Brienne is out of character and surprising. But if we ask whether Jamie Lannister can reliably be counted on to "save people like Brienne of Tarth from torture and defilement" or whether Sydney Carton can reliably be counted on to "do things conducive to the happiness of the woman he loves," then I think our answer has to be rather different. For while Jamie Lannister is very clearly not a good person, his return to save Brienne seems very much in character: he acts exactly as someone who knew him well might expect him to act. The same might be said of Sydney Carton.

Why does Jamie Lannister risk his life to save·Brienne, when he does not seem to care very much when similar things happen to others? As Hursthouse hypothesizes, it is most likely because the value of the V act is—in this particular case—somehow "lit up" for him. Most likely, something in Jamie responds to Brienne's stubborn courage, unflinching loyalty, and noble ideals. He can see the value of preserving Brienne from harm, even though he cannot see the value of preserving similarly situated women. Why does the selfish Sydney Carton give his life to save his rival's? Because love illuminates the value of self-sacrifice and brings him—for the very first time—to value someone else's happiness above his own. They cannot and would not do similar things for others because the illuminating features—empathy in the one case and love in the other—are not present.

But while in Hursthouse's example the features that "light up" the value of the V act are fleeting and external, the features that light up the value of the V act for Jamie and Sydney seem to stem from who they are. For there is a good argument to be made that in both cases it is the agent's character that enables the illumination to be present in the first place. It is in Jamie's character, whatever his other faults, to admire Brienne's virtuous traits. And that admiration lights up for him the value of saving this particular virtuous woman from defilement. So why should we concede that the motivation is not really his? The same might be said of Sydney Carton.

A more likely possibility, and one which would salvage Hurst-house's claim that weak and vicious people are not capable of 22-carat morally right acts, is that—even though their motivations are truly their own—their act will nonetheless fall short of what a truly V act would be for other reasons. Since this will be the case even in cases of sustained changes in behavior—a counter-example that Hursthouse does address—it is to such cases that I will now turn.

Sustained Changes in Behavior

In the examples described above, the weak or vicious person does a single good thing and immediately resumes his more typical behaviors. I have argued that at least some such acts are not so much "out of character" as in character: the most likely explanation is that it is characteristic of such individuals that they only recognize V acts as valuable in certain highly circumscribed situations. But some of those who act out of character do so because they self-consciously reject their vicious ways.[14] Even if it happens rarely, people sometimes do change. They experience a genuine conversion and embrace new values and a new outlook. Shouldn't we grant that these individuals, at least, really do the right thing because it is the right thing to do, and from the first moments of their conversion, even though they have not yet cultivated virtue?

While Hursthouse is willing to concede that genuine conversions can occur, she is not—with one possible exception—willing to concede that the newly converted agent will immediately begin performing 22-carat morally right acts:

> The re-formed character's first V act is not quite the "22-carat morally right act" that was initially imagined—unless by the grace of God. For even if we allow sudden transformation of character, nothing but supernatural intervention could transform someone lacking in virtue into anything better than, say, fairly virtuous.[15]

Such an agent could be no more than "fairly virtuous" because even if her motives and priorities had changed, she would still either have to develop virtue or else have virtue bestowed on her through direct divine intervention. Only then would her act qualify as a 22-carat morally right act. And—unless one supposes it to be bestowed all at once by God—the development of virtue is a lengthy process. It means losing one's old habits, for one thing, and also developing the insight and

---

[14] Although Hursthouse does not acknowledge the possibility, it seems to me that these acts could also be fleeting. What if I whole-heartedly reject my past life and in all seriousness turn over a new leaf, but then experience some tragic event?

[15] Hursthouse, *Virtue Ethics,* 159.

sensitivity that virtue requires: "An adult who has hitherto thought only of himself will be poorly equipped to put his new-found love of his fellow human beings into good practice; one who has hitherto ruthlessly pursued money and power and now sees them as dross is not in the best position to deal with people of modest ambition as he should."[16] While one still suffers from these obstacles, one can perform good acts, but they will still lack something of the fullness a good act should have: they will not (yet) be 22-carat morally right acts.

This latter argument is much more successful. Consider Ebenezer Scrooge, our initial example of an individual who is supposed to have made a sustained moral change. It is fair to suppose that Scrooge, after becoming convinced of the error of his ways, wholeheartedly wants to change his life. But someone who has spent a lifetime hoarding money will most likely have a hard time making a change, no matter how wholehearted his conversion. Part of his problem, as Hursthouse notes, is that he has acquired miserly habits: it will be as difficult for him to begin giving away his money as it would be for a morbidly obese individual to begin an exercise program. But the problems go still deeper. Suppose Scrooge does manage to give away his money. The mere act of giving away money, even when it qualifies as a morally right action, does not yet qualify as a virtuous one. Indeed, it is likely that in many instances he will fail to act as he should, simply because he does not habitually notice occasions for giving. But even if he does, he will have to give away the right amount of money, and he will have to give it to the right recipients. This requires a sensitivity and insight that Scrooge most likely does not have. He simply has not cultivated the ability to recognize which gifts are helpful and which ones harmful, let alone the ability to recognize those in need of his help. But even if he were to do all this, Scrooge would still struggle to perform 22-carat morally right acts. For a genuinely good act should have pure motives, and it is not clear that Scrooge has the ability to have such motives. There is every likelihood that he will feel a slight pang of regret as he makes his generous gift to Tiny Tim; that some part of him will want to hold back; that he will still long to hold on to his money; or, failing all that, that he is at least partially motivated by the desire to mitigate the impression he knows others have of him. So his nascent good acts, while good, will not (yet) be examples of 22-carat morally right acts. This sounds entirely reasonable. Absent any other feature that could explain a 22-carat moral act, Hursthouse's argument seems correct.

This same account also indicates that the good acts of weak or vicious people will fall short. I have argued that we should not deny that Jamie Lannister's motivation to save Brienne is really his motivation.

---

[16] Hursthouse, *Virtue Ethics,* 159.

But there is nonetheless every reason to think that when Jamie Lannister does attempt to save Brienne, his act will still fall short of complete moral rectitude. Indeed, unlike Scrooge, Jamie does not even care about achieving his ends in a virtuous way. If Jamie had to torture and defile to save Brienne from torture and defilement, he would be perfectly willing to do so. So Hursthouse has indeed given us good reason to suppose that non-virtuous agents will be unable to do the right thing because it is the right thing to do.

The Case of Religious Conversion

Hursthouse hypothesizes that the notion that even those who lack the virtues can perform 22-carat morally right acts is most likely rooted in "religious views about the possibility of redemption." She is also demonstrably attentive to religious examples, pointing to Saul's conversion on the road to Damascus, and conceding that in some instances a weak or vicious person might—through direct divine intervention—become capable of performing 22-carat morally right acts.[17] But the supernatural intervention Hursthouse has in mind appears to be quite specific. For she maintains that if a vicious person were to begin producing 22-carat morally right acts immediately upon conversion, then he would also have to receive, immediately upon conversion, virtue. Supernatural intervention could make 22-carat moral action possible, on Hursthouse's view, if what was provided through supernatural intervention was virtue. If Saul, immediately after his experience on the road to Damascus, begins performing 22-carat morally right acts, then this could only be because God not only took away his old habits of acting and reacting and replaced them with new ones but also provided him with the necessary knowledge "about people and life" and gave him "sensitivity, perception and imagination."

The type of divine intervention that Hursthouse envisions could not be a common occurrence. For it enables 22-carat morally right action by removing vicious habits and desires and replacing them with the virtue that is (for Hursthouse) a prerequisite of morally good action. So, suppose that God wishes to enable a committed alcoholic to perform a 22-carat morally right act. Then, on Hursthouse's view, God must first remove the alcoholism and replace it with Aristotelian temperance. I will argue against this view in the subsequent section. For the time being, I only want to point out that such intervention would have to be very rare. For while alcoholics often do undergo conversions, those conversions are not typically accompanied by the immediate disappearance of their alcoholic habits. On Hursthouse's account,

---

[17] Hursthouse, *Virtue Ethics,* -159.

then, we would have to concede that most of those who undergo conversions are not immediately capable of 22-carat morally right acts. And this conclusion, I will argue, runs contrary to the Christian view.

22-CARAT MORALLY RIGHT ACTS: THE CHRISTIAN VIEW

Hursthouse rightly hypothesizes that the notion that the non-virtuous can perform 22-carat morally right acts originates in "religious views about the possibility of redemption." However, I don't think her answer adequately accommodates those religious views. In this section I will examine some examples of 22-carat morally right Christian action and argue that Hursthouse's accommodation is inadequate.

In what follows I will consider three examples, two scriptural and one literary. In all of the following examples, the individual in question is (a) described as having led a sinful (a.k.a. non-virtuous) life and nonetheless (b) suddenly performs one or more acts that are not just good, but exemplary: acts which can only be construed as 22-carat morally right acts. Hursthouse's account, I will argue, cannot sufficiently accommodate these examples.

First, consider Hursthouse's own example: Saul's experience on the road to Damascus. In the Acts of the Apostles, Saul first appears as a zealous and enthusiastic persecutor of Christians. Saul, we are told, "concurred" in the killing of Stephen and actively "harassed" the early Christian church (Acts 8:1-4). Indeed, his very trip to Damascus originates out of a desire to persecute the Christian church there (Acts 9:1-2). But on the road to Damascus, Christ reveals himself to Saul. Saul makes a sudden, immediate change of life (Acts 9:3-22).

A second example can be found in the gospel of Luke. Luke's gospel describes an event at the house of Simon the Pharisee. As Christ reclines to eat, a woman who is a "known sinner" comes and bathes his feet with her tears and anoints them with oil. Knowing his host's thoughts—that a true prophet would know the woman's sinfulness—Christ admonishes Simon, telling him that the woman's many sins are forgiven because of her great love. Christ also calls Simon's attention to the difference between the comparatively small acts of hospitality that Simon has shown him and the actions of the sinful woman: "I came to your home and you provided no water for my feet. She has washed my feet with her tears and wiped them with her hair. You gave me no kiss, but she has not ceased kissing my feet since I entered. You did not anoint my head with oil, but she has anointed my feet with perfume." This, Christ tells Simon, is why the woman's sins are forgiven: her love is great. Little, says Christ, "is forgiven the one whose love is small" (Luke 7:36-50).

To the two scriptural examples described above, I want to add a third, fictional example, namely the example of Graham Greene's "whiskey priest." Although the whiskey priest is fictional, he is the hero of a novel widely recognized for its Christian themes. It is therefore reasonable to assume that the actions ascribed to him are actions that Christians deem possible. Graham Greene's The Power and the Glory tells the story of a whiskey priest, the last priest to remain in Mexico during a time of persecution. The priest is no one's idea of a hero, and he certainly does not meet Hursthouse's criteria for virtue. He is an alcoholic, inclined to self-pity, and has broken his priestly vows: he has fathered a child with his housekeeper. At the same time, he continues to minister to his people. He likewise refuses to obey the government's command that he reject his vocation and marry. Towards the end of the story, the priest finally reaches safety. He has no sooner reached safety, however, than he receives word that a dying criminal wishes to confess. The priest knows that he is being lured into a trap, but when he becomes convinced that there really is a dying criminal who might really wish to confess his sins, he returns anyway.[18] Even when the criminal himself tells him of the trap and urges him to run, the priest tries to complete his errand, urging the criminal to make his peace with God.[19]

At least in Greene's telling, the whiskey priest performs a genuinely good act. He does a genuinely good thing: he returns from safety to certain death to give the sacraments to a dying man. He does this genuinely good thing, moreover, for what are, in Greene's telling, genuinely good motives: he recalls all the evils things the criminal is done and cannot bear the thought of a man dying "with all that on his soul."[20] Faced with a choice between his own safety and the possibility of bringing a sinner to God, the priest has no difficulty choosing the latter; he even, we are told, feels "quite cheerful."[21]

How, if at all, can Hursthouse's account accommodate the examples above? Hursthouse's reply, in each of the examples detailed above, would have to either be that the individuals above perform good acts that are not yet 22-carat morally right acts or else that, if 22-carat morally right acts occur, it is because God has removed bad habits and desires and replaced them with virtue. That is to say, either Saul, the sinful woman and the whiskey priest still perform something that falls short of 22-carat morally right action or all of their destructive habits and desires have been supernaturally removed. But the surrounding context rules out the first option. Christ upholds the acts of the sinful woman as exemplary to those present, claiming that she alone has provided true hospitality. Saul, similarly, is described as

---

[18] Graham Greene, *The Power and the Glory* (New York: Penguin Books, 1940), 180.
[19] Greene, *The Power and the Glory,* 188.
[20] Greene, *The Power and the Glory*, 180.
[21] Greene, *The Power and the Glory*, 180.

making a complete, wholehearted and immediate change from persecutor to disciple. And Graham Greene's whiskey priest, walking into a clear trap on the mere chance of saving a soul, feels "quite cheerful." In each of these cases, I think we have to assume that the acts described are 22-carat morally right acts; i.e. that in each example the agent does the right thing for the right reasons.

On the basis of the preceding, I think we must assume that Saul, the sinful woman and the whiskey priest all perform 22-carat morally right acts in spite of their sinful past. But if this is the case, then Hursthouse can only accommodate these examples by insisting that, immediately prior to their 22-carat morally right acts, God intervenes and replaces all their bad habits and desires with virtue. But this option is equally problematic. In the first place, in at least two of the three examples, this is demonstrably false. The converted Saul (now Paul) admits to a continuing struggle against his previous desires (Rom. 7). The whiskey priest continues to crave alcohol even after he has freely sacrificed his life for another.[22] Moreover, even though we are not told any details, it seems entirely reasonable to speculate that the sinful woman still experienced sinful desires after bathing Christ's feet with her tears. And this is as it should be. If in all these cases God simply intervened and removed their pre-existing habits and desires it would seem to diminish the magnitude of what occurs. For in each case, the power of the story has to do with the power of Christian love; of how it can arise and flourish in the most unlikely places. If the "place" is first altered beyond recognition, the story has considerably less power. The three examples I have described point to a deep Christian intuition about 22-carat morally right action, one which we cannot expect an Aristotelian account of virtue to accommodate. For the Christian holds that it is God's grace, not human strength, which makes the acts described above possible. It is possible for Saul and the sinful woman and the whiskey priest to do the right thing for the right reasons because they are shored up and strengthened by God's grace; and possible for them to find the appropriate acts in the first place because the Holy Spirit guides them. In the final section of this paper, I want to offer some thoughts about how the traditional Christian notion of infused habits could supply what is missing from Hursthouse's account.

ACCOMMODATING THE 22-CARAT MORALLY RIGHT CHRISTIAN ACT

Hursthouse struggles to accommodate virtuous Christian exemplars because her account of virtue is a binary one: there is only one kind of virtue, namely virtue, and to the extent one has the virtues, one

---

[22] Greene, *The Power and the Glory,* 206.

cannot have vicious desires or motivations, and vice versa. On hers and any thoroughly Aristotelian account of virtue, virtuous and vicious motivations are mutually exclusive. This forces one to insist that individuals like Saul, Luke's sinful woman and Graham Greene's whiskey priest either do not act with 22-carat motivations or else that they have had their vicious habits and desires divinely "erased." Both options are unsatisfactory. The first cannot sufficiently accommodate Christian accounts of morally good action, while the second accommodates those claims at the expense of common sense. But it is not at all clear that the options need to be understood in this binary way. Christian theologians have long described the spiritual life in terms of the growth of a "new life" or of the beginnings of a "new man." However, they also do not maintain that this new life immediately drives out the old.

In his Mere Christianity, C. S. Lewis argues that the Christian "is in a different position from other people who are trying to be good."[23] Other people hope to deserve praise from God or men by being good, "but the Christian thinks any good he does comes from the Christ-life inside him."[24] God, Lewis continues, does not love us because we are good, but makes us good because he loves us. Christians say that Christ is "in them" because they mean that Christ "is actually operating through them."[25] Saul, Luke's sinful woman and the whiskey priest are immediately capable of doing good things, not because they have suddenly lost a lifetime of bad habits, but because Christ works through them. What Hursthouse really needs in order to accommodate Saul, and what any Christian virtue ethicist wishing to accommodate examples like Greene's whiskey priest needs, is a theory of how Christ can enable 22-carat morally right action, even in those who possess a lifetime of vicious habits.

Early Christian scholars like Augustine and medieval scholars like Aquinas could accommodate the possibility of 22-carat morally right acts, even in those weighed down by vicious dispositions, because they could appeal to notions like the infused virtues and the gifts of the Holy Spirit: of habits bestowed by God along with grace that enable even those weighed down by vice to perform good acts.[26] And their notion of infused virtue was very different from the exception Hursthouse carves out for the case of divine intervention. Hursthouse speculates that the newly converted might perform a 22-carat morally right

---

[23] C.S. Lewis, *Mere Christianity* (New York: Harper Collins, 2001), 63

[24] C.S. Lewis, *Mere Christianity,* 63.

[25] C.S. Lewis, *Mere Christianity*, 63.

[26] For an excellent discussion of the origins of the notion of infused virtue, see Bonnie Kent, "Augustine's On the Good of Marriage and Infused Virtue in the Twelfth Century," *Journal of Religious Ethics* vol. 41, no. 1 (2013):112-36.

act if, at conversion, God took away all one's existing bad habits and replaced them with Aristotelian virtues. We have seen that this all but rules out 22-carat morally right action in the newly converted: conversion does not in the typical case remove a life-time of negative habits and desires. The traditional Christian notion of infused virtue proposes something rather different: God bestows habits that make 22-carat morally right Christian action possible without removing their destructive habits and desires. There is no need for such a hypothesis, because the convert's 22-carat morally right action is not something he does all by himself, but something he does with God's help. God helps him to see what the right action is and sustains and helps him in the willing and the doing of it.

How could the traditional notion of divinely infused habits provide a way out of Hursthouse's difficulty? Consider two reasons why Hursthouse argued that 22-carat morally right acts are impossible for those with destructive habits and desires. First, the value of such acts might not be "illumined" for them, or at least not by anything in them. Second, even if they desire to act rightly, those who lack Aristotelian phronesis will not have the sensitivity or insight required to "read" situations appropriately. But if God—while not removing destructive habits and desires—nonetheless unites man to himself in friendship, through (say) the divinely given habit of charity, then it seems entirely reasonable to think that the value of acts will be "illumined" in a way they were not before. It is, after all, her "great love" that leads the sinful woman to wash Christ's feet, and Christ's revelation of himself that initiates Saul's conversion. It is, similarly, pity for a man about to be cut off forever from God that spurs the whiskey priest's act of self-sacrifice. In each case, it is reasonable to think that the divine gift of a relationship with God "illuminates" the value these certain actions.

The same Christian tradition can also supply an answer to Hursthouse's worry about phronesis. The Christian tradition has long held that believers receive the help and guidance of the Holy Spirit. Thomas Aquinas held that man was enabled to receive the guidance of the Holy Spirit through divinely given habits which enabled him to receive the help and guidance of the Holy Spirit. Since my goal here is not to defend a specific theory of divinely infused habits, I will not enter into the details of Aquinas's theory here. My point is merely that a habitual ability to receive the prompting and guidance of the Holy Spirit can explain—in a way Hursthouse cannot—how even those with destructive habits and desires are capable of interpreting situations rightly.

I am not proposing that contemporary virtue ethicists simply appropriate some historical figure's account of infused habits as their own. The historical notion of infused virtue has shown itself to be problematic. Those who postulated them did not agree on a single account of exactly what virtues God infused or how they should be understood. Does God provide only faith, hope and charity, or does he bestow other virtues as well? Nor do they agree on any one account of exactly what the infused virtues do. Indeed, even when one focuses on the theory of a specific figure, such as Aquinas, many details remain unclear. Even if Aquinas indisputably recognized infused virtues, he does not offer any clear account of how such virtues relate to Aristotelian virtues. Do they replace Aristotelian virtues? Transform them? Do the two somehow supplement each other?

What I am proposing, however, is that in order to accommodate central Christian examples of exemplary action, contemporary virtue ethics needs something like the traditional notion of divinely infused habits. The examples of Saul and Luke's sinful woman and the whiskey priest point to an important difference between the Christian view and Aristotle's. For the Christian holds that anyone, no matter how weak or vicious he might be, can, with the help of God's grace, perform a 22-carat morally right act. Aristotelian ethics cannot accommodate this possibility. ■

Journal of Moral Theology, Vol. 5, No. 1 (2016): 144-168

Natural Law: New Directions in Thomistic Theological Ethics

Charles R. Pinches

ATURAL LAW, MUCH DISCUSSED OF LATE, has always been
an attractive topic. Part of the attraction lies in what might
be done with it. It would be a fine thing if humans the world
over could share a universal ethic—and perhaps the natural
law can give us that. However, precisely because it is so promising we
do well to be cautious. Natural law has sometimes been wrenched
from its context in Christian theology. It may be useful, but is not really portable. We are repeatedly tempted to carry it here and there to
address the problems, or the perceived problems of the day, forgetting
about its essentially theological location, which is the only place it can
be thoroughly and rightly understood. Recently, we have become
more aware of this theological location, and of the need to honor it.
But how to do this well—particularly given the temptation?[1]

   In what follows I consider three Thomistic thinkers who are helpful
in establishing the proper location of natural law in theological context:
Jean Porter, Servais Pinckaers and Herbert McCabe. Of these, Porter's
work is the most recent and likely the best known. It is helpful, I argue,
but takes a certain turn, following the "promising" temptation. The
work of Pinckaers and McCabe,[2] in that order, helps tether natural law
more thoroughly to Thomas's theologically informed understanding.
Both also thoughtfully open new directions for the further exploration
of natural law today.

---

[1] A sign of renewed attention to natural law, as well as of its temptations, The International Theological Commission of the Catholic Church recently published *In
Search of a Universal Ethics: A New Look at the Natural Law*. As John Berkman and
William Mattison say in their introduction to a recent printing of the document, "a
new look is warranted by the all too often impersonal and ahistorical presentations of
Christian teaching on the natural law in the past" (Grand Rapids: Eerdmans, 2014), 3.
[2] Pinckaers and McCabe were both Dominican friars whose work in moral theology
sparkled brilliantly in the second half of the 20th century, even if it remains unknown
to many. We have yet fully to appreciate its significance. The two were born months
apart, in 1925 and 1926 respectively. McCabe died in 2001; Pinckaers in 2008.

JEAN PORTER ON THE NATURAL LAW

The first of Jean Porter's trio of works on natural law, *Natural and Divine Law: Reclaiming the Tradition for Christian Ethics,*[3] position's natural law historically within the tradition of scholastic theological discussion. Although she treats Aquinas's views often, he does not dominate this first book. This has an important broadening effect; natural law inquiry has frequently rushed to question 94 in I-II of the *Summa Theologiae*. While this is an important and rich question, it cannot be understood on its own.[4] Porter helpfully reminds us that Thomas was commenting on, extending, and critically examining natural law within the scholastic discussion.

This makes room for Porter's second book on the topic, *Nature as Reason: A Thomistic Theory of the Natural Law*. As the subtitle indicates, here Porter focuses more directly on Aquinas on the natural law.[5] This is the book that will most concern us in this paper; it is also Porter's most influential work on the topic. It is followed by a third book: *Ministers of the Law: A Natural Law Theory of Legal Authority*.[6] This is a fine book in many ways, but, as I argue below, its topic suggests a certain trajectory in Porter's work on the natural law that relates to the named temptation: to understand natural law by one of its promising uses. Throughout it she holds firmly, and rightly, to the point that the law's context is always fundamentally moral. As she quotes favorably from Richard Shweder, "the social order is a moral order vigilantly and incessantly sustained by small and large judgments about right and wrong, good and bad, virtue and vice."[7] Laws in a given society, then, cannot but attend to this essentially moral matrix. In this way, a strict legal positivism that conceives of law as whatever happens to be specified by law-making authorities in that society

---

[3] Jean Porter, *Natural and Divine Law: Reclaiming the Tradition for Christian Ethics*. (Ottawa: Novalis, 1999).

[4] As Porter says near the beginning of her second book (and looking in this way back to the first), "Aquinas's account of the natural law cannot be understood, even on its own terms, unless it is placed in the context of the views of his own immediate forbearers and contemporaries, nor is its significance for our time fully apparent apart from this context." Jean Porter, *Nature as Reason: A Thomistic Theory of the Natural Law* (Grand Rapids, MI: Eerdmans, 2005) 47.

[5] As one might guess, not all Thomists agree that Porter gets Thomas right. For instance, Martin Rhonheimer holds that Porter's treatment is principally her own invention, not at all consonant with Thomas's full view of the natural law. "Porter," he says, "disregards the core of Aquinas's concept of natural law. She also fails to consider key points of Aquinas that do not fit into her agenda." *The Perspective of the Acting Person: Essays on the Renewal of Thomistic Moral Philosophy*, ed. William F. Murphy, Jr. (Washington: Catholic University of America Press, 2008), 284-5.

[6] Jean Porter, *Ministers of the Law: A Natural Law Theory of Legal Authority* (Grand Rapids: William B. Eerdmans Pub., 2010).

[7] Porter, *Ministers of the Law*, 111.

will always miss the mark. This point is important and well displayed throughout the book.

In the second book Porter develops a point that arises in her first, namely, that the scholastics assumed an essential connection between natural law and virtue. Both are fundamentally indexed to human happiness or well-being, and therefore must be teleologically understood. As Porter believes, Aquinas inherited this understanding and developed it in important ways.

> What is distinctive about Aquinas's account [beyond his scholastic interlocutors] is rather the way he identifies terrestrial forms of happiness with the practice of the virtues. In what follows I take this connection as a starting point for developing a Thomistic account of the natural law.
>
> More specifically, I will argue that happiness is the proximate origin for the norms of the natural law. The kind of happiness in question is terrestrial happiness, understood in both its natural and graced forms as equivalent to the practice of the virtues. The virtues, in turn, are dispositions perfecting our capacities for knowledge and love, as these are exercised throughout the whole range of activities necessary to sustaining human life. Thus, considered as normative ideals, they stem from and are ineliminably shaped by the natural inclinations and needs of the human organism. Hence, our paradigms for virtuous behavior, together with the reflective ideals grounded in those paradigms, represent the point of connection between well-being and the norms of the natural law—between nature as nature, in Albert's words, and nature as reason.[8]

For Aquinas, Porter believes, natural law is about both nature and reason, and these are intrinsically linked. The link comes in the *telos* of the human person, happiness, to which we naturally and reasonably move. Within this movement, fundamentally grounded as it is in the "needs, desires, projects, and long-standing commitments" which promote the well-being of ourselves and other people, practical reason (or prudence) can do its work.[9] And it is this same practical reason that guides and infuses the natural law.

Porter's work is corrective; as such, it helps open the possibility of a return to natural law that avoids a stultifying modern mindset about natural law, one that ignores the virtues. Indeed, as Porter says, the connection between natural law and virtue "may seem strange to us, accustomed as we are to drawing a sharp dichotomy between natural law and virtue as two approaches to moral reflection. But this dichot-

---

[8] Porter, *Nature as Reason*, 162.
[9] Porter, *Nature as Reason*, 170.

omy was unknown to the early scholastics, and as we will see, it reflects assumptions about the relation of virtue to law that we need not make our own."[10] Particularly in Aquinas's thinking, the connection is based on his assumption that "the end of action which informs and gives structure to the precepts of the natural law is the overall perfection, which is to say, the happiness of the acting person." This happiness, especially understood "terrestrially" (i.e., in this life) is "the life of virtue"—which "provides the goal which informs and gives structure to the various precepts of the natural law."[11]

Porter is right that any further fruitful work on natural law must recognize its essential link with virtue; she has done a great service by bringing this clearly before us. However, there remains a distinction between the two that she perhaps blurs too much.

Rightly accenting what is clear in Aquinas, Porter notes that "the precepts of the natural law pertain to the natural inclinations of the human person, and stand in an ordering to one another determined by those inclinations." As such, even though the natural law is in one sense "external" the "precepts themselves are not imposed 'from without', so to speak; rather, they emerge out of the natural and rational exigencies emerging from the operation of the virtues themselves."[12] However, as Aquinas goes on to work out, natural law and virtue *operate differently* with respect to the natural inclinations, and with respect to our formation towards our true end, happiness in one or the other form.

Unfortunately, Porter does not stop to work on this difference, which might be done by considering specifically what are the precepts of the natural law, what external actions they specify, and how keeping the precepts might form us as human beings.[13] Instead, she moves forward quickly to a discussion of the virtues. As she tells us, she believes

---

[10] Porter, *Nature as Reason,* 50.

[11] Porter, *Nature as Reason,* 50.

[12] Porter, *Nature as Reason,* 176.

[13] Porter refrains from specifying any negative commands that flow from the natural law such as, for instance, "no murder." Yet one can easily hold that specific prohibitions (don't steal, don't murder, etc.) are there for our good, the same good that the virtues equip us to pursue. Given the rich context she has provided it, the natural law need not be understood to be exhausted in such prohibitions. Its principles are broad: for instance, that we have a natural inclination to seek the truth. Naming prohibitions in the natural law need not diminish its connection to virtue.

Porter moves instead to a treatment of the virtues that echoes back on the natural law, marking out "paradigmatic acts" related to the virtues which are identifiable but also always debatable from culture to culture, e.g., regarding acts of courage she tells us that "One society's heroic martyrs are another society's murderous and perverse suicide bombers" (*Nature as Reason*, 334). It is clear that she has an aversion to such prohibitions. I suspect this relates most to what she wants to do with the natural law, namely to carry it forward to a discussion of natural law as the basis of positive law

she has "sketched a naturalistic framework for interpreting and defending the four cardinal virtues" and comments that the cardinal virtues "seem to be almost universally recognized as cardinal, or primary
or fundamental, for a good reason. These represent traits of character
that contribute to human well-being in such basic ways." [14] Importantly for Porter, the cardinal virtues are linked with "paradigmatic
actions," as fortitude, for example, is linked with the willingness to
endure death for the sake of some greater good.[15]

This quick move—from virtues to paradigmatic acts—tells us
something important about how Porter is proceeding. Her interest in
the virtues is not so much in how, operating in conjunction with the
natural law, they move human persons further towards the good, but
rather *what they might help us identify*. In particular, she seems most
interested in searching out "moral norms" that the virtues (or the natural law) might help us articulate, norms that might supply something
like a universal ethic.

As it happens, though, the search must be constantly qualified since,
as Porter holds, paradigmatic acts of the cardinal virtues cannot give
us the specific moral norms for which she seems to be looking. For the
paradigmatic acts turn out to be ambiguous. This point relates to what
Aquinas notes in his discussion of the similitudes of the virtues: the
similitude of fortitude, for instance, is something that looks like fortitude, but is not specifically tooled to the complete life of virtue in
which the virtues are united. And so Porter is led to say, with an air of
perhaps feigned disappointment: "If the paradigmatic virtues are morally ambiguous in this way, then it would seem that we cannot, after
all, derive moral norms from a consideration of these acts. And if this
is so, then it would appear that we cannot derive stable moral norms
from the general parameters of human well-being, from which our
ideas of these paradigmatic acts emerge."[16]

This kind of statement is repeated often in Porter's work, like a
refrain. It reveals a certain dynamic: As she works with the virtues, or
natural law, Porter opens the possibility that we might find the basis
for something like a set of universal moral norms. This, she gives the
impression, is what natural law inquiry is searching for. But, we never
quite find it—or at least what we find is never enough to allow us
specify a set of "stable moral norms."[17]

---

in any society. This explanation is made all the more plausible by the fact that she
notes that the cardinal virtues are "almost universally recognized as cardinal."
[14] Porter, *Nature as Reason,* 181.
[15] Porter, *Nature as Reason,* 183.
[16] Porter, *Nature as Reason,* 186.
[17] For instance, fifty pages after the quote noted here, Porter, referring to Lee Yearly's
work, notes that "he observes that there does seem to be considerable agreement
across cultural boundaries on the values of the central virtues." However, when we

To summarize the point so far made about Porter's treatment, she has rightly and helpfully connected natural law with virtue by rooting both in the teleology of happiness or well-being. This opposes, again helpfully, conceptions of natural law that have dominated previously, such as those proposed by John Finnis or Germain Grisez "whose normative judgments do not depend in any substantive way on more broadly natural or metaphysical—let alone theological—commitments."[18] Yet as her analysis proceeds, Porter says very little about what natural law might contain or how it might operate in a way different from the virtues to which she has rightly connected it. Instead, she presses on with the virtues (and their paradigmatic acts) always in an attempt to find a "universal ethic" or a set of "stable moral norms" that might function in a way similar to those Finnis and Grisez propose. The virtues, in effect, are treated by Porter as a possible means to discover the sort of moral precepts we might have hoped the natural law would provide. What happens—and this seems by Porter's design—is that we repeatedly discover that work with the natural inclinations, the virtues and the teleological structure of happiness can't quite produce these norms. Indeed, much of the latter part of *Nature as Reason* takes on the convention of following out an always incomplete search for a universal ethic. This seems quite unfortunate, for in pursuing this search, Porter's attention is drawn away from how the natural law and the virtues actually function to form us towards the *telos* from which both take their meaning and substance.

The next section of this paper elaborates this critical point. Yet before proceeding there, let us mark two more features to appreciate in Porter's work on the natural law, which will assist us later on.

Early on in *Nature as Reason* Porter tells us that Aquinas believes "human reason is one expression of a more general intelligibility proper to the natural world." Yet she also goes on to say that Thomas and most of his scholastic interlocutors "do not regard actually existing social institutions and practices as the immediate expressions of prerational nature."[19] These institutions and practices come, rather, out of "reasoned communal reflection, giving rise to the laws and customs appropriate to a society of rational men and women."[20]

---

take various complicating factors into consideration "it becomes apparent that the broad consensus on the virtues and the paradigmatic form of practicing the virtues cannot be regarded as a fully universal ethic" (229). This refrain can be also found in Porter's third book. After surveying certain agreements among cultural psychologists, she says: "It may seem that we have now found what so far has eluded us, namely the starting points for a universally valid natural law morality. But this conclusion would be too quick..." (Porter, *Ministers of the Law*, 111).

[18] Porter, *Nature as Reason*, 66-7.

[19] Porter, *Nature as Reason,* 49.

[20] Porter, *Nature as Reason,* 49.

That is to say, as part of creation, the natural world is ordered and therefore intelligible. It moves towards an end—Christians will say an end in its creator. Yet in the case of human beings this movement is not predetermined by nature. Human beings live by and within "social institutions and practices," but these do not follow directly from our "nature," for example from our needs and desires to eat, seek refuge from danger, sexually reproduce, etc. Such features of human life— what Porter calls our "prerational nature"—do indeed help shape social institutions and practices. But they do not predetermine their form. Rather, their form comes through "reasoned communal reflection" which is neither over-against nature nor predetermined by it.

Porter spends less time than she might considering just how this "communal reflection" might go in one or the other society. For instance, as different peoples communally reflect in the quite different environments in which their common life takes shape, they will need to be aware of such things as their peculiar natural habitat. Are they a mountain people or do they live on the seashore, etc.? Yet Porter is eminently clear throughout that the *telos* of this reflection will be well-being, or "terrestrial happiness." As such—and this is a second point to appreciate in her analysis—whatever form their "social institutions and practices" take will relate to prudence. Prudence will operate mainly within the context of the cultural setting of a people, providing them with wisdom about how to live well. Yet prudence also links essentially, with all the virtues, to the nature of the human person, conceived not simply as comprised of certain prerational features of our animal existence spread out as if on a chart, but the very destination of our created nature in human happiness.

Porter's reflection on these points helpfully locates natural law within the complicated mix of human culture—arising, as she has it, from our "prerational nature"—but turns this in any number of interesting ways as the "reasoned communal reflection" of a given people carries it. This implies that signs of the natural law will be spread throughout a given culture; yet to identify them clearly we will need to study that culture. It is possible in this way to think of cultural studies as a kind of natural law inquiry.

This sort of complexification of the natural law in relation to evident differences we discover from one culture to another may appear to crowd out judgment, which the notion of "law" includes. However, the process of "reasoned communal reflection," Porter holds, "can be carried out well or badly."[21] That is, the "moral traditions" that arise as particular peoples engage in reasoned communal reflection...

---

[21] Porter, *Nature as Reason,* 49.

are not impervious to rational critique, or completely opaque or un-persuasive to those standing outside them. We need a more nuanced account of the relationship between specific beliefs and practices, and the moral claims they generate. Because it focuses on the complex relation between social conventions and the natural principles from which those conventions stem, a Thomistic theory of the natural law is well suited to provide a starting point for developing such an ac-count.[22]

This sets a promising agenda. Porter has rightly found in Aquinas (and his scholastic forbearers and contemporaries) a complex linking of na-ture with reason, which gives room for the virtue of prudence to oper-ate from and in relation to the trajectories in nature towards a fuller articulation and specification of what we must do (or not do), and who we must be if we are to live fully human lives. Natural law is to be understood in relation to this complex mix. Inquiry into it needs to be appropriately subtle and flexible.

In this context Porter points out, rightly, I think, that there is not simply one way to be human. She believes this follows from her anal-ysis. "If the Thomistic theory of natural law developed here is valid... [t]here are many ways to be human, including a plurality of defensible and legitimate expressions of the basic inclinations of human na-ture."[23] Porter here and elsewhere complexifies the relation between the natural inclinations and the happy life. They are fundamentally re-lated, since nature is teleological. They set us on the path of being human. But precisely how this goes will vary as the virtues develop and interact with particulars of a given life, lived as it always is in the context of culture and the practices, institutions, and traditions it car-ries. Moreover, as the saints show, goodness diversifies.[24]

One final caveat, though, on this point. As noted, Porter speaks of "reasoned communal reflection" as sometimes going badly. Affirming that there are different ways to be human does not preclude also saying that there are also clear ways to deviate from being human. This devi-ation, especially as it is willful, has been long understood in the Chris-tian tradition under the notion "sin." However, "sin" is not in the index of Porter's book; it may be mentioned, but it plays no central part. This deviates from what appears to be the force of Saint Paul statement, much used within natural law reflection: "For what can be known about God is plain to them ['the Greeks'], because God has shown it to them. Ever since the creation of the world his eternal power and

---

[22] Porter, *Nature as Reason,* 51.

[23] Porter, *Nature as Reason,* 333.

[24] The point has been made often. As C.S. Lewis succinctly puts it: "How monoto-nously alike all the great tyrants and conquerors have been: how gloriously different are all the saints" (*Mere Christianity* [New York: Harper Collins, 2001], 226).

divine nature, invisible though they are, have been understood and seen through the things he has made. So they are without excuse" (Romans 1:19-20 [NRSV]). In this regard, one of the functions of the natural law, is to help identify sin. As we read in the Decalogue (which for Aquinas is essentially coextensive with the natural law): "thou shalt not...."[25]

FURTHER CRITICAL ISSUES—A "NATURAL LAW MORALITY"?

I have meant for my reflections so far on Jean Porter's treatment of natural law to be both appreciative and critical. She has, I believe, steered natural law inquiry away from diversions and eddies that have caught many a craft, particularly those powered by "the new natural law." Yet there is a direction in Porter's work that, I believe, is over determined by what she seems eager to derive from the natural law. This causes her to miss key points about how natural law actually works. I hope to bring this more clearly to the surface in this section.

Recently in this journal Bill Mattison and David Cloutier featured Porter's *Nature as Reason* as one of six books that have strongly influenced the resurgence of virtue in Christian ethics. They admire some of the features of Porter's work so far noted, then pause on a "bold claim" that Porter makes late in the book. As she says there, "a Thomistic theory of natural law is not at odds with a virtue-oriented approach to morality; this theory of natural law is a theory of virtue."[26] The claim is indeed bold; but it also overreaches. It is essential to connect natural law with virtue, yes, but also to note their *difference.* To say that a theory of natural law *is* a theory of virtue risks obliterating this difference.

It is important to recall that virtue modifies character, and law does not. Thomistic ethics is principally about character in the sense that God opens the Trinitarian life to us; God re-makes us into the sorts of beings who can become God's friends. This is ratified by the structure and weight of the *Summa*. Thomas repeatedly draws our attention to virtue since it is what we need to become good—not as if goodness becomes our possession but that it properly describes how we feel and act and live.[27]

For Thomas law is always preparatory, and in this sense secondary, to virtue. "Consequently it is evident that the proper effect of law is to

---

[25] Porter notes that for Aquinas the Decalogue is nothing more nor less than a revealed form of the natural law. And she does not seem to believe he is wrong. See Porter, *Nature as Reason,* 268-88, where she discusses Aquinas on the Decalogue.

[26] David Cloutier and William C. Mattison III, "The Resurgence of Virtue in Recent Moral Theology," *Journal of Moral Theology* 3, no. 1, (Jan. 2014): 245-6

[27] This weight can also be felt in the *Summa* by the fact that Aquinas dedicates some nineteen questions to law, and just one specifically to natural law; virtue in its various forms informs and infiltrates virtually the entirety of the second part.

lead its subjects to their proper virtue: and since virtue is 'that which makes its subject good', it follows that the proper effect of law is to make those to whom it is given, good, either simply or in some particular respect."[28] This point goes relatively unexplored in Porter's work: how law moves us toward virtue. She holds, of course, that law is teleological. Yet if so, how does it move toward its end? And as it moves, how is its movement completed by virtue?

In fact, and as noted above, Porter is more eager to use law—and, indeed, virtue—to *identify* a morality than to consider how it forms us toward virtue. This trouble is demonstrated by the fact that she comes to speak of something called "natural law ethics" or "natural law morality,"[29] and it is compounded when she speaks of not one, but *many* natural law moralities.

> If the natural law in its primary sense is understood in terms of a basic capacity operating through first principles, and if we add, as we must, that these underdetermine the specific norms in terms of which they are expressed, then clearly we cannot speak of *the* natural law ethic, seen as foundational to, or indeed as a contrast to, *the* distinctively Christian way of life. Earlier I remarked that any socially embodied morality can be regarded as a natural law ethics, and the same can be said of the moralities that have emerged through the practice and reflection of the church in its many embodiments.... For this reason, I would suggest that we should extend scholastic flexibility by speaking of natural law moralities in the plural, including some which predominate among "the nations," and others which are distinctively Christian.[30]

---

[28] Thomas Aquinas, *Summa Theologiae*, trans. Fathers of the English Dominican Province (New York: Benziger, 1947), I-II q. 92, a. 1. Thomas also says "the principles of common law are called the 'nurseries of the virtues'" (*ST* I-II q. 51, a. 1). He says this in a question addressing the cause of habits, where he is considering whether habits are natural at their beginning. He believes they are not, but that they arise in connection to principles that are—which, in this case are none other than the principle of the natural law, the appropriate basis of common law. For our purposes here, we need simply note that, for Thomas, law forms us, even nurses us, so that we can come to acquire virtue.

[29] There is no difficulty in saying that Aquinas has a theory of natural law—which is to say that he puts forward views about natural law and how it functions in a broader moral and theological order. But to say that Aquinas has a natural law ethics is to take quite another step. It suggests that if you have Aquinas's theory of natural law, you have his ethics. But this is plainly not true.

[30] Porter, *Nature as Reason*, 330. The term "natural law morality" is used various times in this region. In a couple of cases (333, 339) the term "natural ethic" is used. It is noteworthy that Porter gathers distinctively Christian ethics into the category of natural law moralities. A consistent question for Porter's work is, what difference, really, does the adjective "Christian" make in her "natural law thinking" about ethics? Stanley Hauerwas has recently said, "As far as I can see, in spite of her strong claims

As noted, Porter has repeatedly given the impression that she is on a search for a "natural law morality," which seems to mean that she is searching after set of universal norms. As she apparently discovers, however, any "natural law morality" she finds can't give this, especially in the form we might have been expecting.

In the passage just quoted Porter shifts to speaking of natural law moralities in the plural. In doing so she makes it difficult to see how "natural law," per se, will help us make any discriminating judgments between these moralities. In effect, following her, we have been led on a long search for some apparent thing, some law or moral code, by which universal moral judgments might be made—even if we have never quite been able to find it. Yet now, after repeatedly being disappointed in this search, we are suddenly offered many natural laws, or "natural law moralities," which qualify as such simply because they arise from and within human cultures.

Now, with so many natural law moralities, a question will arise: How do we adjudicate between them when they differ? Porter is aware of this; as she goes on to say, "[i]t stretches credulity to claim that all these moralities are equally sound or desirable. A rational grasp of the exigencies of our nature does offer criteria for distinguishing between better and worse social arrangements."[31] Here I wonder if we have perhaps discovered what Porter has been aiming at all along: a kind of ongoing conversation between and among "natural law moralities" about better or worse social arrangements, informed by some basic human agreements about natural human inclinations.

It is helpful to recall that these passages come to us near the end of Porter's second book on natural law—and there is a third. Another passage from this same region close to the book's end helps display where things might be leading.

> [T]he Thomistic theory of the natural law does identify morally significant constraints in human nature, considered as such. We cannot establish a determinate yet universally compelling moral code on the basis of these constraints, but that does not rule out the possibility of arguing for their moral significance with a reasonable expectation that others will find our arguments persuasive.[32]

---

concerning the necessity of creation to justify a natural law ethic, her theological convictions do no work for her" (*Approaching the End: Eschatological Reflections on Church, Politics and Life* [Grand Rapids: Eerdmans, 2013], 18).

[31] Porter, *Nature as Reason,* 340.

[32] The frequency of this pattern is illustrated by the fact that six pages before this Porter says: "From this point we might seem to have all we need to develop a full-blown substantive set of moral norms which are grounded in human nature and can therefore be justified without any reference to any particular theological, philosophical or cultural tradition. But," Porter continues, "on reflection, that is not so obvious...." And so she goes on to note how different societies define courage differently,

Settled within this framework of reasoned persuasion, within and between cultures, seems to be where Porter most desires to work. In the last section of *Nature as Reason* she considers how natural law as she has described it might help articulate an understanding of natural rights. To be sure, the question of natural rights is today an important consideration for people worldwide. Many of these people are not Christian, nor are they likely to be convinced by the rationalism of Finnis or Grisez's natural law. If Porter is to participate in a discussion with this worldwide audience about rights she will need some recourse to statements that suggest a moral code even if they do not explicitly lay one down. Or, one moral code will need to be tested against another as leaders of governments and societies discuss together what behavior they believe should or shouldn't be tolerated.

Discussions of rights in this sort of context can be important. Further, affirmations such as the United Nations declaration on human rights have had and continued to have good effect.[33] Indeed, when Porter moves at the end of *Nature as Reason* to a discussion of the language of human rights she is following a one clear trajectory in Aquinas, namely from natural law to human law. *Ministers of the Law*, Porter's sequel, carries her analysis precisely in this direction. It is an impressive foray into legal scholarship.

Yet the fact that natural law might help in this way is not to say that this is its true destination, or even its identifying feature. What is this feature? Natural law is not the same thing as virtue, neither is it identified by virtue. Nor is it by itself a morality that can help the human race to agree upon a universal moral code. Rather, natural law holds a place within the Christian tradition of discussion about the beginning of the journey of the human being toward God. In this way, natural law is not a place to stand; it is not a morality in itself. Rather it is a feature of a much larger picture of the moral life, which is nothing more or less than the movement of the human being towards perfection. Most proximately, natural law is on the way to virtue. In the end, this is not where Porter carries it.[34]

Natural law theory, such as it is, needs continually to remain aware of how it functions in relation to the whole. Natural law opens a path;

---

opining that "one society's heroic martyrs are another society's murderous and perverse suicide bombers" (*Nature as Reason*, 334).

[33] See Porter, *Nature as Reason,* 361, where she discusses this and other efforts to build world consensus on human rights.

[34] To be fair, Porter's final section in the final chapter of *Nature as Reason* turns to grace. This is the strongest theological section of her whole book, and a promising last note. However, the turn at the beginning of the chapter sets its framework. Moreover, the theological references of the first section are separated from the theology of the last section by a lengthy consideration of human rights as they might suitably fit within a variety of "natural law moralities," including especially Christian morality.

it helps us begin to articulate what it means to be human creatures whose natural inclinations draw us upward. It is a gateway to virtue, to the discovery that what we should be and do is also what we love. In this way it fits within the pattern of formation and transformation that is the moral life. As law it constrains us with limits; in any larger view of the moral life these constraints will need to find their appropriate context. But we cannot tip the whole of our understanding and vision of the moral life in this direction—as if what we finally need from "morality" is mainly a set of norms; a list of obligations that can be compared with others' lists.

Many things Porter says in *Nature as Reason* and elsewhere suggest this is not all she hopes for; her analysis is consistently richer than that. Nonetheless, there is a consistent strain in her work that suggests such norms, and the comparisons that might be drawn between them, are the target of her analysis.[35] By apparently conducting a search for a "natural law morality," and thereby implying that this is really what ethics is all about, she does nothing to allay this impression.

SERVAIS PINCKAERS ON NATURAL LAW

Servais Pinckaers, O.P., has repeatedly drawn our attention to an important contrast in how morality is conceived, according to two quite different paradigms. The contrast is between a morality of virtue and a morality of obligation. Compared to the former, the latter is a latecomer, even if it emerges as early as the fourteenth century. He calls it "new."

> St. Thomas, like the Fathers, clearly recognized the existence of moral obligations, but he subordinated them to the virtues. In the new conception the relationship was reversed: Obligation is given priority and invades the entire domain of the moral life. This period marks the birth of what can properly be called the "morality of obligation." Later this morality will be embodied in moralities of duty and moral imperatives, for which Immanuel Kant will provide the model in philosophy.[36]

As the morality of obligation takes hold, law becomes prominent. "As the source of morality, law reigns over the entire domain of morality. It is henceforth understood as an edict of a legislative will and no longer as a work of wisdom."[37] For Pinckaers this is not first or even primarily something that happens in the Enlightenment, but rather in

---

[35] I have discussed Porter's work before on another topic with this criticism in mind. See Pinches, *Theology and Action* (Grand Rapids: Eerdmans, 2002), 140-8.
[36] Servais Pinckaers, *Morality: The Catholic View* (South Bend, IN: St. Augustine's Press, 2001), 32.
[37] Pinckaers, *Morality*, 34.

the Church. Post Aquinas, the great weight of Catholic moral reflection shifts from virtue to law. Pinckaers notes, for instance, how the casuist Alphonsus Liguori spends over 900 pages in his major work discussing laws, and 73 on the theological virtues. Moreover, as Pinckaers points out, moral theology came to be separated from other "branches" of theology, like scripture or systematic theology, sacraments or ecclesiology.

For Pinckaers the turn from virtue to obligation had sweeping repercussions; these have set into our habits of moral and theological reflection including up until very recent times including assumptions informing some of the discussions of Vatican II.[38] While Pinckaers thought the new *Catechism* and Pope John Paul II's *Veritatis splendor* marked significant steps forward, even at his death in 2008 he plainly thought the renewal of Catholic moral theology, which on his view corresponded to a reclaiming of the virtues and of the New Law in Aquinas, was a work in progress.

The return of natural law in recent years may or may not demonstrate a sign of that renewal. In truth, signs are mixed. Porter's work displays this quality. As we have followed her, she insightfully shows how natural law must be linked with virtue and teleology, and therefore to our human destination as creatures on their way to the God who created them. But, nevertheless, she falls back into the old (or, for Pinckaers, "new") "morality of obligation" when she searches throughout her treatment for a universal moral code, giving credence to the view that what morality is really all about is to be found in a set of norms that governed human life—and that natural law is most useful insofar as it can help us identify this.

As Pinckaers treats natural law, he begins (like Porter) with the significance of Aquinas's language of the "natural inclinations." Yet he does so cautiously, noting that it is "difficult to speak of natural inclinations today because of the subtle modifications of ideas and associations that have been caused by nominalism." [39] Nominalism, which Pinckaers traces to William of Ockham, can be associated with Divine command theories of ethics, which accent that the good is good because God commands it—and so morality arises precisely from these commands and only from them.

Pinckaers believes that nominalism and the morality of obligation depend on a bifurcation of nature and freedom.

---

[38] See *The Pinckaers Reader*, ed. John Berkman (Washington, D.C.: Catholic University of America Press, 2005), 374-5.

[39] Servais Pinckaers, *The Sources of Christian Ethics*, trans. Sr. Mary Thomas Noble (Washington: Catholic University of America Press, 1995), 400.

Our chief difficulty is caused by our habit of considering nature and
freedom as contraries. If we think of freedom as something dependent
only on our voluntary decision, and totally indeterminate before we
take that decision, then we will be led to think of the natural as something necessarily predetermined. In this view, it is hard to see how we
can reconcile the natural and the free. We will see the natural inclinations of both intellect and will as tendencies both blind and coercive.[40]

But clearly, and as Porter also believes,[41] this sort of understanding of
nature diverges profoundly from Aquinas's understanding. If we do
not see how natural inclinations and human freedom are related, we
will mistake Thomas on morality, and likewise on natural law.

For him [Aquinas], natural law was the expression, in the form of precepts, of our natural inclinations, which were guided by our inclinations to goodness and truth. Thus natural law, imposed externally
when taught, was in reality written in the human heart—that is, in the
very nature of our human faculties of reason and will, at the root of
free action. This teaching on natural inclinations was fundamental for
St. Thomas. It established natural law and provided the basis for morality. Inclinations developed into virtues, which received their beginnings from them and would provide morality with its main categories.[42]

Pinckaers spends considerable space developing the inclinations in
five specific directions, familiar from the *Summa* I-II q. 94. These are
the (1) inclination to the good, (2) to self-preservation, (3) to sexual
union and the rearing of offspring, (4) to the knowledge of the truth,
and (5) to live in society.[43] Pinckaers is prepared, Porter less so, to
specify these as precepts which can and should yield specific direc-
tives for human behavior. Pinckaers, in my view, has the better part
on this point. But what is more crucial to gather from Pinckaers here
is how he relates these precepts to virtue. To see this clearly another
distinction from Pinckaers is needed: that between the "freedom of
indifference" and the "freedom for excellence."

The former arises in connection to nominalism. Since it does not
root the commands of law, God's commands, within any configuration
of natural goods, the law does not correspond to anything in us; it is
wholly from without. That we are free creatures, capable of choice,
has, therefore, no correlation to our natural inclinations. We are made
free to choose, but can find no guidance from within our creatureliness

---

[40] Pinckaers, *Sources*, 400-1.
[41] It is somewhat surprising that Porter does not engage Pinckaers's work at any point
in her three books on natural law.
[42] Pinckaers, Sources, 404-5.
[43] Pinckaers, *Sources*, 407; See also *ST* I-II q. 94, a. 2, whence these derive.

about what to choose. Taken as such, we are creatures who need a law imposed on us if we are to move towards a good end, since our inclinations are of no reliable help.

By contrast, the "freedom for excellence" assumes a correlation. We are naturally inclined to do the good, and, in fact, this is what our freedom is for: so that in what we choose we may move ever further towards our good. To explain, Pinckaers draws out an analogy with hunger, moving further from biological to "spiritual" inclinations.

> A biological inclination such as hunger or thirst directs that appetite in a determined and compelling way. Yet we would hesitate to say that it is contrary to freedom, since by eating we are achieving the physical strength needed for action. Spiritual inclinations in no way limit freedom but rather incite and develop it. Anyone drawn to a person, a virtue, a science, or an art ["spiritual inclinations" in Pinckaers's understanding] realizes that his freedom increases through the love he feels and is not diminished by its determination.[44]

This understanding of freedom assumes a correlation between our natural inclinations and the natural law and so reorients the meaning of law. While law remains in one sense external to us, it is not imposed as if foreign. As Pinckaers says, "natural inclinations form natural law… and they provide the seeds of the excellence that will grow out of the virtues."

When expressed in precepts, the natural law offers commands that seem to (and in one sense really do) "restrict our freedom with the force of obligation." Nevertheless,

> this law is not the work of a will external and foreign to us. Precisely because it is the expression of our natural inclinations, especially the spiritual ones, this law penetrates to the heart of our freedom and personality to show us the demands of truth and goodness. These guide us in the development of freedom through actions of excellence. Thus natural law is an inner law. It is the direct work of the One who has created us to image him in our spiritual nature and our free, rational will. The exigencies of natural law have their source both in God and in our human nature.[45]

Here Pinckaers may appear to operate with too rosy a picture of human nature. And, to be sure, differences will arise on these points between typically Catholic and typically Protestant accounts of how deeply the

---

[44] Pinckaers, *Sources*, 404.
[45] Pinckaers, *Sources*, 452.

acids of sin have eroded the connection between our created nature and the current state of our inclinations.[46]

While these are important debates, they do not affect the essential points Pinckaers (following Aquinas) has laid out about the form and purpose of the natural law. Natural law speaks to our created nature, not contravening it—even in its force as law—but rather affirming it and drawing it forward to its proper end. This means that natural law has a place within a larger picture that is centrally about our formation. As the Christian story unfolds, we may see that this includes our re-formation, indeed, our rescue and redemption. But this does not change the fact that the natural law, and in fact all laws that come from God, are given to draw us towards our rightful and final end.[47]

The clarity with which Pinckaers has laid out this point helps display how law functions in the human movement toward virtue—what morality is all about. "For St. Thomas, virtues are more important than precepts, since they constituted the end and perfection of the inclinations"—which makes law more of a beginning point. Moreover, as the sequence in the *Summa* shows, law also makes way for grace which comes in the form of the New Law given in Christ and so also in the theological virtues (as well as the gifts of the Spirit) that are infused in us as we are transformed by God's love.[48] As Pinckaers believes, "[t]hrough the New Law our inwardness opens to the mystery of the divine inwardness, under that action of the Holy Spirit."[49]

Thomas's reflections on grace in the *Summa* follow appropriately; by the light of grace we are moved beyond our natural end to "participate in the divine nature."[50] Natural law begins a progression; it is a first call upwards, a call which makes sense as a call only because of what lies beyond it. It cannot be separated off as if it might stand on its own—what amounts to the crucial mistake of "casuistical ethics" which takes as its only task the application of precepts given or allegedly derived from the natural law to particular cases.

---

[46] Pinckaers has responded to this point. The substantial argument he makes, albeit briefly, is that without the scheme he has laid out (following Thomas) it is hard to give an account of sin as fundamentally against God. As sin turns us from our own true end, and often as it does also turns others, it also turns from God "since it seeks to vitiate his crowning work, who is made in his own image." *Sources*, 465.

[47] Precisely in this context it is worth remembering that the Decalogue of Exodus 20 is given its context and meaning in chapter 19. "Now therefore, if you obey my voice and keep my covenant, you shall be my treasured possession out of all the peoples. Indeed, the whole earth is mine, but you shall be for me a priestly kingdom and a holy nation" (Exod. 19: 5-6).

[48] This is borne out by the sequence of their treatment in the *Summa*. Natural law, treated in question 94, opens not only to the Decalogue, treated in question 98 and following, but also to the law of Christ, treated in question 106 and following.

[49] Pinckaers, *Sources*, 453.

[50] Aquinas, *ST* I-II q. 110, a. 3.

Pinckaers's treatment of natural law is simpler than Porter's, and perhaps more elemental. Given the complicated nature of the human being to which it applies, natural law may need complicating. (What follows from Herbert McCabe functions partly in this way.) Nonetheless Pinckaers has captured with great clarity the movement in natural law toward virtue and so has secured the place of natural law in a morality of virtue, indeed, in a morality of Christian virtue. Genuinely theological treatments of natural law, particularly ones that follow Aquinas, must always keep natural law in this place.

HERBERT MCCABE ON NATURAL LAW

Herbert McCabe's reflections on natural law, which are sprinkled among his books, some only recently posthumously released, begin with an affirmation of the structure of the position just described in Pinckaers.[51] With Pinckaers (and Porter) he speaks of natural law in terms on the natural inclinations. Borrowing a distinction from D. H. Lawrence between "little needs" and "deeper needs," he affirms that "the deep desires that a man has, the desires he cannot help having, are a manifestation of his human life. His being human consists in having what Aquinas calls 'natural inclinations'. They are the presence to him of the law of his nature, the natural law."[52]

Yet we find in McCabe a stronger contrast between one and the other kind of desire (or inclination) within us: this means the discovery of those which relate to the natural law will be difficult. As he notes, "besides those deep desires that define our humanity, we have also inherited certain deep feelings from our pre-human ancestors which to some extent overlap with our deep human desires but are not identical with them."[53] There is nothing in Aquinas's theory of natural law that denies this. Indeed, as McCabe believes, his theology of natural law predicts conflicts, tragic ones, that will arise as the "deep desires" occasionally clash.

It important to note in this context that Aquinas did not believe the natural law is easily discovered.

> He [Aquinas] thought that it was possible for man with much difficulty, after a long time and with the admixture of many errors to discover, without being told, what the natural law commands. The idea that it is easy to know the natural law or that most men may be expected to understand it or that knowledge of it is something innate in us is quite foreign to his thinking.... Since he thought it rather hard to discover he would not have been surprised to find that small primitive

---

[51] Although their lives were parallel in many ways, one does not find in either Pinckaers or McCabe a clear acknowledgement of the other's work.
[52] Herbert McCabe, *Law, Love and Language* (New York: Continuum, 2003), 63.
[53] McCabe, *Law, Love and Language*, 64.

communities were hazy about it and held bizarre views about sexual morals or the ethics of killing.[54]

The notion here of "discovery" of the natural law suggests some sort of historical movement towards knowledge, even if it is difficult. And, indeed, McCabe believes there is something of this progressive element in Aquinas's theory. However, McCabe adds his own sentiment that, whether Aquinas believed this or not, there also exists the possibility of regress. As he notes, "sophisticated societies" of our time are especially susceptible to an obscuring of the natural law—which is to say an obscuring of the meaning of being human—because of their embrace of capitalism. "A certain distortion of the nature of man is built into the capitalist culture which makes it difficult to recognise ourselves for what we are, to recognise, in fact, what we want."[55] Capitalism does this as it establishes an "alienated form of social intercourse" whereby each of us is in one sense pitted against the other. We become salesmen of ourselves since, after all, in the capitalist view society is understood essentially as a commercial enterprise.

So for McCabe the natural law is difficult (even if possible) for a society to discover, and it can be easily obscured by other currents that exist or arise within that society or in connection to other animalistic instincts that remain within the human creature. Furthermore, while it surely is something to which we are inclined, McCabe does not imagine the natural law is "in" us in the sense that it invariably arises in a human self, by itself. It is true that the natural law defines us as human beings, but being a human being is not something we come to be on our own. Indeed, as the fifth point on Pinckaers's (and Aquinas's) list affirms, our humanity always includes living in society.

In making this point, McCabe means to say more than simply that human beings naturally reach out to one another, and so take up a common human life. Rather, we must see that "our moral perceptions and judgements, like all our other judgements, begin not from our bare experience, but from the society and tradition into which we are brought up." There is, in this regard, no human morality without formation in society. The point is not novel; it has been with us since Aristotle who assumed morality involved the "training" of the "practical intellect, the appetites and even the perceptions."[56] Extending Aristotle's implication, McCabe holds that "we come to recognize, say,

---

[54] McCabe, *Law,* 58-9. When McCabe refers to "being told" the natural law, he is referring to the Decalogue. The Israelites were, in effect, given the natural law at Sinai. This point affirms Thomas's view that the natural law is not different from the Decalogue—although of course it is expressed differently.

[55] McCabe, *Law,* 60.

[56] Herbert McCabe, *The Good Life* (New York: Continuum, 2005), 8.

a generous act as praiseworthy just as we come to recognize a particular move in football or ice-skating as excellent. None of these recognitions simply come naturally. They are all the result of education."[57] In this regard, any view of the natural law that diminishes the significance of moral education within community, as if the natural law could simply be discovered intuitively, without any direction from others, will fail.

Ever a critic of the capitalistic mindset, McCabe suggests that moral education in the climate of capitalism, undergirded as it is by an Enlightenment vision, is virtually nonexistent. We live "in a society whose predominant ideology or theory of itself is that there is not, or should not be, any such tradition of moral education…. Society, says the conventional wisdom, exists to protect us from each other, to keep the peace between people with quite divergent views of the good life…. Friendship and love do not come within the purview of society as such. They are too personal and too sacred for the marketplace."[58] Indeed, McCabe believes that only as this description of society fails is room yet available for the continued existence of "ethics." There is no ethics unless there exist traditions in which people continue to be educated into the "sort of life that is becoming to a human being."

The "liberal ideology" behind this modern vision "is unfair to its world"—indeed, very fortunately, its world exceeds it. McCabe believes that "[t]here is, in fact a great deal of shared moral belief and perception handed down in various groups within our society, although, because it is unrecognized or disowned or sentimentalized, it is undoubtedly being eroded." The handing down of these traditions is not only vital work, but it is complicated and multifaceted. It "is not handed down simply in words. It is handed down in institutions and practices."[59] As such, we receive it critically; and as we do, as we change its words and ideas and practices, we change the fundamental structures of human living.

This last point is one McCabe accents, far more than Pinckaers. A complicated structure supports his *Law, Love and Language*—a book that purports to introduce ethics, all the while that it challenges its typical categories of analysis. McCabe begins by relating ethics to love, then stretches and complicates his initial points as he proceeds through ethics as law and language—and then returns at the end of the book to love. His treatment of ethics as law, then, is not meant to be final. This comes especially clear as he ends the chapter:

---

[57] McCabe, *Good Life*, 9
[58] McCabe, *Good Life*, 10.
[59] McCabe, *Good Life*, 9-10

> The criticism I have to make of this theory of ethics as law will appear in the next chapter [on language]. Its weakness, as I see it, is its too ready assumption that mankind as a unity exists "by nature." It seems to me that human unity is something towards which we move, a goal of history. We need to take seriously that mankind is in one way self-creative, that since our unity is linguistic as well as biological, it is not simply given to us but also made by us.[60]

It is important to see that, for McCabe, natural law cannot simply be about individual or even societal excellence, but must also move us to live together with all other human beings in community.

The "idea of the natural law depends on being somehow able to see humanity itself on the analogy of a society bound together in friendship."[61] This is a high demand. McCabe notes that while it is "implicit in the Christian Gospel," it is "not philosophically perspicuous."[62] One might note, for instance, that even though Aristotle believed that friendship was the glue that held states together, he did not think that all members of the human species were required to see all other members as friends. Indeed, his claims about friendship applied most explicitly to Athenians—even *some* Athenians. (After all, Aristotle advocated for the infanticide of deformed infants.[63])

For McCabe, this unity is a new kind, since human beings relate to one another in a new way, not simply biologically as a species (in the sense that we are born from one another or can reproduce with one another), but as language users. All sentient animals communicate; this is because they see things in the world as significant to them—as sheep (rightly) see a wolf as dangerous—and respond to this. However, this reaches a new level for members of the human species: With them, "communication reaches the point of being linguistic, that is to say, man is able to some extent create the media through which he makes his world significant. These media have their roots in the sensuous life of man and their creation is the history of a community leading into biographies, which are themselves the histories of minor communities."[64]

For McCabe, an animal species is a unity, or community; it is not simply a logical class in the way that all red things belong to the "class" of red things. We manufacture or stipulate the unity of the class of red things with our minds; by contrast, an animal species is "a physical structure extending over time and space, beginning in evolutionary history and spreading throughout some area of the world." Within the

---

[60] McCabe, *Law,* 67.
[61] McCabe, *Good Life,* 13.
[62] McCabe, *Good Life,* 13.
[63] Aristotle, *Politics*, trans. Ernest Barker (Oxford: Oxford University, 1995), 1335b.
[64] McCabe, *Law,* 90.

species it makes sense to say that individual members have a function vis-à-vis the species: "a particular member of the species exists by being born of that species and its function can be seen as preserving and transmitting the genes that characterize the species."[65]

Animal species are governed by laws related to the form of their life and its continued existence. As Aquinas would have it, this is none other than God's eternal law to which all contingent beings are subject. Importantly, there is no correspondence between this law and what sometimes might appear to be a law imposed upon such creatures by human beings.[66] While we may care for, or, often enough, abuse non-human animals, we do not give them laws. "Man cannot impose laws on irrational beings, however much they may be subject to him. But he can impose laws on rational beings subject to him, in so far as by his command or pronouncement of any kind, he imprints on their minds a rule which is a principle of action."[67] In this last sentence Aquinas is referring to human or positive law which extends the natural law in human governance. And of course, natural law is the means by which God rules us (as opposed to God's other creatures); it is the eternal law extended to fit the particular kind of creatures human beings are.

This distinction between the sort of species or grouping we human beings are as compared with other created species is important to McCabe. The difference comes with language, which also comes with rationality. "It is characteristic of human animals to deploy symbols, to live in the structure we can broadly call language. What we call 'mind' is having the capacity to live in such structures."[68] But, importantly, language is not static; far from it, since, after all, it is a symbol system we have made up. This, in fact, is a further implication of the distinction between the human species and other animal species we are otherwise familiar with. Animals, such as sheep, *find* things in the world meaningful (e.g., wolves are dangerous and so the smell of

---

[65] McCabe, *Good Life*, 66.

[66] This is an important point particularly when we are called to consider in our own time, much more than in Aquinas's: What is the right sort of relation between human beings and non-human animals? Its implication is that non-human animals are never our "subjects." We do not rule them in the manner of law: they receive their laws directly from their maker. Of course we can understand some of the laws by which they live, perhaps better than they can (conceptually better, of course, not experientially) and as such assist their specie's life. But when we do this, we do not become their lords. This is one reason why the intentional creation of entirely new species, particularly if this is done for human benefit, should give us pause.

[67] *ST* I-II q. 93, a. 5.

[68] McCabe, *Good Life*, 67.

a wolf is frightening). By contrast, "[w]e make meanings; we do not just find the world meaningful in certain ways."[69]

That we have this distinctive relation with language, and with one another through language, makes the human species different. For one, it makes us free in the sense that we can, through language, represent the world to ourselves in more than one way, and so also choose what we do based on one or the other representation. It also makes us more dependent, since we cannot have this freedom, which gives us each our distinctiveness, without receiving it. "A linguistic community is a special sort of grouping in a very radical sense, for it changes the meaning of the word 'grouping'…. In the new kind of grouping… what the part receives from the whole—language and rationality, the symbols in which she can represent herself to herself—are precisely what makes possible her specifically human kind of individuality."[70]

Like Pinckaers, McCabe sees Enlightenment ideas of politics and sociality as looming obstacles to any truthful articulation of who we are and how we are related. Such thinking always mistakenly begins by positing "individuals" who "come together initially for mutual support and protection to form a society." But "such a view is incoherent because it supposes these individuals to be already in possession of what only society could provide—institutions such as language, contract, agreement, and so on."[71] By contrast, McCabe's view—which seems paradoxical at first, but becomes much less so upon reflection—is that we become individuals only by more fully belonging.

> It is through belonging to the community that you can make of yourself the kind of person you are—so that you are not just passively made but actually make yourself, determine your life and character. In this way you make yourself the kind of person who can yet more make herself, whose life is more and more her own. This is, to speak generally, the role or task or function that belongs to being human. It is the task of entering more into the life of the community so that you can enter yet more.[72]

McCabe does not believe that individuality separates one off from community life. To the contrary, individuality properly understood always includes the life of virtue, for virtues are precisely those dispositions that one needs to live well as the specific kinds of creatures we are, in our dependency and individuality. Expressed in this context, "virtues are dispositions to enter into community, not to be absorbed in some lifeless way by a collective, but to develop those specifically

---

[69] McCabe, *Good Life*, 68.
[70] McCabe, *Good Life*, 27.
[71] McCabe, *Good Life*, 26.
[72] McCabe, *Good Life*, 28-9.

symbolic, linguistic, rational relationships with others which we can sum up in the word 'friendship' and which are characteristic of the grouping of human animals."[73]

We return here to the notion of friendship which McCabe connects essentially to the natural law: "The idea of natural law depends on being somehow able to see humanity itself on the analogy of a society bound together in friendship." To "see" this unity, however, is not to claim it already fully exists. Indeed, natural law thinking can be plagued by a "too ready assumption that mankind as a unity exists 'by nature'."[74]

Natural law, we must recall, is not static but rather developing; it is always on the way to virtue. So it is that the promise of natural law is both extended and complicated by the features of the linguistic human animal McCabe has worked to display. This is partly because "as communication becomes more intense, it becomes more isolated"—a point that is illustrated by the fact that "the development of communication, the growth of human culture, is not a simple or a single story."[75] The story of Babel in Genesis 11 marks this point—and the story of Pentecost in Acts 2 acknowledges it, at the same time that it treats it as not the final word.

McCabe refers us at this crucial point to the "biblical view" in which we are presented "with the idea that man is *summoned*, that he is called to a destiny, that, in fact, his history has meaning." With this comes the idea of autobiography, of having a story, one that each of us has individually, and also which tribes or nations might write. But this story is importantly not at present write-able or tell-able. In fact, "the biblical view of man is that he *will be able* to write a history of mankind."[76] In the terms of Christian theology, this is an eschatological affirmation. Expressed in McCabe's language:

> Men are called to become mankind, that in Christ we are able to create mankind. "In this way we are all to come to unity in our faith and in our knowledge of the Son of God, until we become the perfect Man, fully mature with the fullness of Christ himself" (Eph. 4:13). However fragmented the human race may be at the moment—and this fragmentation which amounts to a deafness to the summons of God is seen as sin—it is moving towards a unity, a point of view from which its history will be intelligible. Such a moment can only take place through what I have earlier called revolutionary change; not by mere progress

---

[73] McCabe, *Good Life*, 29.

[74] Both of these points are quoted above. They are from, respectively, McCabe, *The Good life*, 13, and *Law, Love and Language*, 67.

[75] McCabe, *Law*, 111.

[76] McCabe, *Law*, 112-13. The translation of Ephesians is from the Jerusalem Bible.

along established lines, but by radical transformation of the lines themselves.[77]

It is perhaps most fitting to see natural law as like a *summons*. This summons does not come to us in opposition to our created natures; indeed, it resonates with the basic needs and desires of the human animal.

In this way, law evidently does not oppose virtue; as Porter repeatedly points out, virtue and natural law are inextricably linked. As Pinckaers makes clearer, however, the summons is the first term in a long series, in the long process of formation that is the moral life. The natural inclinations to which the law speaks are seeds that must develop, in a distinctively human way, which is also for Pinckaers a "spiritual" way. This draws the natural law forward, not only to the Decalogue but to the new law in Christ. As McCabe's treatment has just illustrated, however, we cannot suppose that this comes simply as a matter of course, following on our human nature, given as a biological species. The unity to which the law ultimately points is not given but rather developing; indeed, it is eschatological. The change it requires of us along the way is not only creative and, as such, free, it is also revolutionary. [M]

---

[77] McCabe does not shy away from the longstanding Christian claim that to ignore the summons is to sin, as St. Paul indicates in Romans 1:19-20.

Journal of Moral Theology, Vol. 5, No. 1 (2016): 169-189

R e v i e w   E s s a y
O n   t h e   S o c i a l   P r o b l e m   o f   F a m i l y

Homes for Conviviality

David Matzko McCarthy

N HIS *TOOLS FOR CONVIVIALITY*, IVAN ILLICH proposes that institutions reach a turning point (a watershed) in their development
and dominance when they become the source of as many social
ills as they, at one time, set out to resolve.[1] His analysis comes to
mind in relationship to the contemporary American family, especially
after an examination of Robert Putnam's *Our Kids: The American
Dream in Crisis*.[2] In Catholic social thought, family—in the post-industrial era—is understood to be in crisis, but it is defended and hailed
as a focal institution for the renewal of a just society.[3] However, families, according to Putnam, reflect and magnify an ever increasing social inequality in the United States. If families were at some point a
solution, they now have become part of the problem.

This essay presupposes that household, family, and marriage have
a social vocation—a natural, outward trajectory in forming networks
of families, extended kinships, and neighborhood networks.[4] A notable example of this view is provided by Julie Hanlon Rubio who has
done considerable work on "the social significance of practices in the
home."[5] In Rubio's phrasing, the preposition "in" is indispensable; the
social role is internal to the flourishing (self-actualization) of the
household. In the words of John Paul II, "far from being closed in on
itself, the family is by nature and vocation open to other families and

---

[1] Ivan Illich, *Tools of Conviviality* (New York: Harper & Row, 1973), 1-9.
[2] Robert D. Putnam, *Our Kids: The American Dream in Crisis* (New York: Simon and Schuster, 2015).
[3] See Leo XIII, *Rerum Novarum* (Vatican City: Libreria Editrice Vaticana, 1891), nos. 13-14.
[4] This essay is a consideration of the thesis of *Sex and Love in the Home* (Eugene: Wipf & Stock, 2011) in the sense that this social role of family is "natural."
[5] Julie Hanlon Rubio, *Family Ethics* (Washington, D.C.: Georgetown University Press, 2010), 56. See also, Rubio, "Does Family Conflict with Community?" *Theological Studies* 58, no. 4 (1997): 597-617; "Animals, Evil, and Family Meals," *Journal of Moral Theology* vol. 3, no. 2 (2014): 35-53.

to society."[6] In other words, household and family have a social purpose, which is embedded in the nature of family.

If this outward trajectory of family is assumed as a given, the difficulty for Catholic social thought and task of this essay is to determine in what sense (if at all) this vision of the household is both natural and credibly social. To evaluate the "natural" family as social, this article will review an account of family offered by Paul Bloom, a psychologist and cognitive scientist, who places himself within the materialist stream of evolutionary biology. In *Just Babies,* Bloom frames the inherent value of kinship in terms of "genetic overlap" (genetic survival), and he frames social, in-group connections in terms of "mutual benefit" (ultimately for genetic survival).[7] By his account, the nature of family is internally directed. In other words, insular kinship relations are natural, and external/social relations are based on their utility for serving kinship/genetic relations.[8] In sum, claims embedded in Catholic thought about a natural social role of family do not seem plausible within the account of nature developed by Bloom (and a whole tradition of cognitive/evolutionary science).

Putnam's *Our Kids* presents similar problems for outwardly directed, social demarcations of family life. The problem is not that he makes a case for naturally inward-looking family. Putnam's immediate concern is social inequality as it affects childhood development and continues to increase amid the disintegration of poor families and the evaporation of opportunities available to poor children.[9] Putnam shows that, in contrast, good working, healthy families are organized for (we could say "regulated by") the purposes of the upward mobility of their members, that is, governed by socio-economic success. Embedded within his narrative (but not directly articulated by him) is the social detachment of the upwardly mobile family. By definition, mobility requires detachment. Historically, the social mobility of the in-

---

[6] John Paul II, *Familiaris consortio* (Vatican City: Libreria Editrice Vaticana, 1981), no. 42.

[7] Paul Bloom, *Just Babies: The Origins of Good and Evil* (New York: Crown Publishers, 2013), 178.

[8] The terms and phrases with which Bloom articulates his inferences from science give weight to Michael Hanby's historical and philosophical explication that the intellectual framework of evolutionary materialism comes from a preceding tradition of political philosophy. See Hanby, "Creation Without Creationism: Toward a Theological Critique of Darwinism," *Communio* 30 (Winter 2003): 654-94. Bloom frames familial and social relations—constructed in terms of survival—in a way that is at least as old as Thomas Hobbes's *Leviathan* (1651). See Hobbes, *Leviathan,* ed. Richard Tuck (Cambridge: Cambridge University Press, 1991), 117-121.

[9] Putnam, in *Our Kids,* attributes an increasing family-based inequality on "the collapse of the working class family" (244) and a "stagnant economy that has seen virtually no real growth in decades for the less educated part of our population" (246).

dustrial and post-industrial middle class requires leaving behind a "positional" structure and stable social roles.[10] Although Putnam's concerns are admirably social, he frames family as an interpersonal institution that is driven and judged by self-interest.

One way to provide a contrast to a socially detached family is to frame the family as a social agent. This approach, generally speaking, is characteristic of Catholic social thought; the family has a role that is framed by the common good. To be fair to Putnam, he presents obvious and commendable concerns and solutions pertaining to the social inequality of families. But, in his account, families are merely private. To call the family a social agent points to an important difference. When individuals (rather than families) are agents, they develop a sense of belonging to a household and a sense of interdependence that we identify as family. Family, in this frame, is a free-standing unit (that may need the assistance of social services if it cannot stand on its own). Putnam draws on this common view that families send individuals out into social and economic life to be agents. When families are agents, in contrast, they develop a sense of belonging to a neighborhood and community-formed place. Families, if interdependent, are connected to other intermediate (subsidiary) institutions.

An illuminating metaphor for this kind of corporate agency is the workshop and the craft that is developed within it. Far from imagining family as a romantic place of interpersonal love, the workshop names connections based on common work, common standards of judgment, and the membership cultivated through common life in a place. Far from imagining family in an ideal world, the metaphor of workshop highlights elements of family life that are often present—in various degrees—in ordinary life. Certainly, parents are concerned to equip children for what they will need to earn a good living. But there is more. There is present within family an often unarticulated Aristotelian understanding that faring well in the market is hollow and self-defeating if one does not also live well.[11] Living well, however, is typically conceived in a personalist, privatized manner—often reduced to matters like loving one's family. In this privatized context, it is as important as ever to see within family a generative social role, as place where social interdependence and engagement is produced.

---

[10] The outline of the "positional" family structure is developed by Mary Douglas in her *Natural Symbols: Explorations in Cosmology* (New York: Pantheon Books, 1982), 19-36. A historical account of the social detachment of the middle class can be found in Hannah Arendt, *The Origins of Totalitarianism* (New York: Schocken Books, 2004), 167-209.

[11] Aristotle, *Nicomachean Ethics*, trans. Martin Ostwald (New York: Macmillan Publishing, 1962), Bk 1.7-9.

Catholic social thought gives us resources to identity and promote the convivial nature of the household. In his *Tools for Conviviality*, Illich uses the term conviviality to refer to sociability, interdependence, and social capital, which strengthen the bonds necessary for human flourishing.[12] He makes "tools" the subject of conviviality because he is concerned to understand the social function of technology. He sees conviviality as the benchmark by which to judge the usefulness of tools. When any given form of technology extends to a point where it undermines conviviality, it has reached its limit of usefulness. This measure of conviviality is applicable to family (and this idea of sociality as a measure is where my use of Illich's *Tools* will end). American culture by and large is at a point where family is as likely to disengage from social membership as it is to cultivate it. As a tool for upward mobility, family is self-referential; it is inclined to be only temporarily fixed within a place or bound with specific sets of social relations. As a context for conviviality, family is much more like a workshop; it is set within reciprocal roles and in a place. This tension between the detachment/mobility of family and fixed social engagement provides the perspective from which to consider works of natural and social scientific considerations of family.

NATURAL FAMILY

In considering *Just Babies* by Paul Bloom, I hope to present a standard type of view from the perspective of the natural sciences (i.e., cognitive science and evolutionary biology).[13] Bloom fits the purpose.[14] He draws on standard research in cognitive psychology. He claims scientific materialism as indisputably true, and he assumes the moral perspective of cosmopolitanism.[15] In each regard—basic scientific claims, a materialist philosophy, and moral universalism—Bloom

---

[12] Illich, *Tools for Conviviality*, 10-45.

[13] Bloom, *Just Babies*, 1-6. Also Bloom's *Descartes' Baby: How the Science of Childhood Development Explains What Makes Us Human* (New York: Basic Books, 2004), xi-xii.

[14] See a review of *Just Babies* by John Whitfield: "Psychology: The Appetite for Right," *Nature* 502, no. 7473 (October 31, 2013): 622-623. Whitfield notes that Bloom represents standard research, compliments him, and then does not comment on the book much further. Renee M. Borges, "Just Babies: The Origins of Good and Evil," *Current Science* 107, no. 2 (July 25, 2014): 306-307, has two criticisms. The first is that he holds too closely to accepted views. She is interested in an alternative approach. The second criticism is that Bloom strays from the research to inquire about broader moral implications. Both criticisms indicate that Bloom is a good source for the discussion in this section. In addition, if TED talks are an indication of cultural currency, Bloom has given two. See www.ted.com/speakers/paul_bloom.

[15] In a general way, he takes the approach of Kwame Anthony Appiah, *Cosmopolitanism: Ethics in the World of Strangers* (New York: Norton, 2006). See Bloom, *Just Babies*, 129-30.

represents the achievements, limitations, and the moral framework of a prominent approach among scientists.[16]

Further, Bloom's *Just Babies* presents a moral perspective that parallels Catholic social thought. Catholic thought understands the family as formed by natural, internal bonds, but it also holds that the caring and loving relations of kinship ought to be directed outward. They ought to form the fabric of wider (but still local) institutions and to invest in the social good. Good families form the foundation for good people, who work for the common good. Bloom begins in the same place. But, for him, our natures and the natural bonds of family become problems to be overcome; our familial bonds, because naturally directed inward, will have to be countered by a commitment to rational principles. Bloom's view—although materialist—appeals to a form of reason that is untethered from material relations. He must shift from materialism to idealism in order get where he needs to go. Our reason (set within an otherwise non-rational reality) must trump our natures.

From a consideration of Bloom's framing of the problem, this section considers scientific findings about families and early childhood development. The findings are striking for a moral theologian: Bloom finds that it is indelibly part of our natures to see and experience moral order; we naturally know the world as ordered to moral ends. He finds that we are natural Aristotelians. This section also takes a critical look at the limitations of Bloom's philosophical assumptions. An extended look at Bloom's presuppositions and anti-metaphysical claims is necessary in order to disentangle his presumptions from the findings of his research. Finally, I suggest that theology is well suited to draw on Bloom's conclusions, where ironically he is not. The fundamental point of contention is whether or not human material nature (not an abstracted/idealist rationality) is ordered to ends that we reason to be good. In other words, the issue in contention is the natural law.

Concerning moral order, there is, within Bloom's project, a tension between science and the goals of his moral cosmopolitanism. As noted, the tension corresponds to the challenges of and call for a social role of family (in Catholic social thought). On one hand, evolutionary and cognitive science indicate that we humans are parochial. We have a

---

[16] Bloom represents not all scientists or even a majority, but a prominent, perhaps the most prominent, line of thought about human nature. A 2009 Pew study finds that a slight majority of scientists believe in God. See "Scientists and Belief," Pew Research Center (November 5, 2009), www.pewforum.org/2009/11/05/scientists-and-belief/. The implications of this belief obviously vary according to individual scientist. In any case, scientific materialism cannot be claimed as *the* scientific view. The interesting conflict is not between science and religion, but among scientists about materialism as a philosophy and the limits of science as a discipline. Also see Elaine Howard Ecklund, *Science vs. Religion: What Scientists Really Think* (Oxford: Oxford University Press, 2010).

natural kin and in-group insularity, complemented by hostility to strangers. On the other hand, Bloom's cosmopolitanism pushes us (his readers/human beings) to a recognition of universal human community and a universal moral framework—detached from particular communities and founded on principles of impartiality. The goal of universal moral standards is, in fact, more than Bloom's "push." It is the very frame for his analysis. He devotes an entire chapter to the problem of our natural prejudices and parochialism, titled "Others." At the end of the chapter, he calls us to use our intelligence and will to "overcome those [natural] gut feelings and appetites."[17]

This tension in Bloom's work is representative of a stream of cognitive/evolutionary science in at least two ways. First, he thinks of natural human morality in terms of feelings as opposed to what might be called rational inclinations. He frequently cites Adam Smith's *The Theory of Moral Sentiments*; he proposes that cognitive psychology is a good fit with the moral philosophy associated with David Hume.[18] Bloom's own moral reasoning will suffer from the same difficulties associated with Hume. (On this point, more will be discussed below.) The second way that Bloom represents a well-established stream of scientific thought is his push toward a seemingly unnatural universalism. Scientists strive for a view of things that is abstracted from particular social, cultural, historical points of view. Molecules do not have a social context. The same will be the case for human beings, if a scientist were to claim no other point of view for understanding human life (and most do have some other standpoint). Inevitably (but ironically), scientists who claim a thoroughly scientific point of view for morality will eventually embrace idealism (i.e., reason is constructed apart from our bodily natures). The human beings of this kind of scientific observation are abstracted from particular contexts and changing variables. In this frame of reference, the rational human being will be best understood when set free of particularities.

In sum, Bloom represents a scientific approach—predicated on detachment—that is unavoidably in opposition to what it finds as the natural attachments of family. As a scientist, he knows that natural bonds establish hostility to outsiders. But also as a scientist, he is committed to abstracting the human being from particular contexts and parochial bonds. This scientific frame matches his moral cosmopolitanism, so that our parochial natures (kinship bonds) establish *the* basic moral problem of human life.[19] Bloom explains that "the amoral force

---

[17] Bloom, *Just Babies,* 130.
[18] Bloom, *Just Babies,* 208.
[19] As an aside, it is worth noting that John Paul II attends to the issue of family and moral formation in his *Letter to Families*, but without a introducing a natural hostility

of natural selection might have instilled within us some of the foundation for moral thought and moral action."[20] Genetic survival takes the lead; "there is a strong reproductive benefit to being biased to favor friends and family over strangers, and one would expect this to be incorporated as part of an innate moral sense."[21] How will we move from natural parochialism to tolerance and a universal ethics? Bloom's work has a penetrating and pioneering tone: He sets the origin of morality (kinship) against common human morality.

However, Bloom's analysis would have appeared far less probing and avant-garde were he to have engaged Stephen J. Pope's *The Evolution of Altruism and the Ordering of Love* as well as his *Human Evolution and Christian Ethics*.[22] In *The Evolution of Altruism*, Pope shows the connections between evolutionary theory and Thomas Aquinas's order of love (e.g., *Summa Theologica* II-II q. 26). Pope observes that the shift from a narrow in-group perspective, "love our friends and hate our enemies," requires a commitment to the human community—a recognition of a common bond (and being) that is both reasonable and a matter of conviction.[23] That is, the teleological claim about the good of human community exceeds empirical evidence but accords with our ordered, rational nature. Within Christian theology, such a claim about nature and human community is made sacramentally and eschatologically.[24] The fraternal and sororal bonds provide a metaphor for wider relations and the unity of humanity as whole. Natural human community is believed to be ordered to an end in human community, an outward trajectory of completion, which both transcends nature as we have it and brings nature as we have it to its fulfillment. This kind of analogical transition (a form that is patterned inward and outward) is not an option for Bloom. His options are philosophically narrow.

In any case, Bloom's findings about the natural bonds of family appear to be cutting edge, philosophically, because he engages only utilitarians and deontologists. He deals almost exclusively with philosophers who set the moral life in terms of abstract relationships—

---

to non-kin. "[T]he genealogy of the person is inscribed in the very biology of generation." John Paul II, *Letter to Families* (Vatican City: Libreria Editrice Vaticana, 1994), no. 9.

[20] Bloom, *Just Babies*, 16.

[21] Bloom, *Just Babies*, 172.

[22] Stephen J. Pope, *The Evolution of Altruism and the Ordering of Love* (Washington, D.C.: Georgetown University Press, 1994); *Human Evolution and Christian Ethics* (Cambridge: Cambridge University Press, 2007).

[23] Pope, *Human Evolution and Christian Ethics*, 309.

[24] Herbert McCabe, *What is Ethics All About?* (Washington, D.C.: Corpus Publications, 1969), 145-53.

that "[develop] general and abstract principles... by thinking about examples with strangers, and then [extending] these principles to family and friends."[25] Why does Bloom not deal with any other approach? My first thought was that he was simply reproducing what he knew of moral philosophy from a course he took as an undergraduate. Then I noticed an endnote where he directs readers to Michael Sandel's *Justice: What's the Right Thing to Do?* for a clearer understanding of utilitarianism and deontology.[26] If he has drawn on Sandel for understanding these theories, then he also knows that Aristotelian alternatives exist and could have been pursued. The reason for his focus on utilitarianism and deontology, one discovers at the end of *Just Babies*, is that these theories provide the theoretical setting where the book is intended to lead us—to "a commitment to impartial principles"—principles that are rational apart from (and to a degree in opposition to) our natural inclinations.[27] Here, he cites Peter Singer, who introduces a counter-structure of abstract reason to lay on the top of natural inclinations.[28]

Bloom, in *Just Babies*, follows the path provided by Singer in *The Expanding Circle*.[29] In terms of a scientifically framed natural causality, bonds of kin and the basis of morality are not the result of the agency of persons. They are caused by a natural drive of genes to survive and carry on.[30] As far as I can tell, this claim about genes and a natural bonding of kin is not, strictly speaking, empirical. It is a logical inference: If there is a genetic drive to replicate and survive, then it makes sense that kinship bonds are a drive of genes to advance themselves. From here, it is an empirical observation that in-group (non-kinship) bonds are often set up as a perimeter, an outer ring of defense against strangers. At this perimeter, natural drives are confronted by Bloom's scientific reasoning, with its obvious preference for thinking

---

[25] Bloom, *Just Babies*, 171.
[26] Michael Sandel, *Justice: What's the Right Thing to Do?* (New York: Farrar, Strauss, and Giroux, 2009).
[27] *Just Babies*, 217.
[28] Peter Singer, *The Expanding Circle: Ethics and Sociobiology* (New York: Farrar, Straus, and Giroux, 1981), 87-124.
[29] Singer, *The Expanding Circle*, 54-86. The criticisms here of Bloom have already been directed at Singer's *The Expanding Circle*. See Philip Hefner, "Sociobiology, Ethics, and Theology," *Zygon* 19:2 (June 1984): 185-207. Hefner asks of Singer, "What could it mean to transcend our genes, turn against them, or be freed from slavery to them—particularly since the organism that turns against is thoroughly dependent on genetic evolution?" (198).
[30] Bloom's sets of questions and problems correspond to the approach developed by Richard Dawkins in his *The Selfish Gene* (Oxford: Oxford University Press, 1976), who begins by announcing the scientific discovery that the meaning of life is the good of the gene.

as opposed to reflexive feeling and its universal point of view as opposed to parochial attachments. Bloom asserts (claims as a rational imperative) that "we can use our intelligence to override our coalitional biases when we feel that they have started to run amok."[31] He does not spell out how we manage to "feel" that our natural affections are in error. In any case, our reason knows which feeling is right.

Bloom seems to notice, but quickly passes over, the philosophical tangles introduced by his rational call to override our natural inclinations and desires. In Bloom's view, there is a clear grounding for natural affections but no natural (i.e., material) basis for moral rationality.[32] Later, I will ask if it is possible to take his findings in an Aristotelian rather than his own Humean direction. The point of this question is an observation that is likely to be obvious to a moral theologian set anywhere within the broad Aristotelian and Thomist traditions. Bloom finds that human beings have naturally teleological habits of thinking, but he has little means (within his own frame) to understand them as anything other than odd and useless (scientifically speaking). In short, he excludes (but needs) the ability to establish a moral teleology—moral purposes and ends. He sees natural capacities in terms of a genetic goal (survival). But what we might think of as natural, but rational tendencies and goals, he sees as accidental, albeit sometimes useful byproducts.[33] In other words, a moral theologian who takes natural capacities at face value (as capacities that direct us to real ends) is more likely than Bloom to be able to follow (and not gloss over) his findings about natural moral reasoning.

Before attending to the scientific findings about the moral life of babies, a few more points should be made about Bloom's philosophy. It has already been noted that Bloom's fundamental claim about morality is not based on testable evidence (to determine what genes want)[34] as much as it is an inference from what is evident: Reproduction and biological inheritance create a special bond (a claim held also

---

[31] Bloom, *Just Babies*, 129.

[32] See Bloom, *Just Babies*, 208-9.

[33] See Bloom's distillation of his *Descartes' Baby* in "Is God an Accident?" *The Atlantic Monthly* 296:5 (December 2005), 105-12.

[34] In making his claim that genetic drives form the basis of morality, Bloom has to personify genes. "There is no hard and fast difference, insofar as genes are concerned, between an individual and its blood relatives. In this way, selfish genes can create altruistic animals, animals that love others just as they love themselves" (*Moral Life of Babies*, 16-17). Apart from the intention and creativity given to genes, it is hard to know how Bloom uses "love" in a way that applies to all animals. His grammatical and semantic structure parallels a nineteenth century Romantic. Nature is the agent, and its works inspire wonder. "I marvel how Nature could ever find space / For so many strange contrasts in one human face..." (William Wordsworth, "A Character," *William Wordsworth: The Poems*, Volume One, Edited by John O. Hayden [New Haven: Yale University Press, 1977], 261).

by the Catholic tradition, particularly Thomists).[35] Bloom admits that, philosophically, his own claims are driven by his commitment to materialism, which he does not argue for, but takes as self-evident.[36] Before he explains his findings in *Just Babies*, Bloom introduces a second presumption about morality. A core of morality can be found that "transcends space and time,"[37] and morality is, at its core, based on "emotions and desires" and "gut feeling."[38] In short, as already noted, he takes the side of the Scottish Enlightenment.

Bloom's appeal to David Hume and Adam Smith seems to be simply a matter of course for him,[39] but there are reasons, given his experiments and set of findings, to wonder if Smith and Hume are as well suited to his project as he seems to think. Already mentioned is the tension between affective kinship and Bloom's cosmopolitanism, which sets rational control over our natural in-group feelings. The point that I want to get to now is about his actual findings. He reports on the results of experiments that do not necessarily evince an affective foundation for ethics. If we were to start with the findings of cognitive science, we would move in an Aristotelian or Thomist direction.

For instance, Bloom reports on experiments pertaining to justice and fairness (experiments performed by others and by him and his colleagues). Some of the experiments attempt to elicit an emotional reaction, when, for example, children become distressed because they are denied candy as a reward.[40] But other experiments display no affective component *per se*. Some experiments measure whether babies reach for a puppet who displays helping behavior over a puppet who displays obstructing behavior.[41] No one will claim that the reaching of a baby is a matter of rational principle. But, likewise, the reaction of these babies, as described by Bloom, is not obviously affective either. In an adult, we would say that choosing to avoid an obstructing agent is rational. Likewise, with babies: Watch a baby who grasps for objects to put into her mouth. The action looks much more like a nascent use of intelligence (investigation through the senses) than it does an

---

[35] Stephen Pope, *Evolution of Altruism*, 77-92.
[36] Like many materialists, he is against a theological view that theologians also hold to be untenable. See Bloom, *Just Babies*, 188-9.
[37] Bloom, *Just Babies*, 10.
[38] Bloom, *Just Babies*, 9, 13; see also, 4-6, 40-1, 56-7.
[39] Bloom offers no reason for his turn to Smith and Hume. I can suppose that Bloom prefers the Scottish Enlightenment for two reasons. First, Hume claims the new Newtonian science for himself. Second, modern science overcomes Aristotelian science, so that it would take an independent and considerably creative scientist to reject Aristotelian science on one hand and yet support an Aristotelian/teleological view of the human being on the other. We do have such scientists among us; they tend to be physicists or they draw heavily on quantum physics (which moves far beyond Newton).
[40] Bloom, *Just Babies*, 78-80.
[41] Bloom, *Just Babies*, 97-8.

affective response to her surroundings. The reaching of the babies seems to indicate a capacity to know, which implies an intellectual capacity to judge good and bad. In sum, the experiments and observations of babies that are described by Bloom offer interesting findings, but they do not support his philosophical claims—his materialism, his defense of Smith and Hume, or his cosmopolitanism.

Bloom finds (through his own studies and those of others in the field) that we have moral capacities and tendencies that come as "natural endowments," prior to social and cultural formation. In sum, they are:

- a moral sense—some capacity to distinguish between kind and cruel actions
- empathy and compassion—suffering at the pain of those around us and the wish to make this pain go away
- a rudimentary sense of fairness—a tendency to favor equal divisions of resources
- a rudimentary sense of justice—a desire to see good actions rewarded and bad actions punished.[42]

Bloom's findings are striking for their similarities to accounts of natural law that are framed by basic capacities which are developed as virtues. Not only do items on Bloom's list appear to be as proto-rational as they are affective, but they also suggest a natural teleological sense: We see order and purpose as an integral part of our experiences and knowledge of the world.

This natural sense of internal design and purpose is the topic of an earlier work by Bloom, *Descartes' Baby*. In that work, Bloom sets out to explain why materialism—although patently evident to the evolutionary biologist—does not come naturally to human beings.[43] Bloom, in other words, hopes to undo and recast the interpretation of ourselves and our world that comes most naturally. We are natural Aristotelians. We are naturally inclined to think of who we are in terms of a soul—an inner self that is greater than and gives structure to our material parts.[44] Bloom finds that we naturally understand people and things in terms of intentions, purposes, and an internal "structure"[45]—what to me looks like a sense of form (an essential *telos*) which is not reducible

---

[42] Bloom, *Just Babies*, 5.
[43] Bloom, *Descartes' Baby: How the Science of Child Development Explains What Makes us Human* (New York: Basic Books, 2004), xii-xiii.
[44] Bloom, *Descartes' Baby*, 54-61.
[45] Bloom, *Descartes' Baby*, 16-19, 46-48.

to material elements.[46] Bloom refers to this sense as our "intuitive dualism," but he is overstating the case. One need not posit a separate spiritual world in order to identify purpose in our natures (or purpose in nature in general according to physicist Paul Davies).[47] The issue of understanding Bloom and the findings of cognitive science (at least his version of them) is not that he reduces what we can know to matter, but that he has a reductionist view of matter and human material life itself.

At this juncture, the question about Aristotle can come to the fore: What might Bloom's findings offer if they were set within an end-oriented rather than Humean frame? As noted, Bloom reports on experiments that show natural human perception and understanding to be far more Aristotelean (teleological) and far less Humean or materialist. Hume, it is worth noting, did agree on this point—that we might be natural Aristotelians. In "Of the Passions" (Book Two) of *A Treatise of Human Nature*, he explains that a "strict philosophical eye" is needed to see the passions in what we normally (naturally) see and experience as originating from a faculty of reason. "When... passions are calm, and cause no disorder in the soul, they are very readily taken for the determinations of reason, and are suppos'd to proceed from the same faculty, with that, which judges of truth and falshood."[48] Ironically, Hume—who usually belittles various theoretical glosses on experience—holds that a "strict philosophical eye" is needed to re-interpret what plainly seems to be the case. He holds that what appears to be reason is not. Why? The question of origins, reason or passions, is also a question of purpose. For Hume and Bloom, an appeal to the passions takes purpose out of nature. "Reasoning" is the description we give when identifying a teleological ordering of our intuitions and desires.

This point about reason is accentuated when we consider what Hume takes to be "these certain calm desires and tendencies" which tend to look like reason but are not. "These desires are of two kinds; either certain instincts originally implanted in our natures, such as benevolence and resentment, the love of life, and kindness to children; or the general appetite to good, and aversion to evil, consider'd merely as such."[49] In effect, what Hume calls subtle passions, Aquinas calls natural inclinations, which—because ordered to ends—are rational.[50]

---

[46] For a modern retrieval of a Platonic sense of "form," see Julius Kovesi, *Moral Notions* (London: Routledge & Kegan Paul, 1967).

[47] Paul Davies, *Cosmic Jackpot* (Boston: Houghton Mifflin Company, 2007), 228-39.

[48] David Hume, *A Treatise of Human Nature*, ed. Selby-Bigge (Oxford: Clarendon Press, 1965), 417.

[49] Hume, *A Treatise of Human Nature*, 417.

[50] A good comparison to Hume's discussion of appetites and will is Aquinas's discussion of the internal act of the will in *Summa Theologica* I-II q. 19 a. 3. However, the

The difference is not the moral dispositions that are identified (e.g., appetite to good), but whether or not these tendencies are ordered and capable of being formed (or re-formable) to a purpose.[51]

Bloom's work fits this Humean set of problems precisely. His reason for pulling our moral reasoning out of nature is determined by his commitment to a particular version of evolutionary science. Only genes have genuine goals and purposes. In terms of family, our genes draw us to kin and in-group coalitions; we are naturally hostile to others. However, a "commitment to impartial principles" comes into play in the last pages of *Just Babies*, like a *deus ex machina*, in order to "trump our self-interest."[52] Impartial principles solve the problems of our natures, but Bloom offers no reasons why the problem is a problem. Why is hostility to strangers a problem (if that is what our genes want)? Bloom makes gestures to real evils of racism and genocide, but no more than gestures. He would, no doubt, hold that racism and genocide are irrational. But rationality simply appears on the other (good) side of the gap from our natures (which are inclined toward the evil of racism). In *Just Babies*, moral idealism simply appears in an otherwise materialist world.

Although Bloom's *Just Babies* has obvious philosophical problems, its findings about the moral lives of babies are not only interesting for how we understand moral inclinations, but also important for how they put focus on family as the problem. Cognitive science confirms that human beings have natural capacities for justice and compassion. As far as I can tell, there is no reason (based on his research) to stay with Bloom's claim that affections form the only basis of natural morality. In fact, Bloom's overarching concern to correct our natural parochialism implies the question, "What are these moral capacities for?" Given his own philosophical groundwork, he cannot articulate this question

---

general point about the structure of the inclination is found is the treatise on law, such as *Summa Theologica* I-II q. 90, a. 1; q. 91, a. 6; q. 94, a 2.

[51] In *A Short History of Ethics* (Notre Dame: University of Notre Dame Press, 1998), Alasdair MacIntyre argues that the basic problem with Hume is that he "is for the most part avowedly engaged in explaining why we have the rules that we do and not in any work of criticism" (175). Hume is after the "givens" without any serious consideration with how passions might be (ought to be) developed. Likewise with Adam Smith, "the whole difficulty is engendered by the way the discussion is carried on in two stages. First, human nature is characterized; and moral rules are introduced as an addendum, to be explained as expressions of... the already specified nature. Yet the human nature specified is individualist human nature, unamenable to moral rules" (*A Short History*, 176).

[52] Bloom, *Just Babies*, 217. I use the phrase *deus ex machina* because impartial principles come into play at the end—without knowing where they come from—after a series of other options are shown to have inconsistent results: interpersonal interaction, story, religious belief, and community. Impartial reason resolves the tension without any difficulties, and the book ends.

beyond the drives of gene replication. But as should be clear by now, his inability to connect nature to human reason undermines his own hope to move, morally, beyond our natural parochialism. In short, Bloom resists questions of human ends and purposes. The question of purpose, "What are capacities for?," introduces the possibility of order from the beginning of human life—that human nature is ordered (reasonably) to human community. If, with this point, we take the findings about natural familial bonds seriously, family is the social system where human moral capacities are ordered and ought to be ordered rationally for a broader human good.

In one sense, this claim about the social role of family is common sense. In another, it is not. The findings of cognitive science point to family as a workshop for moral development. The family is characterized by strong ties of membership, which shape the world where our moral capacities are put to work. The common sense is that family provides the place and sets of relationships where a person's moral development is cultivated and expanded. Bloom calls for this expansion, but he does not look to family. Indeed, a striking omission of his research is that he does not think that it is important to take into account the family systems of his test subjects. In his overall cosmopolitan project, he assumes that family is a naturally and inherently self-interested unit. Kinship and in-group ties are the basic problem. This insular view that family is the problem forms another kind of plain sense. Here, we turn to Robert Putnam's *Our Kids*, where family is found to be the context of training for personal advancement and, for this reason, a significant source of social inequality.

SOCIAL HOME

Putnam writes *Our Kids* in order to describe the current crisis of social inequality as well as the contributing social and economic patterns, which have been developing for a number of decades and seem to be continuing unabated. He also proposes constructive responses, based on the evidence.[53] The trends in social inequality are well-known; it is clear that absolute mobility—whether children fare better than their parents—has stalled.[54] Putnam's thesis is that opportunities for social mobility are, not simply stagnant, but "poised to plunge in the years ahead, shattering the American Dream."[55] He hopes to get ahead of conventional research, identifying the coming plunge by

---

[53] For example, Putnam notes that various "marriage policies" have not worked: "I see no clear path to reviving marriage rates among poor Americans." The way forward is to support parents, especially single parents, through anti-poverty programs. *Our Kids*, 244-7.

[54] Putnam, *Our Kids*, 44.

[55] Putnam, *Our Kids*, 45.

looking at current realities—at the institutions and social networks through which social mobility and inequality are mediated. Family is the hub of these networks and institutions. The personal and social development, social capital, education, and life skills that are (or are not) mediated through families to children tend to be determinative for the social and economic opportunities available to them. The crisis of social mobility is also a crisis of families.

My claim, in this section, is that Putnam's *Our Kids* reveals a problem with the prevailing view of the model family. He describes a dissolution of poor and working class families, but he also presents a narrow view of good working families. They are loving and encouraging, but show little concern for the collapse of social and community networks that dominates Putnam's concerns. In Putnam's own analysis, the "plunge" of social mobility and the entrenchment of social inequality present no problems for successful families or how he defines their success. However, if we begin with the common sense findings of cognitive science—that family is the primary moral world for children and that basic human moral capacities are developed there—then the "model" family will cultivate an outward, social orientation. Familial love will be oriented to justice; personal happiness and material success will have as their ends social engagement and community building. Putnam frames the "goods" of family in terms of personal development and well-being.[56] In contrast, Catholic social thought thinks of personal fulfillment in terms of social responsibilities.[57] In this frame, the happy home is oriented to the common good.

Putnam's research poses a challenge to this social conception of family. He shows how families and networks of families mediate, rather than relieve, social inequality. In fact, he admits that marriage and a stable family unit are no longer useful categories in setting out a way forward.[58] For the poor and working class, the operative category is not "family," but the mother.[59] Among the disadvantaged, women raise their children alone or while cohabiting, with no consistent engagement or support of fathers or partners. In contrast, middle and upwardly mobile couples have the means to maintain a stable household, and because of family life, they are better off—personally, economically, socially. Marriage continues to be an aspiration for poor women

---

[56] See, for example, Putnam's description of "Andrew and His Family," *Our Kids*, 50-4.

[57] See John XXIII, *Pacem in terris* (Vatican City: Libreria Editrice Vaticana, 1963), nos. 8-38.

[58] See the studies reported by Andrew J. Cherlin in *The Marriage-Go-Round: The State of Marriage and the Family in America Today* (New York: Vintage Books, 2009), and "Demographic Trends in the United States: A Review of Research in the 2000s," *Journal of Marriage and Family* 72 (June 2010): 403-419.

[59] Putnam, *Our Kids*, 74.

and men, but they lack the means or stability of means to establish and sustain a household. "[M]oms in this context seek romance over marriage as a respite from their everyday poverty and uncertainty."[60] In this context, family stability is hardly a practicable choice. If family is the hub of advantageous social networks, the problem for many of our kids is that this center point is fragmented beyond repair.

I see no reason to dispute Putnam's analysis of the social and economic crisis. Indeed, my point is to extend the analysis from the dissolution of the poor and working class families to the failure of the stable and good working ones. Putnam lists well-known causes for our predicament: the economic stagnation of our postindustrial era, individualism and a lack of investment in local networks and institutions (including marriage), deflation of social capital, social and economic segregation of neighborhoods and schools, and the fact—not only of segregation—but that poor and socially disadvantaged children live in unstable and unsafe neighborhoods (threatened by violence, drugs, and crime) and attend inferior and poorly funded schools.

There is little reason to dispute Putnam's proposals for change. On a possible point of dispute, he does not think that it is worthwhile to pursue policies that attempt to increase the marriage rate and to keep parents together. He explains that there is not much evidence that "even well-designed, well-funded public programs" have had their intended effects.[61] The argument could be made (in response to Putnam) that such marriage policies cannot stand on their own, but can still be effective if part of a whole set of programs and policies (the kind which Putnam outlines). In any case, Putnam recommends aid and tax relief to parents and families. To slow the incarceration rate and restore parents (mainly fathers) to their place in home, Putman joins the call for a reform of our court and prison systems and an emphasis on rehabilitation and restoration—education, job training, and an emphasis on social responsibility. He emphasizes the need for preschool education programs and a corresponding "professional 'coaching' of poor parents."[62] For schools themselves, he finds that "the most promising approaches... involve moving kids, money, and/or teachers to different schools."[63] In this regard, he looks to the success of Catholic schools: Students from poor backgrounds attain high levels of

---

[60] The quotation is a citation by Putnam, *Our Kids*, 74, from Linda M. Burton, "Seeking Romance in the Crosshairs of Multiple-Partner Fertility: Ethnographic Insights on Low-Income Urban and Rural Mothers," *ANNALS of the American Academy of Political and Social Science* 654 (July 2014): 185-212.
[61] Putnam, *Our Kids*, 245.
[62] Putnam, *Our Kids*, 249.
[63] Putnam, *Our Kids*, 251.

achievement, attributable "to the social and moral community within which parochial schools are embedded."[64]

This theme of "social and moral community" is an undercurrent throughout the book. In his chapter on community, Putnam explains that "neighborhood poverty is bad for kids for many reasons, but probably the most important is [a scarcity of] social cohesion and informal social control... cooperation among neighbors... 'collective efficacy'... 'rooted in trust'."[65] Later in the chapter, he will offer two clear solutions: financial, job-generating investments in poor neighborhoods and programs that "move poor families to better neighborhoods."[66] However, in his section on what to do about our social segregation, Putnam begins with schools. "At the permeable boundary between schools and community are afterschool activities, mentors, and above all extracurricular activities." In this regard, he tells the reader, "Close this book, visit your school superintendent." We are to call for an end to "pay-to-play" policies, which limit participation in extracurricular programs and to ask the superintendent what we can to do help the schools "serve poor kids more effectively."[67]

In effect, Putnam recommends a formal, institutional approach. Earlier in the chapter on community, he notes that informal mentoring and networking are important features of stable neighborhoods. But later, he warns that, in fragmented communities, occasional and informal mentoring—the kind prominent in well-functioning neighborhoods—will not work. Informal mentoring depends upon (is "a by-product of") already existing social capital. His analysis makes sense. Informal mentoring cannot carry the burden of "social and moral community." Its occasional character draws on, but does not stabilize, social connectivity. Putnam holds that disadvantaged children and youth need consistent, formal, trained, institutionally supported mentors—from social service organizations and churches. To attend to the gap between advantaged and disadvantaged neighborhoods, families, and schools, Putnam advocates for federal and state programs and policies as well as for consistent, institutional support from stable community organizations like churches.

Well-situated and exemplary families, however, are missing from any part of a solution. *Our Kids* is engaged and compassionate, realistic and practical. For this reason, an unsettling undercurrent runs throughout the book. The aspirations of Putnam's model families are entirely self-referential. In one of his case studies, a mother—indisputably and proudly a helicopter parent—makes a case that contradicts

---

[64] Putnam, *Our Kids*, 255.
[65] Putnam, *Our Kids*, 218.
[66] Putnam, *Our Kids*, 260.
[67] Putnam, *Our Kids*, 258.

Putnam's own thesis. She is from "an affluent in Michigan family" and "is proud of standing up for her kids at school."[68] Toward the end of Putnam's description of this mother and her family, he includes her commitment to the fiction of the "self-made" American.

> "You have to work if you want to get rich," she [the mother] insists. She's skeptical about special funding for educating poorer kids. "If my kids are going to be successful, I don't think they should have to pay other people who are sitting around doing nothing for their success."[69]

Putnam then turns to the story of David, who "has clear educational aspirations" and "feels great responsibility for his diverse brood of younger half-siblings." But with an absent mother and frequently imprisoned father, he has no education and no options or opportunities. The "bad name" of his mother and father has meant that "townspeople were disinclined to treat him with any sympathy." Putnam concludes, "In the most fundamental sense, David has had to fend for himself this entire life."[70] The gap between David's opportunities and those of the upwardly mobile children is supposed to be unsettling. But also disquieting is Putnam's apparent agreement—or at least lack of criticism for the view—that good families simply take care of their own.

Whether or not Putnam takes this self-referential family as normative is not the point. The point, more troubling, is that he assumes, descriptively, a contrast only between fragmented parenting and inwardly-oriented, upwardly mobile families. There is no third way. "Good" families develop bonds only in terms of private fulfillment, with no wider "good" at stake (no common good or broader conception of justice). About a young man from a well-off family in Bend, Oregon, Putnam concludes, "Perhaps the most striking feature about Andrew's view of life is the exceptional warmth he feels, even as a late adolescent, toward his family."[71] Another case study ends when an interview with a parent is interrupted by a call from a college-age child—for advice about missing car keys. "Afterward she [the mother] points to her phone and says, 'Proof perfect, right? You always are there for that support, that advice, that voice of reason. As a parent, it

---

[68] When her daughter did not receive a year-book scholarship, she threatened a high school principal with going over his head to the school board. For whatever reason (power, connections, potential shame and embarrassment for the principal?), the threat immediately worked. See Putnam, *Our Kids*, 24-5.

[69] Putnam, *Our Kids*, 25.

[70] Putnam, *Our Kids*, 28.

[71] Putnam, *Our Kids*, 54.

never ends'."[72] Good families promote the good of their members apart from the good of other families or communities.

In short, families are a problem. On one hand, poor and working class families are going through a process of degeneration. On the other hand, good families are oriented to their own success, so that their regeneration contributes to a cordoning off of resources— "social, economic, cultural and spiritual."[73] I have no doubt that Robert Putnam knows of some, and hopes for more, of another kind of family, what *Gaudium et spes* refers to as "a kind of school for deeper humanity."[74] In Catholic social thought, the family is considered "the foundation of society." Here, a basic vocation of family is to cultivate virtues of wisdom and justice and a desire to contribute to the common good.[75] If Putnam has encountered these kinds of families (and surely he has), he does not expect them to play a role in creating an advantageous environment for struggling children and their parents.[76] Perhaps it would be too moralistic if Putnam, as a sociologist, were to call upwardly mobile families to raise their children better. Perhaps it would be reaching too far into metaphysics if he were to propose that families orient their lives to a higher good, a common good of human beings.[77] But even if he were to do so, the fact remains that "good" families in the United States are too often oriented only to their own success. The fact that model, upwardly mobile families are not part of the solution is a crisis for the American family.

CONCLUSION

In Catholic social thought, the family is understood to be ordered to the common good. This ordering of family has a direct (and inverse) relationship to the successful families in Putnam's *Our Kids*: The common good is defined by shared opportunities and access to personal

---

[72] Putnam, *Our Kids*, 92.

[73] Paul VI, *Populorum progressio* (Vatican City: Libreria Editrice Vaticana, 1967), no. 13. In this phrase, "social, economic, cultural, and spiritual," Paul VI is attempting to include the whole of the problem of human development.

[74] Vatican II, *Gaudium et spes* (Vatican City: Libreria Editrice Vaticana, 1965), no. 52.

[75] In the family, generations of members "help one another grow wiser and harmonize personal rights with the other requirements of social life" (*Gaudium et spes*, no. 52).

[76] Families that are "schools for deeper humanity" are absent from *Our Kids* perhaps because they have no measurable, salutary effect on the problems of social inequality and the fragmentation of disadvantaged families. We could, I suppose, criticize Putnam and the tools of sociology for the limits of the discipline's ability to measure salutary effects. But this criticism gets us—and the failure of families—of the hook too easily.

[77] For the metaphysical turn in sociology, see Douglas Porpora, *Landscapes of the Soul* (New York: Oxford University Press, 2001).

and social development.[78] Family—by nature and vocation—has a social role in forming networks with other families and creating a fabric of engagement and participation for the good of society as a whole. At the end of my treatment of *Our Kids*, I introduced the question of whether or not Putnam, as a sociologist, could have called his successful families to be responsible for the common good: It is striking that he does not turn any criticisms toward the complacency of upwardly mobile. He proposes a set of programs and policies to alleviate social inequality and to provide opportunities for disadvantaged children, but absent is an appeal to the advantaged to raise children who see justice, beyond their own success, as a higher good. In any consideration of family, this goal of justice (within family relations and outward) is the place to begin.

Bloom's work, as philosophically tangled as it is, presents a clear case that we human beings have a natural sense of justice and compassion and that these natural capacities are formed within family. Family is a place, a workshop, where the craft of living well is formed. The evidence provided by Bloom in *Just Babies* pertains to the contemporary crisis of family in two senses. First, the fragmentation of family among the poor and working class not only undermines opportunities for social and economic development, but also creates obstacles within a basic avenue for moral development—the setting of family where one learns to order one's life in relationship to others and to various goods that leads to a fulfilling life. Second, the self-referential character of Putnam's model families not only perpetuates social inequality, but also puts their own success in crisis. These upwardly mobile families attain their success by diminishment, by narrowing their social and moral purview. The crisis of family is its framework of achievement.

Catholic social thought conceives of family and household, not merely the individuals within them, as social bodies and agents. In *Familiaris consortio*, John Paul II gives a summary of the tradition:

> The family has vital and organic links with society, since it is its foundation and nourishes it continually through its role of service to life: it is from the family that citizens come to birth and it is within the family that they find the first school of the social virtues that are the animating principle of the existence and development of society itself."[79]

---

[78] The common good is "the sum of those conditions of social life which allow social groups and their individual members relatively thorough and ready access to their own fulfillment" (*Gaudium et spes*, no. 26).

[79] John Paul II, *Familiaris consortio*, no. 42.

Families, networks of families, and neighborhoods have the capacity to sustain generative social economies.[80] Doing so is no easy task. But some of Putnam's successful families might not be far off from getting to work. Insofar as families create a social world to which individuals are responsible—a "family whole," which decenters the individual—the task becomes, not one of unraveling the family or parochial bonds, but one of expanding their shared world.[81] It is by this expansion that the family is a social agent—expanding the bonds necessary for wider human flourishing.

Is their hope for families? It is conceivable that some households will become committed to a place, unlike the suburbs, where social and economic divisions are blurred, where the family can sustain the kind of stability needed to extend opportunities and moral community. It does happen that families, virtually isolated in their comfortable worlds, raise children who desire to live with the poor—to teach school, coach, form scout troops, and put in the common labor needed to maintain a neighborhood. It is not impossible for the advantaged and disadvantaged to become friends. As a tool for upward mobility, family is self-referential; it is inclined to be only temporarily fixed within a place and only provisionally bound within specific sets of social relations. As a context for conviviality, family is much more like a workshop; it is set within reciprocal roles and in a place. This tension between the detachment/mobility of family and fixed social engagement provides the perspective from which to consider natural and social vocation of family. ∎

---

[80] McCarthy, *Sex and Love in the Home*, 120, 228.
[81] John Wall, *Ethics in Light of Childhood* (Washington, D.C.: Georgetown University Press, 2010), 145-51.

CONTRIBUTORS

Lucas Briola is currently a doctoral student in systematic and historical theology at The Catholic University of America in Washington, D.C. He holds a MTS from the Boston College School of Theology and Ministry. Lucas's primary general research interests include questions in ecclesiology, modern theology, theology and culture, and sacramental theology. His work has also appeared in the *Downside Review*, and he has contributed to dailytheology.org.

David Cloutier holds the Knott Professorship of Catholic Theology at Mount St. Mary's University in Emmitsburg, MD. He is the author of *The Vice of Luxury* (Georgetown Univ. Press, 2015) and *Walking God's Earth: The Environment and Catholic Faith* (Liturgical Press, 2014). He is the editor of catholicmoraltheology.com, blogs at dotCommonweal, and is the president of the Board of Directors of the Common Market, Frederick, Maryland's food co-operative.

John S. Grabowski is Associate Professor and Director of Moral Theology/Ethics at The Catholic University of America. He is the author of *Sex and Virtue: An introduction to Sexual Ethics* (CUA Press, 2003). His articles have appeared in *Nova et Vetera, The Thomist, National Catholic Bioethics Quarterly,* and *The Linacre Quarterly.*

Christopher K. Gross is an Assistant Professor at the Institute for the Psychological Sciences of Divine Mercy University. He earned his Ph.D. from The Catholic University of America and specializes in sexual ethics and virtue theory. His articles also have appeared in the *National Catholic Bioethics Quarterly.*

Angela Knobel is Associate Professor of Philosophy at the Catholic University of America. She earned her Ph.D. from the University of Notre Dame, and specializes in Aquinas's moral philosophy. Her articles on virtue ethics have appeared in *Nova et Vetera, Christian Bioethics, The Thomist, International Philosophical Quarterly, American Catholic Philosophical Quarterly,* and *Studies in Christian Ethics.*

Erin Lothes is assistant professor of Theology at the College of Saint Elizabeth, Morristown, NJ and a former Earth Institute Fellow at Columbia University, which is an interdisciplinary postdoctorate in sustainability studies. She is the author of *Inspired Sustainability: Planting Seeds for Action* (Orbis 2016) and *The Paradox of Christian Sacrifice: The Loss of Self, the Gift of Self* (Herder and Herder, 2007). She has published articles on Catholic energy ethics as well as interdisciplinary analyses of faith-based environmentalism.

David Matzko McCarthy is the Fr. James M. Forker Professor of Catholic Social Teaching at Mount St. Mary's University in Emmitsburg, MD. His works in progress are *Saving the World and Healing the Soul: Romance and Action in Film*, with Kurt Blaugher (forthcoming 2016), *Moral Vision*, with James M. Donohue, C.R. (2017), and *The Natural Law of Membership*, with Charles R. Pinches.

Elaine Padilla is Assistant Professor of Constructive Theology at New York Theological Seminary. Her theological analysis constructively interweaves current philosophical discourse with Christianity, Latin American and Latino/a religious thought, mysticism, ecology, and gender. She is the author of *Divine Enjoyment: A Theology of Passion and Exuberance* published by Fordham University Press, and co-editor of a three-volume project with Peter C. Phan, *Theology and Migration in World Christianity* being published by Palgrave MacMillan. These are entitled: *Contemporary Issues of Migration and Theology* (2013), *Theology of Migration in the Abrahamic Religions* (2014), and *Christianities in Migration: The Global Perspective* (2015).

Christiana Z. Peppard is Assistant Professor of Theology, Science and Ethics in the Department of Theology at Fordham University, where she is affiliated faculty in Environmental Studies and American Studies. She is the author *of Just Water: Theology, Ethics, and the Global Water Crisis* (2014), co-editor of *Just Sustainability: Ecology, Technology, and Resource Extraction,* and author of articles in *Journal of Environmental Studies and Sciences*; *Journal of Feminist Studies in Religion*; *Journal of Catholic Social Thought*; and *Journal of the Society for Christian Ethics.* Her research engages religious environmental ethics at the intersection of Catholic social teaching, ecological anthropology, natural law theory and the scientific fields of hydrology and geology. Her public media work includes venues such as *The New Republic,* Public Radio International, *The Washington Post,* TED-Ed, MSNBC, and CNN.com. Professor Peppard holds a Ph.D. in Ethics from Yale University, Department of Religious Studies.

Matthew Petrusek, Ph.D., is an assistant professor of theological studies at Loyola Marymount University in Los Angeles. Dr. Petrusek's interests and specializations include meta-ethics, the intersection of philosophical and theological ethics, Christian ethics, ethics and political theory, natural law, virtue theory, distributive justice, and human dignity. He has published in the *Journal of the American Academy of Religion*, the *Journal of Moral Philosophy*, and *Philosophy and Theology*, and has served as an on-air analyst for Notices MundoFox, CNN Españo, and KCal.

Charles Pinches is Professor and chair of the Department of Theology/Religious Studies at the University of Scranton in Scranton, Pennsylvania. Among other books, he is the author of *Theology and Action: After Theory in Christian Ethics* (Eerdmans, 2002) and *Christians Among the Virtues* (with Stanley Hauerwas; University of Notre Dame Press, 1997). Most recently he has been collaborating with David Matzko McCarthy on a new book on natural law.

Jame Schaefer serves as Associate Professor of Systematic Theology and Ethics at Marquette University where she constructively relates theology, the natural sciences, and technology with special attention to religious foundations for ecological ethics, directs the Interdisciplinary Minor in Environmental Ethics, and advises Marquette Students for an Environmentally Active Campus. Among her publications are *Theological Foundations for Environmental Ethics* (Georgetown University Press, 2009), *Confronting the Climate Crisis: Catholic Theological Perspectives* (Marquette University Press, 2011), and the inaugural "Animals" entry in *New Catholic Encyclopedia* (2013).

Matthew A. Tapie is Assistant Professor of Theology and director of the Center for Catholic-Jewish Studies at Saint Leo University, FL. He is the author of *Aquinas on Israel and the Church* (Pickwick, 2014), and co-editor of *Reading Scripture as a Political Act: Essays on the Theopolitical Interpretation of the Bible* (Fortress Press, 2015).

Articles available to view
or download at:

www.msmary.edu/jmt

The

Journal of Moral Theology

is proudly sponsored by the

Fr. James M. Forker Professorship
of Catholic Social Teaching

and the

College of Liberal Arts

at

Mount St. Mary's University

MOUNT ST. MARY'S UNIVERSITY
College of Liberal Arts